HOW TO GET STARTED IN YOUR OWN FRANCHISED BUSINESS

The Latest Shortcuts To Profit And Independence

by

DAVID D. SELTZ

FARNSWORTH PUBLISHING COMPANY, INC.
Rockville Centre, New York 11570

© 1980, David D. Seltz.
All rights reserved.
First printing, February, 1980.
Published by Farnsworth Publishing Co., Inc.
Rockville Centre, New York 11570.
Library of Congress Catalog Card No. 79-27945
ISBN 0878631720.
Manufactured in the United States of America.

Library of Congress Cataloging in Publication Data

Seltz, David D.
    How to get started in your own franchised
business.

    Includes index.
    1. Franchises (Retail trade)—Management.
2. Small business—Management. I. Title.
HF5429.S47 1980   658.8'708   79-27945
ISBN 0-87863-172-0

About The Author

David D. Seltz is known, both nationally and internationally, as an authority and spokesman for the franchising and marketing fields. He is President of his own consulting firm, Seltz Franchising Developments, Inc.

Mr. Seltz has been Chairman or Featured Speaker for important franchising seminars throughout the United States and abroad. He served as Chairman of the International Franchise Congress in Zurich, Switzerland, for two consecutive years. During this time he was also Featured Speaker at seminars in England, France, Italy and other countries. He is the author of 16 books and approximately 2,000 magazine articles. Mr. Seltz has received wide recognition in articles and columns appearing in *Nation's Business, Business Week, Wall Street Journal* and *The New York Times*. Columnist Sylvia Porter referred to the Seltz Organization as "foremost in the franchising field."

FOREWORD

The first edition of this book was prepared in the mid-60s when the franchising concept was becoming popular and was about to commence its meteoric rise. At that time this book was highly regarded and was considered one of the foremost franchisee advisory books in the field.

Since then, the entire franchising field has undergone great changes. The franchisee is now protected by Federal regulations, by rigorous regulations in many states, and by varying provisions even in non-regulatory states. New Federal disclosure regulations became effective October 21, 1979.

That's why the entire book has undergone major revisions, making it "in effect" a new book. Reading the first chapter, "Franchising Updated," you will note that it discusses new forms of business association between franchisor and franchisee. Initially, there was a "vertical" relationship, something like this:

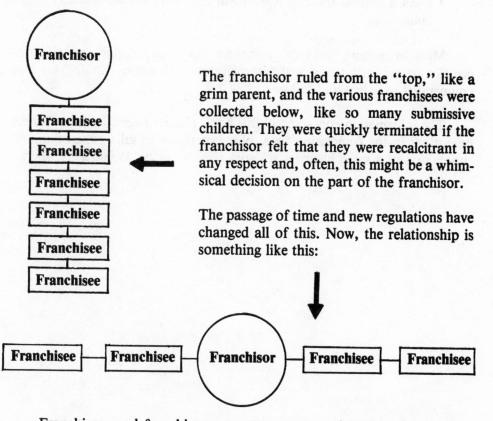

The franchisor ruled from the "top," like a grim parent, and the various franchisees were collected below, like so many submissive children. They were quickly terminated if the franchisor felt that they were recalcitrant in any respect and, often, this might be a whimsical decision on the part of the franchisor.

The passage of time and new regulations have changed all of this. Now, the relationship is something like this:

Franchisors and franchisees operate on an equal level, with the franchisor, in the center, providing sophisticated managerial assistance. To the extent to which this is performed well, the franchise business becomes profitable and payment of continuous residual fees becomes justified.

i

Is a franchised business desirable? In our opinion, definitely, "Yes." As a franchisee you are investing in a proven business, receiving the benefits of expert training and guidance and can by-pass many years of expensive "trial and error."

A franchised business offers many opportunities and you, as a franchisee, can be the beneficiary. However, as will be explained in detail in this book, you can't expect "certified success" from the franchisor or the franchisee program—just as you cannot be guaranteed success in **any** type of business. A great deal depends on *you*.

The purpose of this book is to provide the information needed to help franchisees to:

- select the franchise most compatible with their qualifications;
- select a franchise with excellent potential for success;
- select a franchise within their financial capacities;
- select a reliable franchisor who will perform his contractual obligations.

Most important, once the franchise has been selected, certain procedures are set forth which will favor success. "Things not to do" are also enumerated to help avoid failure.

The information contained in this book reflects over 20 years of direct operations in the franchising field, plus experience in sales promotion and supervision of a small business advisory service having 35,000 subscribers.

TABLE OF CONTENTS

1.

FRANCHISING UPDATED

Franchising has an ambiguous image. It is viewed alternatively as saint or sinner; as the "All American" Dream or the Great American Disillusionment; as a millionaire-maker or aspiration-forsaker.

Through the years franchising has epitomized all these contradictory roles, yet cannot be identified as any of them.

In many ways franchising resembles the fable of the nine blind men describing an elephant. The one who touched the trunk, for example, described the beast as resembling a tree. The one who touched the tail thought he had contacted a snake. Each understood only that part he had experienced.

It is necessary to understand what franchising is to understand its status today. Even the Federal Trade Commission often "wrestles" with an exact definition, so it is best to state first what franchising is not. Franchising is *not* a trade, profession or industry. It is instead, a marketing format or "vehicle" designed to distribute a particular product or service to its market in the quickest, most economical and profitable way.

The California Franchise Investment Law describes franchising as:

"A contract or agreement, either expressed or implied, whether oral or written, between two or more persons, by which: a franchisee is granted the right to engage in the business of offering, selling or distributing goods or services, under a marketing plan or

7

system, prescribed in substantial part by a franchisor and the operation of the franchisee's business pursuant to such a plan or system substantially associated with the franchisor's trademark, service mark, trade name, logotype, advertising or other commercial symbol, designating the franchisor or its affiliate.''

Many faces and facets characterize the franchising field. These range from multi-million-dollar institutional enterprises, such as Holiday Inns, to moderate investment service-type businesses.

Name any business that comes to mind and it's probably franchised! The automotive aftermarket is thoroughly franchised, with gross sales exceeding billions of dollars. Virtually every part of the automobile, including fenders, radiators, seat covers, transmissions, and mufflers is franchised. There are also dozens of successful service businesses developed around the car, including do-it-yourself repairs and such esoteric services as painting, rust-proofing, detailing, and bodywork.

Of course, there are literally hundreds of food businesses (fast and slow service, standup and sitdown, full-menu or specialty, structurally ornate or austere) that are franchised. These include the well-known McDonalds, Kentucky Fried Chicken, and Burger Kings, plus a plethora of well-known and lesser-known names.

Franchising can also be a gas station, a municipal transportation system, a sports team, or a bottling works.

Franchising has evolved from the frenetic ''everything goes'' era of the '60s, when regulations were minimal, to the sobering, tightly-regulated '70s. During this initial ''laissez faire'' period, many franchisors sold ''geography'' rather than businesses. They literally ''sliced up'' the country (and even the world) into so many pieces of a ''pie'' which they proceeded to sell for varying, arbitrarily-established sums of money.

The emphasis was on the amount of quick ''front money'' that one could grab, rather than the achievable profits from a network of successful franchisees that the franchisor had helped to establish. The rationale and objectives were short-range rather than long-range.

There were also examples of more and more franchisors entering the field on a financial ''shoestring.'' In many instances, the franchisee's investment was used to cover corporate expenses and there was no money left to fulfill commitments to their franchisees. Quite often the franchisor would go out of business in a short time, taking their franchisees with them. Others failed to prove the validity of their business, or expanded more rapidly than their ability to absorb and train franchisees.

Today's ever-increasing number of state laws have been enacted to prevent these practices, to protect franchisees and to impose controls over franchisors.

In essence, these controls are designed to assure that the franchisor:

- is properly capitalized (so that he can meet his obligations to his franchisees);

- has made full disclosures of all aspects of his business and company;

- doesn't compel purchase of his products or other supplies as a "tie-in" sale;

- doesn't unreasonably restrict the franchisee's territory;

- doesn't terminate franchisees without good cause;

- dosen't create a "pyramid-type" structure, one that encourages continuing resale of the franchise rather than product sales. [As a result of "pyramids," the eventual bottom-level franchisees (very similar to the chain-letter principle) run out of salable population and usually lose their investment.]

As a consequence of these stringent regulations, major conceptual changes in franchising have taken place.

Foremost among these are philosophical changes. Franchising is no longer viewed as a "vertical" structure with the franchisor, like a stern parent reposed grimly at the top, and his franchisees, like so many errant children, nestled meekly below. Now it functions in a "horizontal" format. Both franchisor and franchisee are equals. The franchisor is, in effect, "employed" by the franchisee to provide the management expertise—the methodological "software"—needed to run the franchise network effectively. To the extent that he does this effectively, so will the business endure and both he and the franchisees will reap the desired profits.

This concept is very similar to the operation of a "condominium." It also resembles, in many ways, the Wholesaler-Retailer Cooperative concept, under which individual businesses band together (usually under the sponsorship of a wholesaler) forming a multi-unit cohesive chain—both regionally and nationally—resulting in enhanced management sophistication.

The stringent regulations have also spurred a search for "alternatives" to franchising. Essentially these seek to create a relationship that, on one hand, may be "non-franchised," thereby avoiding many of the regulatory restrictions of franchising . . . but, on the other hand, one that helps to achieve the many outstanding benefits of franchising. The principal benefit is the ability to recruit dedicated entrepreneurial management, willing, able and qualified to invest in their own future.

Central among possible alternatives is the "partnership" concept. Based on this concept, both franchisor and franchisee share in the business in varying proportion (depending on their respective investments) with the franchisee frequently able to acquire more and more participation in future earnings as a result of predesignated performance factors.

This concept gives the entrepreneur an equity in, or ownership of, his own business with a minimum investment. It also combines the franchisee and the franchisor into "one team pulling together."

There are various partnership formats, both general and limited. These lend themselves to numerous variations and applications. This concept also enables younger entrepreneurs—who have the ambition but lack the required substantial capital to invest (as much as $150,000 for some fast food franchises)—to invest a smaller sum initially and to benefit in the future business expansion achieved through their efforts.

One case in point is that of a well-known variety store's program. These heavily-inventoried stores—in expensive rent locations—would, normally, require an investment of $100,000 and more. To attract younger, dynamic management, the parent will often participate in a form of joint venture. This is done selectively, based on the outstanding qualifications of the applicant. According to this concept, the franchisee invests a lesser sum—e.g. 30% of the capital requirement, and the parent will invest approximately 20% (taking a minority interest). A separate corporate entity is established in the franchisee's name. It's his business for all intents and purposes; however, the licensor retains majority voting rights and installs two of its members on the board until the indebtedness is paid up in full. Together they will approach an outside financing source to produce the capital balance for operating the business. The fact that the franchisor is a participant confers a financial clout that persuades banks to make the loan.

A successful restaurant chain is also a case in point. For an investment of $10,000 to $15,000, the franchisee receives an earnings participation— usually 5%—in the profits of a $250,000 (and up) business, plus a basic salary (paid even while in training), plus the ability to buy shares in other nearby operations. And, to top it all, he can receive a return of his original investment any time he seeks it.

Another interesting development in franchising is to attract the multi-unit franchisee, as contrasted with the single-unit franchisee. This multi-unit franchisee is also known as a "controller," or a "distributor." Normally, he commits himself to the operation of a "cluster," or group of units within a contiguous area, averaging six units per controllership. The controller is, in effect, a sub-franchisor: he co-participates in many of the normal functions of the franchisor for his area, inclusive of: recruitment, training, on-going advice and even warehousing. He will, in some instances, operate one unit while managing his other units and share franchise fees and royalties with the franchisor.

One notable benefit of such controllerships is that the franchisor is able to deal with a sophisticated individual, having executive capabilities and adequate capitalization. The trend towards controllership has been escalating. Horn & Hardart of New York, for example, has become a multiple-unit franchise of Burger King (currently 22 former Automat stores have been converted into Burger Kings). Other examples include Big Boy, Arthur Treacher, and Shakey's Pizza. A collateral benefit of controllerships is that this type of franchise is deemed more likely to succeed than the less sophisticated, single unit franchisee, who tends to "run scared" in assuming a business of his own. Those franchisors espousing the controllership concept consider that there is less possibility of problems or failure.

There has also been a trend towards "buy backs." Franchisors frequently offer, contractually, to buy back the franchise, in the event of dissatisfaction, refunding all or most of the investment within a designated period. They will also, in many instances, provide a "buy back" formula whereby, contractually, they will commit themselves to buy back the business for book value or four times earnings, whichever is the greater, or on some other agreed formula.

In today's new climate of franchising, greater stress has been placed on the quality of franchisee support and "back-up." These services are no longer administered casually. A systematic and conscientious effort is made by the franchisor to assist the franchisee to succeed and to include him as part of the "team." Many franchisors have established franchisee associations to advise them on ways to best meet franchisee needs and objectives. In the employment agency field, for example, Manpower Company has established a number of sub-committees in addition to their franchising consulting committee and its sub-committees. Members of these sub-committees advise and counsel with the Home Office on strategies, long-range planning, recruiting needs and other corporate policy matters.

Other franchisors provide a formula enabling selected franchisees to obtain "shares" in the franchisor's corporation, permitting them to grow as the corporate structure grows. One popular plan today is the ESOP concept, under which franchisees purchase company stock, thus participating in and benefiting by the company's growth.

Indicative of the new emancipation of franchisees in today's regulatory climate, is this "magna carta" promulgated by a McDonald's franchisee association, known as the McDonald's Operators' Association (MOA). This group, in effect, constitutes a "rump caucus" of McDonald franchisees. As such, it differentiates from McDonald's company-organized "National Operators' Advisory Board (NOAB)." This latter group is not a policy-making body, it is a two-way communications conduit.

The points expressed in this so-called "Magna Carta" are:

1. No operator should be summarily terminated, there sould be an automatic right of renewal.

2. Relationships between business partners regarding renewals or expansion should not be disrupted.

3. New units in an operator's market should be offered to the operator first.

4. New units which reduce revenues of existing stores should never be opened.

5. McDonald's Corp. should pay for unit structural changes, except for interior improvements.

6. Original leases should include all items needed to maintain McDonald's high standards.

As noted from the above points, the franchisees were concerned about and sought to preclude "market saturation." Also indicated is the feeling of long-established franchisees that franchisors should provide, at their own expense, the same new-design structure that new franchisees are getting.

One prominent franchisor referred to the "Franchisee Realities of the Seventies," as comprising new "realities" as follows:

Reality #1 Franchisees have rising demands similar to emerging nations. They demand professionalism. They expect the franchisor to bring into his marketing strategies in the management of his business the highest possible competence. They will not settle for incompetence and mediocrity.

Reality #2 The franchisor/franchisee relationship should be one where the parties deal with each other similar to labor and management over a bargaining table. Sell the franchisee on the merits of the proposition rather than dictating to him. Take him into your confidence; be sincere.

Reality #3 Franchisees seek self-improvement programs for improving their management capacities and their profits. They also seek help in personal financial budgeting. Manpower Company has provided a correspondence course and postgraduate courses on the subject.

Reality #4 Franchisees seek effective advertising coverage on a national and regional basis. The type of coverage sought is that which they could not afford "on their own."

Reality #5 The franchisee expects that the franchisor will maintain his reputation on the highest level. Any reduction in franchisor's status can also affect the franchisee and his substantial investment.

Reality #6 Franchisees want to participate in future plans. They've developed their own expertise and seek that it be used. They want to be consulted and their advice included in the planning of the company. Communication must be "a two-way street."

Reality #7 Franchisees want their family to have a vested interest in the business. A franchisor should establish a program that assures continuity, in the event of his death, under proper management (or the option of selling their franchise). General Business Services has for years espoused a program to help franchisees sell their business, when desired.

Reality #8 Franchisees like their company to expand. They resent a business that is on a treadmill. Hence, innovativeness is required.

Reality #9 Franchisees seek diversification, for add-on profits and add-on earnings, and to ensure that the business is constantly upgraded, in conformance with current needs. This is particularly pertinent in view of today's escalating overhead costs.

There have been many examples: McDonald's has introduced breakfast (constituting an add-on business for essentially the same overhead), also new structural formats in conformance with community needs. The Ben Franklin stores converted from the small five-and-dime "Mom and Pop" type of variety store to the sophisticated shopping center type of store with a potential sales volume three or four times greater than the original store.

Reality #10 Some franchisees want money *now* from the business they built. They also seek monies beyond salaries and dividends, (ordinary income), and want the opportunity for capital gain. There should be a phased-in plan to help attain this goal, commingling his interest with the company's interest.

Reality #11 Franchisees want to be assisted in becoming VIPs in their community. Help them become "joiners," prepare speeches that they can make, local newspaper columns that can be inserted. Have photos taken with influential community backers. Prepare success stories about them.

One prominent franchisor expresses today's franchisor views in this manner:

"The day of the franchisee as a junior partner is over. Now the franchisee and the franchisor are equal partners in a mutually beneficial investment; the franchisee furnishes a time and money investment; the franchisor, the expertise. Each expects the other to live up to certain expectations."

This franchisor has promulgated a set of such "expectations" as follows:

THE FRANCHISEE EXPECTS:

1. That the franchisor will strengthen the organization as a whole through a well-thought-out expansion program. The quality of new franchisees interests him as well. He considers solid expansion the goal rather than an increasing number of pins in a map.

2. That the franchisor will do for him what he cannot do for himself. This includes researching and developing new promotions, ideas, and products and the tools to help implement them. The net result is a building and publicizing of a corporate image.

3. That the franchisor will express concern for the franchisee's personal growth by providing self-improvement tools such as

workshops on management, communications, and personal finances. The franchisee also seeks self-improvement tools in the non-business area that will assist in his everyday understanding of himself and the people around him.

4. That the franchisor will assemble a competent, informed staff on which the franchisee may call for assistance in problem solving. He further regards this staff as an extension of his own staff; no matter how demanding he may be, the staff must realize that through his franchise fee he is paying for and has a right to expect instant professionalism in return.

THE FRANCHISOR EXPECTS:

1. That the franchisee will put his best effort into his business, adapting the programs that the franchisor has found of value and working for their mutual success. In every endeavor the franchisee will uphold the good name of the organization by ethical conduct and high standards.

2. That the franchisee will evince an interest in the organization as a whole, sharing with other franchisees the results of his experiences. When a new approach is tried by the franchisee, the franchisor has a natural interest in the outcome.

3. That the franchisee will constantly think of himself as part of a larger whole. When he is approached with intelligent plans and instructions, he will cooperate enthusiastically so that the entire organization benefits from unified action.

4. That the franchisee will be a walking advertisement for the franchise concept in his own community by taking part in public service ventures. Becoming an active member of business associations, making non-commercial speeches about the business, providing expertise in the field to those who need it, all of these add to the value of the company name, locally and nationally. "For both franchisee and franchisor, the written agreement is the smallest part of the contract. It is the unwritten agreement that binds each to the other in mutual prosperity. Like partners in a good marriage, each must expect to give and take."

Despite restrictive regulations, franchising is growing. In one year alone, there were over 11,000 new franchise units in this country with total sales of over $12 billion. Sales of goods and services through franchised outlets grew to 8.9% in 1978 to $149.6 billion according to the U.S. Commerce Department survey of 1051 franchisors. These represent an estimated 99% of all U.S. franchising sales. The number of franchised establishments increased by 3.7% during 1978 to 457,693 units. This rate should accelerate as business recovers from the depths of recession.

The fear of another recession has given new impetus to the urge for going into business for oneself. The insecurity of salaried jobs, regardless of seniority, has been dramatically pointed up, with an ever-increasing number of individuals seeking to master their own economic destiny. Women are now active candidates for business ownership. Even persons currently employed are actively seeking businesses of their own as future unemployment insurance.

What is the lure of franchising? It is based on following a "success formula." When Mr. X has a successful business and a well-known trade name, you can share his training, continuing guidance and success by becoming his franchisee, all for payment of an establishment fee and continuing royalties. This fee implies that Mr. X will enable you to avoid the usual trial and error of going into a business of your own by "coat-tailing" onto his success. Since he is already earning well, the business obviously offers good earnings potential. It also must be the type of business that provides favorable self-identification.

The U.S. Department of Commerce's "Franchising in the Economy" indicates that the following are the fastest growing franchises:

printing and copying services
personal services and business services
   (tax preparation, recordkeeping, automated bookkeeping and billing, collection systems, tax services, computer schools)
background music
engineering
marketing consultants
recreation (particularly campgrounds)
entertainment
travel
non-food retailing
convenience stores
full- and part-time job agencies
construction, home improvements, and maintenance
   (water conditioning, burglar and fire alarms, floor care, pavement and driveway concreting, and porcelain maintenance)
cleaning services
equipment rental
automotive products and service
   (auto and trunk rentals, car washes, parking services, brake parts and diagnostic shops)

carpeting and upholstery of homes, offices, plants and institutions
lawn care
selling and construction of swimming pools
educational services
dietary and exercise training centers
day-care centers
hotels and motels

The most extensive franchises, in terms of dollar sales, remain the auto and truck dealerships, gasoline service stations and soft drink bottlers. Gasoline service stations, in many cases, are moving toward the low-overhead self-service station.

Minority businessmen are finding success in the areas of auto products and services, fast foods, non-food and food retailing, as well as laundry and dry cleaning services. The ever-expanding minority franchisees are benefiting from the franchise method in all areas. A worthwhile book, the "O.M.B.E. Funded Organizations Directory," can be obtained from the Office of Minority Business Enterprise (O.M.B.E.) which provides financial, technical and managerial aids.

The following checklist has been prepared for use by prospective franchise investors by the Small Business Guidance and Development Center in Washington, D.C. It is all-inclusive and the best possible guide for those interested in franchising.

1. For how many years has the franchisor firm been in operation?

2. Has it a reputation for honesty and fair dealing?

3. Will firm assist you with:

a. management training program

b. employee training program

c. public relations program

d. capital

e. credit

f. merchandising ideas

4. Will firm assist you in finding a good location?

5. Is firm adequately financed so that it can carry out its stated plan of financial assistance and expansion?

6. Has franchisor shown you any certified figures indicating exact net profits of one or more going firms which you have personally checked yourself?

7. Is franchisor a one-man company or corporation with experienced management, trained in depth, so that there would always be an experienced man at its head?

8. Exactly what can a franchisor do for you which you cannot do for yourself?

9. Has franchisor investigated you carefully enough to assure itself that you can successfully operate one of its franchises?

10. Did your lawyer approve franchise contract after he studied it paragraph by paragraph?

11. Does franchise call upon you to take any steps which are, according to your lawyer, unwise or illegal in your state, county or city?

12. Does franchise give you exclusive territory rights for the length of franchise, or can franchisor sell a second or third franchise in your territory?

13. Is franchisor connected in any way with any other franchise-connected company handling similar merchandise or services?

14. If answer to the last question is "Yes," what is your protection against this second franchisor organization?

15. Under what circumstances can you terminate franchise contract and at what cost to you, if you decide for any reason at all that you wish to cancel it?

16. If you sell your franchise, will you be compensated for your goodwill or will the goodwill you have built into the business be lost to you?

17. Are you prepared to give up some independence of action or secure advantage offered by the franchise?

18. Do YOU really believe you have the innate ability, training, and experience to work smoothly and profitably with the franchisor, your employees and customers?

19. Are you ready to spend much or all of the remainder of your business life with this franchisor, offering his product or service to your public?

20. Have you made any study to determine whether product or service which you propose to sell under franchise has a market in your territory at the price you will have to charge?

21. Will population in the territory given you, increase, remain static, or decrease over next five years?

22. Will product or service you are considering be in greater demand, about the same, or less in demand five years from now than today?

23. What competition exists in your territory, already, for the product or service you contemplate selling?

    a. non-franchise firms

    b. franchise firms

2.

BUYING A FRANCHISE

When You Buy a Franchise, What
Should You Expect for Your Money?

What is the significance of a franchise fee? What is meant by "royalties?"
To what extent are they justified?

When you buy a franchise, you are "buying a business." This usually
means a rather substantial investment. You are going to part with a considerable portion of your life's savings . . . for the opportunity to make a
good living. A better living than ever before, you hope . . . and maybe even
the chance to get rich.

Exactly what are you paying for? What should you expect for your
money? What you want and ought to know is: (a) How much is the prospective franchise business worth? (b) Just what are you going to get for the price
you pay? First, of course, there's the actual merchandise and material you
get, which can be measured in dollars and cents. Then there are the "in-
tangibles" which aren't so easy to evaluate yet which can be far more important than the merchandise and material in determining the ultimate success
or failure of your venture.

Under the category "franchise fees" you are, in effect, reimbursing the
costs that franchisor incurred in recruiting you as a franchisee and in getting
you effectively established in your business. This would include:

• Recruitment costs

• Operations Manual

- Instructional Materials and Supplies

- Flow and Control Forms

- Advertising and Promotional Materials

- Publicity Kit

- Recordkeeping System

- Administrative Costs

- Home Office Training Program

- Grand Opening Program

- Site Selection, Lease Negotiation

The above does not include inventory, lease hold improvements, equipment, construction, etc.

Category 2, "royalties," (usually a percentage of franchise's gross sales) acts to compensate the franchisor for those continuing services performed on your behalf, to provide needed guidance to help assure your continuing success. These include:

- **Continuing national advertising**

- **Continuing field support**

- **Continuing sales and promotional assistance**

- **Regional and national clinics**

- **Continuing use of trade name**

- **Refresher training**

- **Newsletters and bulletins**

- **Management Advisory Services**

Many franchisors assess a percentage of gross sales or a minimum monthly fee (whichever is the greater) for franchisee advertising. This constitutes the amount franchisor judges that the franchisee should budget for advertising needs; in other instances, this fee is collected by the franchisor and placed into a "segregated fund" to be used as an advertising pool, participated in by all franchisees on a proportional basis.

Additional fees may be charged by franchisors for supplementary services: for example, submitting a monthly computerized "Business Health Audit" assessing franchisee's business strengths and weaknesses.

Remember that in seeking to purchase a franchise, the applicant seeks something he feels he needs. He wants to become part of a successful operation. He seeks to avoid the risks of going into business independently and desires to benefit from a proven success formula. He seeks the "shelter and support" of a parent organization to instruct him in what to do, how to do it, and when to do it, to make a success of the operation.

That is why he is willing to pay for a franchise. That is why he is justified in paying for a franchise. If he gets these benefits, he is well on the way to success. If he doesn't, no matter how little he has paid for the franchise, he isn't getting what he has paid for and his chances for success, or even survival, are small indeed.

Thus, "franchise fees" are not something to be avoided. They are "success insurance" and may be the promise of better days and of good business—provided the promise is implemented with a sincere desire, on the part of the franchisor, to assist in the franchisee's SUCCESS.

19 Ways a Franchise Can Help You.

9 Ways It Can Hinder You.

Franchising has attained a spectacular success. In 1977 franchised businesses totaled $212 billion in annual sales, which was equal to 31% of all retail sales in the nation. More than 500 companies offer franchises. Their outlets number nearly 400,000. Gross business done by franchise operations aggregates billions of dollars—nearly 10% of the gross national product. It is estimated that current failures among independently-operated small businesses will total as high as 50%, as compared with a failure rate of only 9% for franchised businesses. These statistics further attest to the specific benefits of franchising.

Generally speaking, there is a franchise opportunity to fit any desire, capacity, or financial ability. Usually, specific experience is not essential. In fact, it is preferred that the franchise prospect should have a good, general sales and business background, rather than specifically related experience. In most instances, operating a franchise business results in a "head-start" as contrasted with operating independently. In effect, the business is "clothed" with the experience of the selected franchisor. Should this be a 37-year-old organization, the franchisee in effect commences as a 37-year-old business—from the very first day of operations.

As in most other things, there are negative aspects as well as positive factors. Under certain circumstances, a franchise business can hinder rather than help, depending on the franchise selection and the market. Below are listed ways in which franchising can help you, followed by ways it can hinder you.

19 Ways in Which a Franchise Can Help You

1. You gain the benefits of your franchisor's expertise, which has been acquired after extensive and expensive "trial and error."

2. You benefit from your franchisor's success formula.

3. You benefit from continuing guidance by the franchisor.

4. You are equipped with sales "tools" and administrative procedures which have been proven for maximum results.

5. You are trained in administrative procedures—assuring most effective work flow and controls.

6. You obtain thorough schooling and "follow-up training."

7. You receive the benefits of significant economies through volume purchases.

8. You receive benefits of cooperative advertising. Your normal advertising expenditures can be shared with a large number of franchisees.

9. You receive the benefits of site selection, lease negotiations, and store layout performed on your behalf by professionals.

10. You commence your business with a nationally-known name and so avoid usual "start-up" problems.

11. In many instances, the franchisor also assists you in your financing needs.

12. Also, economies can be achieved in insurance requirements. For example, blanket franchisor insurance policies can be made available to franchisees, locally—at greatly reduced cost.

13. You benefit from the constant interplay of new ideas resulting from franchisee local, regional and national conferences and conventions.

14. You receive continuing motivation—as a result of being part of a "big family."

15. Tested advertising is supplied to you, initially and continuously thereafter.

16. Publicity campaigns which project your firm's "image" are provided by the franchisor. You "get known" in your area in minimum time.

17. Public relations guidance enables you to utilize important areas of influence to help further your business.

18. Grand Opening Program—provided to you as a "package" by the franchisor—generates an immediate traffic flow.

19. You receive the benefits of a pre-tested product or service.

9 Ways in Which a Franchise Can Hinder You:

1. Selection of an improper franchise; for example, one that doesn't fit your qualifications.

2. Selection of an improper franchisor, who fails to fulfill his contracted commitments.

3. Inadequate financing, that prevents you from fulfilling the financial requirements of your business.

4. Failure to absorb instructions . . . or to cooperate with your franchisor.

5. Inadequate dedication to your business, your attitude remaining that of a wage-earner rather than the enthusiasm and self-motivation of an entrepreneur. Thus, you are not fulfilling the basic requisites of a franchisee.

6. Selection of an improper location for your business which can seriously impede your business progress.

7. Improper arithmetic—paying too much for franchise or other factors that act to reduce earnings.

8. Failure to "apply yourself" toward continued self-improvement in the field of your choice.

9. Absentee ownership, or part-time ownership, to the extent that you are not in proper control and supervision of your own business.

TO SUM UP . . .

Whether franchising constitutes a boon or a bane to *you* depends on:

You, your abilities and *your* outlook.

3.

GETTING ADVICE
ON SELECTING A FRANCHISE

Whom to Ask—What to Ask

If you are considering the purchase of a franchise, you know how very important it is to you and how much rests on your decision. Often, a substantial portion of your life savings may be involved. Moreover, you plan to devote all of your energies to reach success. Naturally, this is a matter of great concern. It makes it essential that no mistake be made and that you select the precise franchise opportunity suitable for you, your talents, and specific needs. What is more, it must provide you with the maximum assurance of a good current income.

Most of us seek some advice when we contemplate taking a really important step. A person about to buy a building will generally enlist the advice of an "authority" in the building field. A man buying a car will seek the judgment and advice of a competent mechanic. In purchasing a franchise, one should discuss the prospective deal with persons in whose judgment one has faith. It is too momentous a step to take without seeking good, sound advice.

It is extremely important, however, to be selective about whom to consult. So we try to suggest the type and quality of advice to seek, how to evaluate it and how to put it to proper use.

Many good opportunities are lost, with subsequent regret, because of too much conflicting advice. Others were lost because of improper advice . . . still others, because of inadequate and incompetent advice . . . and, yet, others because of "out of context" advice. Hence, the *quality* of the advice you obtain, and its *interpretation* are highly important.

Now, let us consider to whom you should turn for intelligent advice on any prospective franchise. The people to consult should include:

(1) Your imediate family—particularly your wife

(2) Your business counselors, such as your attorney and accountant

(3) Interested friends whose business acumen you respect and whose loyalty can be relied upon

(4) Other franchisees actively engaged in the same business. In addition, seek the advice of knowledgeable people with an understanding of and a sensitivity to the type of business you are considering. For example:

(a) People and firms in related fields (even if not franchised). Interviews with such organizations can give you a perspective on the industry and its potential. They can also alert you to possible pitfalls.
(b) Government and research reports on the market potential of your area and its relationship to the field you are contemplating entering.
(c) Trade publications covering the particular business or industry.

Several factors must now be kept in mind. First is the type of advice you obtain from these sources. Second is the "context" (by whom the advice was given, under what circumstances and with what objectives). Third is the dimensions of the advice offered; in other words, did the advice emanate from a vital source of "first rank" importance or from a comparatively minor source of more or less questionable worth?

For example, your lawyer's advice should be given the greatest consideration in view of his legal knowledge and business sophistication. Special regard should be given those aspects of his advice pertaining to matters of legal importance. Similarly, your accountant's advice should be considered in the light of its "arithmetical" approach. This professional advice should be combined with the more imaginative, broader factors to be considered in a franchise proposition.

As to your family's advice, it is most important that it not be minimized and under no circumstances should it be disregarded. Your family lives with you and with your business. Your failure is their failure; your success is their success. However, you must recognize that their perspective may be more emotional than logical and thus more subject to modification through your own logic. Under no circumstances should you go into any business against your family's wishes—for no matter how great the potential for your success, you cannot pursue it, successfully, without their cooperation and encouragement.

Friends generally mean well in giving advice. However, their advice must stand the test of your own process of logic and should not be accepted in entirety, no matter how well intended. Remember, that even the most sincere friend's advice is colored by his own experiences and prejudices, which often have no relationship to your particular situation.

Other franchises can comprise a very important and highly valuable source of advice. They are actually involved in the operation. They have already committed their finances, their energies and their aspirations, in the same way you are now considering. Here again, regard their advice thoughtfully. Franchisees often suggest the fable of the nine blind men who, when asked to describe an elephant, each responded with a different description based on that portion of the elephant that he touched.

People in related fields should be asked for advice, too. They can "fill-in" the gaps in your conception of the contemplated franchise. They can:

(a) Supply you with latest statistical facts concerning the business.

(b) Inform you as to current rates of failure or success.

(c) Give you their opinions of your particular franchise offer.

(d) Alert you to possible pitfalls.

Once you have completed your "advice gathering" in the various ways and from the miscellaneous sources described, it is up to you to evaluate that information carefully. A good idea is to prepare a "pro" and "con" chart. For example, your chart might start out something like this:

"PRO" factors: Huge market potential. Income continuity appears assured, after break-even point has been reached. Solid parent company; good "track" record.

"CON" factors: Pilot operation not conclusive. Training program inadequate. Takes long time to reach break-even point.

As stated, your chart might start something like the above, but could, and should, include many more factors on both the "pro" side and the "con" side. Even all this might not give you a reliable assessment and judgment of the franchise affiliation under consideration because each franchise situation must be considered in the light of these considerations:

(1) Facts and figures

(2) Company history

(3) *YOU*—the franchise situation as it relates to your personal situation.

You must remember that, in the final analysis, no one can make the decision for you. It is *you* who will have to judge the quality of all the advice sought and received. Weighing all the "evidence," you must ask yourself, whether or not the proposition is suited to you. Is it something you would like to do? Are you capable of doing it? Is the franchisor organization equipped—both in personnel and in motivation—to give you the cooperation, the training and the long-range, continuous support that you need? Seek advice but don't let too much advice, from too many persons, confuse you or negate your own good judgment.

Whatever your decision, the best of luck to you!

4.

HOW TO JUDGE A FRANCHISE— AND A FRANCHISOR

Let us suppose that for some time you have been searching for a franchise opportunity. You've been looking at ads, have made numerous inquiries and have received a great deal of literature on a variety of franchises. Some don't appeal to you, some look pretty good and then one appears that looks like "this is it!"

You are exultant and you hurry home to announce to your wife and family that, at last, you have the right franchise deal! You bring home letters, brochures and the contract! You have with you all the information you've obtained about the company, the product and what kind of investment is required in order to secure the franchise for your area. You have made careful notes and written an analysis of the proposition indicating why it appeals to you, and what makes it "just right" for you.

But—is it really? Maybe the company's advertising agency has done a wonderful job? Maybe they've painted a "glowing" picture that's a Madison Avenue masterpiece? Now, let us say that perhaps it is a "teriffic" deal. However, the question of greatest importance is this: Is it the right deal for *YOU?"*

The thing to remember is that there is such a thing as compatibility. With compatibility, most marriages succeed. Without compatibility, with no community of interest, a marriage is "doomed to failure!"

As with man and wife, so with man or woman and business. Just as a person seeks the congenial mate, he seeks the business he can get along with, too. He has to consider the opportunity from all "angles." Does he like the business? Is there "room" for that product or service in his area? How much of an investment is required? Can he afford it? Even if he can pay the price, does it offer reasonable assurances of the kind of future income he needs?

What about the franchisor? Does he command respect—both as a person and as a businessman? Can you find enduring compatibility in his business, under his guidance? How well have others fared under similar circumstances? Contact other franchisees—get their opinions.

This chapter contains a self-evaluation chart to help you consider the franchise proposition as it relates to YOU. Your own particular compatibility is all-important. The fact that somebody else is "making a fortune" with the same deal doesn't mean that *YOU* are going to do similarly. On the other hand, if there exists genuine compatibility between you and the particular business, it is quite possible that you will do even better at it than the next person.

Consider that you may have to adjust yourself to a new way of life. You'll probably have to forget all about eight-hour days. You may have to live on less money for a while—perhaps for a year or two—until you've got your new business firmly established. Your wife may have to work alongside you and be your partner in business as well as in life. Can she do it and will she do it?

QUESTION	*YES*	*NO*
Can I handle the financial requirements of the franchise without undue strain?	☐	☐
Am I well-equipped from emotional, mental and experience standpoints?	☐	☐
Is there a realistic enduring need for this business in my area?	☐	☐
How well does this type of business (and the specific franchisor) rate with such community agencies as the Better Business Bureau, Chamber of Commerce, and with banks?	☐	☐
How good are my chances for meeting proposed sales quotas?	☐	☐
Are my qualifications sufficient for promoting this business properly?	☐	☐

QUESTION	YES	NO
Has there been a good percentage of success among franchisees of this company?	☐	☐
Does my wife approve of this venture?	☐	☐
Can I expect the help and cooperation of my wife in this business?	☐	☐
Have I a good chance to meet local competition successfully?	☐	☐
Is the company's national standing in the field good?	☐	☐
Does the franchisor offer a good course of training?	☐	☐
Is the franchisor equipped to give me proper backing?	☐	☐
Is there a good potential for success in the territory offered me?	☐	☐
Does the company offer a good advertising program?	☐	☐
Has the prospective franchisor's interest in me been genuine and sincere?	☐	☐
Is there a good chance of attaining the income I require?	☐	☐
Does the contract offer me sufficient time in which to become established and make a success?	☐	☐
Does my lawyer consider the contract adequate as to safeguards and protection of my interests?	☐	☐
Are the obligations placed on me fair and reasonable?	☐	☐
Do I possess the energy and initiative necessary to run this business?	☐	☐

There are 21 questions above. Figuring 10 points for each "Yes," the maximum score is 210. If you cannot achieve a score of at least 140 points, you had better not proceed with the particular franchise you are considering.

JUDGING FRANCHISE FEASIBILITY

The *16-Point Feasibility Criteria* described below contains suggested "guidelines" to consider in evaluating and selecting a franchise business.

Criteria No. 1. *The Franchise Organization:* is the present operation successful? Can the product or services generate adequate earnings? Bear in mind that in buying a franchise you are buying a *pre-proven* success "formula" and the ability of the franchisor to project this formula to you to help achieve success in your proposed trading area.

Criteria No. 2. *Is There Assurance of Business Continuity?* The parent company represents the trunk of a tree, the franchisees the various branches. If the trunk withers and decays, so will the branches. Make sure that the business has "enduring" qualities. Products and services based on temporary "fads" (for example, trampolines) or temporary impulse-demand products (such as CB radios), may produce spectacular short-term profits but not long-term income.

Criteria No. 3. *What is Franchisor's Financial Position?* Ample finances—exceeding franchisee investments—are needed to sustain a franchise program. Assess the financial strength of the franchisor through Dun and Bradstreet and other financial services. An under-capitalized franchisor cannot provide assurance of franchise program continuity.

Criteria No. 4. *Can Franchisor's Production Facilities Meet Your Sales Needs?* Is franchisor adequately equipped to fill your orders promptly? One of the things that can nullify franchise sales efforts and devastate morale is insufficient production. This can result in damaging delays and increased expense. Check out the franchisor's business fulfillment capabilities.

Criteria No. 5. *Does the Franchisor Have Sufficient Personnel?* Does he have the depth of personnel required to implement a franchise program? Or is he "short-staffed" with everyone too busy handling existing work to devote adequate attention to franchisee needs. The franchisor requires an in-depth Table of Organization.

Criteria No. 6. *Analyze Your Products or Services;* are they "positioned"? Do they fill a needed "niche" in the industry? Are they distinctive, differing from other related products—whether in packaging, merchandising, servicing or structure?

"Wendy's"—a hamburger chain—is an example of a company that succeeded because it "positioned" itself between McDonald's and Burger King by offering a "fresh and juicy" hamburger, rather than pre-frozen meat hamburgers. They also introduced a drive-through window.

Criteria No. 7. *What is the Recurrent Sales Factor?* Do your products or services generate "repetitive" needs which can assure repeat patronage? A "one-time sale" item is incompatible with the franchise concept of continuous business growth.

Criteria No. 8. *Is Your Profit Margin Attractive?* Is the profit margin high enough to support a desirable living style for you? This is extremely important because a business that yields a bare-subsistence living style is a business that lacks economic justification.

Criteria No. 9. *Is the Business Too Technical for You to Learn?* The business should be "learnable" even though you have had little or no experience in that particular field. Perhaps the training is at fault. Curiously, it has been found that a franchisee who had non-related business experience is more easily trained and is more likely to succeed, than one who has had extensive experience in that specific field.

Criteria No. 10. *Does the Product Require Installation?* If so, can needed installation work be economically sub-contracted to local labor? Or, conversely, must you stop all further selling—and earning more money— and attend to the product installation yourself?

Criteria No. 11. *Are Freight Costs a Factor?* Does the product involve the shipment of heavy, bulky items? Will freight charges add to costs and make the product non-competitive in this particular market? Weigh this factor carefully.

Criteria No. 12. *Is There a Sound Financing Plan?* In most operations, financing generally attaches to all or some of these factors:

(a) Land

(b) Structure

(c) Equipment

(d) Inventory

(e) Modernization

Financing is generally accomplished by means of one or any combination of the following methods:

(a) The Franchisor—financing the structure, lease or inventories.

(b) The Lessor—in many instances he will subordinate his land and build to suit. Builders and contractors will also build to suit, based on a certain rent yield.

(c) Local Banks—generally know the parent company and the potential of a particular franchise program in their trading area and, if attractive, they may be inclined to offer favorable loan terms.

(d) *Governmental Lending Sources* include Small Business Administration, Federal Housing Authority, and the Department of Housing and Urban Development, to name a few. Such loans have been minimal in recent years because of the limited availability of funds but may "open up" again soon.

(e) *"Disadvantaged" Financing Sources* are available under various government programs designed to put "disadvantaged" minority groups into business. The MESBIC program, an anacronym for Minority Enterprise Small Business Investment Company, operates through private small business investment corporations which are financed by a combination of government and private capital. Objective of this program is to finance worthy business ventures where 51% of the enterprise is held by a "disadvantaged" group member—socially, ethically, physically, or economically "disadvantaged."

Criteria No. 13. *How is the Franchise Fee Structured?* It should be priced to reimburse franchisor's costs incurred for establishing you as a franchisee in his business and putting you into a successful position. The franchise fee, in other words, should cover "value received" by you, the franchisee. The large profits that the franchisor seeks (and is justified in receiving) should result from his continuing efforts on your behalf and from the increasing number of franchisees included in the program.

Criteria No. 14. *How Good are the Training Facilities?* There should be ample initial training (both in-house and in the field) followed by "refresher" training (approximately 6 months later). Most important, there should be a comprehensive Operations Manual to serve as a primary training guide.

Criteria No. 15. *Your Franchise Agreement,* is it "top heavy" with negatives? Does it stress a preponderance of things you can't do and few things that you can do? The agreement is often a reflection of the franchisor. Does it convey basic "fairness" or "unfairness" in his views towards the franchisee? It can also provide clues as to the "comfortableness" and pleasantness of the prospective business association.

Criteria No. 16. *Your Franchisor's Philosophy.* This is an intangible, yet we consider it most important. Are his views as a franchisor short-range or long-range? Is it a matter of how much "front money" he can extract from franchisees? How much "geography" he can "cut up?" Or,is it how many *successful franchisees* can be established within a reasonable period? The high profits a franchisor seeks should be attainable as a result of the multiplicity of successful franchisees he has helped to create.

SPECIFIC FACTS TO EXPLORE ABOUT THE FRANCHISOR

AND THE FRANCHISE BUSINESS

Who Is The Franchisor?

If the franchisor is well known, has a good reputation, and has a successful franchising operation, you can, naturally, proceed with confidence.

You should find out everything you can about the operation including:

1. number of years it has existed;

2. whether the franchisor has the successful franchisees he claims;

3. whether he has a reputation for honesty and fair dealing with his franchisees.

A personal contact with franchisees is an excellent way to learn about the franchisor. Obtain the names and addresses of a representative number of franchisees in the particular area in which you are interested, travel to see them and learn all aspects of their operation.

Take the opportunity to view samples of the franchise products or services, equipment, advertising materials, etc., and to obtain profit data and other pertinent information about the operation.

Beware of a franchisor who will not give you the names and addresses of his franchisees freely!

Consult Dun and Bradstreet and the Better Business Bureau to learn the financial standing and business reputation of the franchisor.

Sometimes, a dishonest promoter will deceptively use a franchise name and trademark that is similar to that of a well-known franchisor. Be certain you deal with the particular franchise organization you are interested in and that the individual representing this franchise has authority to act on its behalf.

Be skeptical of franchisors whose major activity is the sales of franchises and whose profit is primarily derived from these sales or from the sale of franchise equipment or services. This may be the "tip-off" to an unscrupulous operator.

The Franchise Commodity

You should determine the length of time the commodity or service has been marketed and if it is a successful promotion. Is it a proven product or service, and not a "gimmick?"

Decide whether you are genuinely interested in selling the commodity or service. Be skeptical of items which are untested in the marketplace. For future market potential decide whether the commodity or service is a staple, luxury, or "fad" item.

If a product or service is involved, be certain it is safe, that it meets existing quality standards and there are no restrictions upon its use. Is the product or service protected by a patent? Does it have liability insurance? Will the same protection be afforded to you, as the franchisee?

If the product is to be manufactured by someone other than yourself, identify the manufacturer and learn how your cost for the item will be established. If a guarantee is involved, determine your responsibilities and obligations as the franchisee.

Under the franchise agreement, will you be compelled to sell any new products or services which may be introduced by the franchisor after you have opened the business? Will you be permitted to sell products and services other than the franchise commodities, at a future date?

The Franchise Cost

Find out the total cost of the franchise. The franchise promotion may only refer to the cash outlay needed to purchase the franchise with no mention made that it is only a down payment and other charges and assessments may be levied against you to operate the franchise.

If other monies are involved, how is the balance to be financed? How much will the interest be? Establish what the down payment is purchasing. Is it a franchise fee? Or does it purchase any equity interest?

Where do you purchase equipment and fixtures necessary for opening the business?

Franchisors often attempt to secure income on a continuing basis through the sale of supplies to their franchisees. If this is part of the proposed agreement, how will the price of these supplies be established? What assurance do you have that the prices will be reasonable and competitive? The franchise agreement cannot prohibit you from purchasing equal quality supplies from another source at a lower price.

Franchisors also charge franchisees royalties based upon a percentage of gross sales on a continuing basis; in some instances, franchisors assess franchisees an additional percentage of gross sales to cover advertising costs.

Think of franchise costs in the light of your financial position. Consider the operating capital you will need to get the business going and to sustain it during the months when profits are small and expenses high.

What Profits Can Be Expected?

Many franchise arrangements provide excellent income-producing opportunities but not all yield the fantastic profits promised. Many produce less profits than represented.

Since "profits" are the overriding motive for entering a franchise business, don't accept the promoter's word. Verify the profits for accuracy. Ask to see certified profit figures of franchisees who operate on a level of activity on which you expect to operate. Utilize personal contact with franchisees, quiz them regarding their financial status and evaluate their profit figures in the light of the territory and size of operation you have under consideration.

Training and Management Assistance

Most franchisors promise to train their franchisees. The type and extent of training varies.

Inexperience and lack of training can produce disappointing results. Clearly understand the specific nature of the training.

1. Will the training include more than a manual of instructions or hearing lectures?

2. What is the length of the training and where do you go to receive it?

3. Who will pay your expenses for the training?

4. Will the training include an opportunity to observe and work with a successful franchisee for a period of time?

5. Do you believe that after taking the training you will be capable of operating the franchise successfully?

6. Will the franchisor furnish management assistance after the business is established?

Describe their assistance in detail in your contract. If advertising aid is promised, will it be in the form of handbills, brochures, signs, radio, TV, or newspaper advertising?

If you are required to furnish money for a franchisor-sponsored advertising program what advertising benefits can you anticipate and at what dollar cost?

Some franchisors promise management assistance with periodic visits by the supervisory personnel of the franchisor. Find out the specific nature of assistance, the frequency of visits, and whether they will be available in time of crisis or when unusual problems arise.

The Franchise Territory

This a critical factor in evaluating a prospective venture. Here are some good questions to ask:

1. Do you have a choice of territories?

2. What specific territory is being offered?

3. Is it clearly defined?

4. What is its potential?

5. What competition will you meet in marketing the commodity today? Five years from now?

6. Has a market survey been made of the area?

7. Who prepared it? Ask for a copy and read it carefully.

8. What assurance is given that your territory is an exclusive one?

9. Are you protected from the franchisor selling additional franchises in your territory at a later date?

10. Does the contract allow you to open other outlets in your territory, or another territory, at a future date?

11. Has the business site in the territory been selected? If not, how will this be done?

Termination, Transfer or Renewal of Franchise Agreement

Some termination provisions can cause unexpected and sometimes severe financial loss to a franchisee.

Franchise agreements may provide that at the end of, or during, the contract term, if in the opinion of the franchisor, certain conditions have not been met, the franchisor has the right to terminate the agreement.

The contract generally provides the franchisor with an option to repurchase the franchise. Under these circumstances, if the contract does not provide a means whereby a fair market price for the franchise can be established, the franchisor could repurchase the business at a low and unfair price.

On occasion, franchisors include a provision in the agreement that the repurchase price will not exceed the original franchise fee. This means that a franchisee who spends considerable effort and money building the business could be faced with selling it back at the price he paid for it.

Does the contract give the franchisor the right of cancellation for almost any reason or must there be a "good cause"? Beware of contracts which, under the threat of cancellation, impose unreasonable obligations such as a minimum monthly purchase of goods or services from the franchisor or unrealistic sales quotas.

Understand the conditions under which the agreement could be terminated and your rights in the event of termination.

Keep these points in mind:

1. How will the value of the franchise be determined in the event of termination?

2. How can you terminate the agreement and what would it cost you?

3. Does the contract contain a provision that would prohibit you from engaging in a competitive business in the franchise territory in the event termination occurs?

Have a clear understanding of contract provisions dealing with your ability to transfer, sell, or renew the franchise.

What would happen to the franchise in the event of your death?

Some reputable franchisors provide for an arbitration clause which allows for a fair evaluation of the franchisee's contribution in the event of termination. Under this agreement, the franchisee would recoup his initial investment or make a profit.

Franchise and a Personality Name

When a "name" personality is connected with a franchise consider his participation in the business. Is he a figurehead with no capital investment? Will he make contributions of time and effort to promote the business? What guarantees do you have that he will make appearances at your business? Does he have a name of lasting value in identifying your franchise with the public? How sound is the franchise operation without the prominent name?

Promoter Selling Distributorships

Be wary of promoters who primarily sell distributorships for some "new wonder product." Exaggerated promises are common in these promotions. In this promotion plan, the distributors solicit sub-distributors and salespeople to sell the product from door-to-door. The idea is that a large portion of the distributor's profits will come from a percentage of the sub-distributor's sales. Unfortunately, some distributors and sub-distributors find that after making sizable investments of money, time and effort, there is little profit and they hold a large stock of unsalable products.

5.

18 THINGS YOU CAN EXPECT A FRANCHISOR TO DO FOR YOU — 7 THINGS YOU MUST DO FOR YOURSELF

Remember the saying, think not what your country will do for you, rather what you can do for your country. Similarly, the franchisee, on one hand, should ask and is entitled to know, what the franchisor can do for him. Secondly, however, the franchisee must also ask himself what it is that he, as the franchisee, can do to insure the success of the enterprise into which he is stepping.

Obviously, in associating himself with an organization on a franchise basis, the franchisee is drawing on the strength and resources of the parent organization. Accordingly, he has a perfect right to expect certain things. By the same token, the franchisee should not expect to have the company do everything for him. It is essential that the franchisee contribute generously and unstintingly of his own talents and capacities as well, if he wishes to make a success of the "combined" venture.

As to what can and should be expected of the parent company, there follows a listing of some of the things which, if properly accepted and utilized, can do much to insure success.

First—and a basic and absolutely essential element—is the important item of HOME OFFICE TRAINING. This course of training may take anywhere from 3 to 30 days, depending on the complexity of the franchise operation and the variety of subjects in which the franchisee needs teaching.

Next in line is the matter of FIELD TRAINING. This generally embraces actual on-site sales experience. Customarily this training is given by one of the company's executives, probably a specialized Home Office trainer. Or, it may be conducted by a successful franchisee who can give the new franchisee-recruit the benefit of a veteran's experience. Besides, there is usually a period of RE-TRAINING. Ordinarily this re-training commences some 60 days after the franchisee has actually started in business. This gives the franchisee the opportunity to "fill-in" on training omissions . . . to ask about and get the answers to specific problems which may already have arisen. Also it gives the franchisee an opportunity to correct any "false" starts.

Among other things the franchisee should expect from the parent company or Home Office are the following:

REGIONAL SALES CLINICS—conducted at varying periods. This enables franchisees from various regions to gather together for an exchange of viewpoints and selling ideas . . . and to "air" common problems and to seek their solution.

PROMOTIONAL TOOLS—Most franchise organizations have available and provide their franchisees with pre-tested, proven sales promotional "tools." As a rule these include descriptive brochures, presentation booklets, sales manuals, direct mail material, "door-opening" plans, and similar material. Their purpose is to aid the franchisee in prospecting, in attracting the prospect's attention, in building his interest and then, in closing the sale.

Also to be expected is continuous advice from the Home Office, which should include product information and technical and sales advice, to follow up and review previous training, as well as to help the franchisee handle any new and special problems that may arise. Frequently, in this area of assistance one finds "trouble-shooters" who are expressly trained to help individual franchisees cope with and overcome vexing problems.

The company interested in "building up" its franchisees usually sends out periodic house organs and occasional "flash" bulletins to advise on current and recurring subjects and special situations. The house organs, generally, not only carry important suggestions from the executive departments but also present an interchange of news, views and ideas from the various franchisees.

So much, for the time being, of what the franchisee can expect from the franchisor. Now let's discuss what should *not* be expected from the franchisor.

The franchisee must not expect the Home Office to run his local organization for him. He must recognize that the basic idea of the franchise is to make him "his own boss" and that he, himself, must assume responsibility for developing systematic, business-like habits and conducting business on a methodical day-by-day basis.

The franchisee should not and cannot expect the parent company to *guarantee* his success. Even a franchise with the biggest success potential can prove to be a failure for the franchisee who does not "apply" himself with proper dedication, devotion, intelligence and energy. At the same time, it often happens that an operation with little likelihood for success *does* succeed when the franchisee applies himself with diligence, initiative and zeal.

He cannot count on the Home Office to keep "on top of him," constantly, and to "drive" him into going after business. He must do this on his own initiative and cultivate the habit of perseverance and persistence.

The franchisee should not expect the parent company to impart information to him by "thought waves," "hypnosis" or other magic process. Whatever material and literature the company supplies, he, the franchisee, must read, study and absorb and then put to use in the most effective way.

He cannot expect the company to do his selling for him. Using all available material and drawing on his own experience, he should carefully prepare his sales "story" attuned to his personality. He should then recite it over and over again, aloud—perhaps into a tape-recording machine—and then listen to it several times in order to eliminate any flaws. Even after that, he should try his "talk" on his friends and neighbors.

Upon selecting the appropriate franchise, he must decide (regardless of what the company tells him) that this is a business he will like and enjoy. If he likes what he is doing, his chances for success are immediately enhanced. He will then apply himself enthusiastically and diligently to his tasks and create an "air" of confidence and exuberance that will transmit itself to his staff and to his prospective customers with beneficial results.

If both the franchisee and the franchisor recognize that theirs is a "two-way street," and cooperate unstintingly with one another, then they are well on the way to success. They should both recognize that theirs is a common "destiny"—that they must constantly work together in order to achieve the success they both earnestly desire.

To Sum Up: 18 Things You Can Expect a Franchisor To Do for You
7 Things You Must Do for Yourself

18 Things a Franchisor Should Do for You

1. Train you thoroughly, so that you become familiar, in every way, with the operation of your business.

2. Give you continuing guidance.

3. Provide regional sales clinics.

4. Provide pre-tested promotional tools.

5. Provide initial and continuing field training.

6. Provide periodic re-training.

7. Give you benefit of house organs, instruction bulletins and "Flash" bulletins.

8. Assist in designing and structuring the physical aspects of your operation—whether store, office or institution.

9. Provide financing advice, as related to your franchise business.

10. Provide assistance in site selection and lease negotiation.

11. Chart all pertinent administrative procedures, assuring the smooth flow of your business.

.12. Provide a co-ordinated national advertising program.

13. Provide publicity and public relations.

14. Give you continuing advice on inventory and inventory control.

15. Provide a "grand opening" program—one that gives you a quick, favorable "image projection" in your area.

16. Supply a constant flow of new ideas, to help set a dynamic tone to your business and to assure its continuing success.

17. Provide recommendations of supply sources usually enabling you to achieve significant operating economies.

18. Provide continual "trouble-shooting" to help eliminate problems.

7 Things You Must Do for Yourself

1. Motivate and dedicate yourself.

2. Study materials and instructions supplied to you by the franchisor

3. Establish a proper community "image"—achieving the trust and liking of people in your area.

4. Establish a proper customer "image"—achieving the respect and patronage of your customers to the extent that they will keep buying from you and refer other customers to you.

5. Obtain helpful publicity on a local level

6. Perfect your sales approach to conform to the needs of *your* customers in your *area*.

7. Follow all precepts and procedures set forth by the company.

6.

YOUR FRANCHISE AGREEMENT — SOME TIPS BEFORE SIGNING

This chapter concerns that *moment when* you have concluded your investigations, have carefully checked references and "case histories" of other franchisees and have arrived at the momentous decision that this is, precisely, the business you want to get into. You are now ready to sign the contract.

However, before you put your signature on that paper, stop and think! Are there any potential "danger spots?" Remember that signing a contract is like taking the marriage vows. There is a finality about it and once you have signed on the "dotted line," your status is one that is quite permanent and not easy to change.

Certainly, the act of signing is, in itself, simple enough. Writing out your own name in your own handwriting takes little time and virtually no effort. Yet this one little act may embody your lifetime ambitions . . . signal your transition from one career to another . . . perhaps entail your lifetime savings. Also it may mean a drastic departure from your past way of doing things and the beginning of an entirely new way of life.

Please remember (and I say this sincerely and advisedly) that the majority of franchise operations are basically honorable. At this moment of decision, your preliminary investigation has, no doubt, already confirmed its honesty and validity. Our "cautions" in this chapter simply bear on those few instances where there might be a difference between what the prospective franchisee *thinks* he will be getting and what he *actually* is going to get.

Frankly, any franchise contract has two basic purposes. The first is to serve as documentation, to all concerned, of the terms of the agreement and a comparison between claims and commitments. Second, it serves as a protection to all concerned parties and establishes a firm basis for all operations and the resolution of any possible future disagreements or disputes.

A contract, of course, is a binding legal instrument. It is vital, therefore, that before signing you obtain professional, competent legal advice. As a layman, you may not recognize terminology that might in effect cancel out a good portion of the contractual benefits you expect to receive.

While on the subject, it might be a good idea to discuss the extent to which you should depend on your lawyer and the extent to which you should not. By all means, heed carefully your attorney's advice in every respect *where legal matters are concerned.* However, when it comes to matters *pertaining to the franchise opportunity itself* depend on your own good judgment. After all, no one knows better than you what your own innate capacities really are. Only you know your innermost aspirations . . . your own potential and capacities, as far as the particular franchise proposition is concerned. No one else can be depended upon to advise you at this point. In this respect you must be the sole judge. The points which follow require most careful analysis and serious consideration:

PARAGRAPH TITLES OF

BASIC PROVISIONS CONTAINED IN MANY

FRANCHISE AGREEMENTS

1. Introduction

2. Definitions, as used

3. Intent of agreement: duration of agreement

4. Licensor representations and warranties

5. Representations of licensees

6. Obligations and duties of company

7. Obligations and duties of licensee

8. Description of property to be licensed

9. Location of property

10. Building alterations

11. Terms of license, fees and costs

  (a) initial

  (b) renewal

12. Trade name and trade marks

13. Use of property

14. Hours of operation

15. Lease

16. Leasehold improvements

17. Fixtures, signs and equipment

18. Termination, severability of license

19. Transfer of license

20. Abandonment or surrender of license

21. Severability

22. Licensor withdrawal from retail business

FRANCHISE AGREEMENTS ANALYZED

This chapter contains specimen franchise agreements representing five different types of franchise operations, as follows:

  1. A service-type franchise (General Business Services, Inc.)

  2. An office-type franchise (Edu-Center, Inc.)

  3. A restaurant-type franchise (Sir Pizza International)

  4. A retail-business franchise (Ben Franklin)

  5. A sales-type franchise (Groutlock Corp., Canton, Ohio)

You will note, in the instance of Sir Pizza, the existence of two types of franchise offerings: 1. *Commissary franchise;* 2. *Store franchise.* For your clarification, the commissary franchise constitutes, in effect, a "prototype" of the franchisor's own operation, projected regionally. This commissary franchisee functions as a "supplier" for retail franchisees within his designated area. Since this type of dual franchise operation is characteristic of many types of franchise offerings, we are including both in this chapter.

In studying these franchise agreements, you will note the following common factors:

1. Protected territory

2. Performance quota designation (usually set at a conservative figure—one that is readily attainable by the franchisee). Failure to meet this quota may act to nullify the franchise agreement.

3. Generally, there is allowance for a "grace" period for the franchisee to "get established" before his quota performance commences (usually three months).

4. A clear stipulation of materials and services that the franchisor commits himself to give to the franchisee.

5. A similarly clear listing of the conditions and performance governing the franchisee's committment to the franchisor.

6. "Assignable rights" of the agreement by the franchisee, wherein permission to assign or sell will not be "unreasonably withheld" by the franchisor.

The franchisee, in analyzing the agreement, should take the following things into consideration:

1. Is the performance quota realistically attainable?

2. Does the contract provide for indefinite continuity of the franchise, provided its provisions are adhered to?

3. Does it allow ample territory, enabling the franchisee to achieve adequate earnings?

4. Does it stipulate receipt of varied materials and services conforming to the original sales representation?

5. Does it stipulate franchise "package" and royalty payments, in conformance with original representations?

In assessing a franchise agreement, first of all consider its general "fairness." Does the franchisor strive to incorporate provisions that basically help rather than hinder your business progress? In connection with this, consider the franchisor's point of view: it is important for the protection of himself and other franchisees that you are subject to basic, reasonable "controls," clearly specified.

Are you definitely the "entrepreneur" you should be, as a franchisee? Or are there clauses which may over-restrict you, and nullify your rights and prerogatives, thereby placing you in the role of an employed "wage earner" instead of that of a franchisee?

7.

SAMPLE CONTRACTS

Relative to the franchise contract examples contained herein, it should be understood that they are intended to provide ideas as to general copy, style, and format. They are not intended in any way to claim conformance to pertinent legalities, to state and federal regulations, etc. It is imperative that you consult legal counsel relative to preparation of your own planned franchise agreements.

Ben Franklin Franchise Agreement
    Schedule A

Exclusive Franchise Agreement
    Groutlock Corporation

Franchise Agreement
    Edu-Center, Inc.

Store Franchise Agreement
    Sir Pizza International, Inc.
        Schedule A

Commissary Franchise Agreement
    Sir Pizza International, Inc.
        Schedule A
        Appointment of Area Director
        Addendum *#1—Territory, 2—Subscriber Materials, 3—General Business Services Price List, 4—Operating and Advertising Supplies.*

BEN FRANKLIN
FRANCHISE AGREEMENT

THIS AGREEMENT, made this_____day of_____
19___, by and between CITY PRODUCTS CORPORATION, an Ohio corporation,
having its principal place of business at 1700 South Wolf Road, Des Plaines, Illinois.

(hereinafter called the "Distributor"), and_____

of_____(hereinafter called the "Owner").

WITNESSETH:

WHEREAS, Distributor is engaged in the business of distributing merchandise to merchants who own and operate retail variety stores, and out of its knowledge and experience gained through many years has developed a merchandising and store operating and service program, known as and designated *The Ben Franklin System*, which it offers to such stores as meet the standards required by Distributor; and

WHEREAS, in connection with such merchandising and store operating and service program, Distributor is the owner of the mark "BEN FRANKLIN" registered in the United States Patent Office and under the laws of various states;

WHEREAS, the Owner desires to avail himself of the advantage of the aforesaid retail system in his store at_____
(STREET)

_____, _____,
(CITY)   (STATE)

which system consists of a complete retail operating and promotional service and selected basic stock lists of merchandise for Ben Franklin Stores:

NOW, THEREFORE, in consideration of the foregoing and of the mutual covenants and agreements hereinafter contained, the parties hereto agree as follows:

1 The Distributor agrees to furnish to the Owner for use in his store the merchandising services outlined above known as the Ben Franklin System of Variety type Retail Store Operation. The Owner agrees to receive such services and follow the practices prescribed thereby in the operation of his store as a Ben Franklin Variety type Retail Store to the best of his ability as long as this agreement shall remain in force.

2 Distributor agrees to furnish the Owner for use in his store basic stock lists of merchandise to be known as the merchandise check list and through supplemental and seasonal check lists to keep it adjusted to conditions, markets and consumer demand. Distributor will also supply general listings of other merchandise which may be desired by the Owner to supplement the basic stock merchandise to be carried by the Owner.

Distributor agrees that said lists at all times during the term of this agreement will be sufficiently complete in its judgment for the successful operation of a modern efficient Ben Franklin Retail Store as contemplated by this agreement. Prices, terms of payment and delivery shall be those quoted by the Distributor from time to time in accordance with its current practices to like stores and the credit standing of the Owner, as to which the Distributor shall be the sole judge.

Owner agrees to purchase merchandise of the type and quality offered by Distributor from time to time pursuant to the aforesaid Ben Franklin Retail System.

3 The Distributor agrees to furnish to the Owner the retail merchandising, operating and promotional services composed of the instructions, aids, materials, and personal services furnished by the Distributor to all Ben Franklin Stores Franchise holders of the class of the Owner herein. Such instructions, aids, materials, and personal services, and the charges therefor, and the extent to which the name "Ben Franklin Stores" may and shall be used by the Owner herein, are set forth and described in substance in Schedule A, attached hereto, which by reference thereto is hereby made a part of this agreement. The said service, and each part thereof and charge therefor, except the extent to which the Owner may and shall use said name "Ben Franklin Stores," may be altered or modified by the Distributor from time to time, in its discretion, to meet changes in conditions affecting the operation of Ben Franklin type Retail Stores, but no such change or modification shall impose any substantially greater financial burden upon the Owner than may be reasonably contemplated at the date hereof, without the Owner's express consent.

The extent to which the name "Ben Franklin Stores" may be used by the Owner, as set forth in Schedule A, shall not be altered or changed during the term of this agreement, or any renewal term, except as provided in said Schedule A, or by mutual agreement of the parties hereto. All of the literature and materials furnished to the Owner by the Distributor in connection with said merchandising services shall be and remain at all times the property of the Distributor, and shall be returned to the Distributor by the Owner within 30 days after termination of this agreement.

4 The Distributor agrees, to the extent specified in Schedule A, that the Owner shall have the right to conduct and advertise the Owner's retail store referred to under the name of "Ben Franklin Stores," and the Owner agrees that he shall conduct and advertise his store under said name, and that he shall not use such name in any way, or to any extent, not so specified in Schedule A.

5 The Owner agrees that so far as practicable his store will be arranged, and his merchandise laid out and displayed in conformity to the standard plans for Ben Franklin Stores and that he will not materially change the physical layout or arrangement without written approval of Distributor.

Owner agrees to a complete relay of the merchandise display and layout, at any time after the first year of the term of this franchise, if the need for such relay is so determined by the Distributor. Distributor agrees to furnish the necessary Store Layout Specialist to plan and supervise this relay work. Owner agrees to reimburse Distributor for these specialized services in accordance with Schedule A, paragraph 4.

 Owner agrees to use the standard Ben Franklin accounting records, or records providing similar information, as approved by Distributor.

a. Where a store becomes newly franchised hereunder, the Owner hereby covenants and agrees to immediately execute the Distributor's regular form contract for the Ben Franklin Mail Accounting Program.

b. If this franchise is issued to an Owner of an existing Ben Franklin Store and if Owner is not currently using the Ben Franklin Mail Accounting Program, Owner hereby covenants and agrees to furnish Distributor on or before the 20th day of each month, the total gross sales for the preceding month during each year of the term of this franchise. Owner further covenants and agrees to furnish Distributor each month, the amount of his ending inventory at sell, if available.

7 It is mutually understood and agreed that the Owner is not the Agent of Distributor for any purpose, and that Owner retains full responsibility for the financing, management and operation of the Owner's store. Owner acknowledges that he may have been given or seen sales forecasts and other projections provided by the Distributor or its employees, either referring to the location covered by this franchise or otherwise, but the Owner hereby stipulates and agrees that neither such materials nor any statement made by the Distributor or any employee thereof is intended to be or shall be deemed to be a representation, warranty, guaranty or indemnity of any nature, regardless of by whom or how asserted, and the Owner agrees that the Distributor shall not be responsible for the results obtained in the operation of said store or liabilities incurred thereby.

8 The Ben Franklin Stores standard sign, and all other signs, insignia, etc. (not including other store fixtures, equipment, and supplies not bearing the name "Ben Franklin Stores" or otherwise exclusively related to the Ben Franklin System of Variety type Retail Store Operation), if the Owner shall have acquired title thereto, shall immediately upon the termination of this agreement, by lapse of time or otherwise, become the sole and exclusive property of the Distributor, and the Distributor agrees to pay the Owner therefor the cost thereof, less depreciation at the rate of ten per cent (10%) per annum, in case of said standard sign; and at the rate of twenty per cent (20%) per annum in the case of all such other signs, insignia, etc.

9 Upon termination of this agreement, whether by lapse of time or otherwise, the Owner agrees that he will promptly remove the Ben Franklin Stores standard sign from said store, and will promptly discontinue the use of all other signs, insignia, etc., relating to or in any way connected with the Ben Franklin System of Variety type Retail Store Operation and that he will within thirty (30) days after such termination return to the Distributor said standard sign and other signs, insignia, etc. (upon payment or tender of payment by the Distributor to the Owner of the depreciated cost thereof as provided in Paragraph 8 hereof), together with all promotional literature, materials, manuals of instruction, Ben Franklin Merchandise Check list, and other literature or materials which may have been delivered to him by the Distributor pursuant to this agreement, all at his own cost and expense.

If owner shall fail or refuse to deliver to Distributor the said standard sign and all other signs and insignia bearing the mark "BEN FRANKLIN" Owner agrees that from and after the date of termination of this Franchise Agreement and until Owner shall so deliver said signs and insignia, that he will pay to Distributor, as rent for the use of the said sign and as a fee for the continued use of the mark and all insignia relating thereto, a monthly rent in the amount of Five Hundred Dollars, payable on the first day of each and every month. In addition to the right to collect the rental herein stipulated during such continued use of the sign and the mark "BEN FRANKLIN," Distributor shall have the right, with or without process of law, to remove and repossess said standard sign and other signs, insignia, etc., and said promotional literature, materials, manuals of instruction, Ben Franklin Merchandise Check List, and other literature or materials delivered to the Owner by the Distributor pursuant to this agreement, and the Distributor shall have the right to enter upon and have free access to the premises of the Owner, with or without process of law, for the purposes aforesaid, and the Owner agrees that he will pay, promptly on demand, all costs and expenses, including reasonable attorney's fees, suffered or incurred by the Distributor in exercising or enforcing any of its rights aforesaid.

 The Owner further agrees that upon termination of this agreement, whether by lapse of time or otherwise, he will not thereafter use the name "Ben Franklin Stores," or any similar name or names, on his store or in his advertising, or on any merchandise or otherwise or will not in any wise infringe upon or attempt to appropriate Distributor's right, title and interest under the registered mark "BEN FRANKLIN."

 The term of this agreement shall be for a period of five (5) years and ____months, beginning_____ , 19____and ending December 31, 19____, subject, nevertheless, to termination upon the following conditions: (a) Either party may at the end of any full calendar year terminate this agreement by giving notice to the other party not less than sixty (60) days before the end of any such full calendar year, and in the event of any such termination by Distributor, Distributor shall not have an option to purchase as hereinafter provided in paragraph 12. (b) Distributor may, at its option, cancel and terminate this franchise at any time upon thirty (30) days' notice if Owner shall become delinquent in the payment of any indebtedness due to Distributor on any account including, without limiting the foregoing, the franchise fee provided for in Schedule A. (c) Distributor may, at its option, cancel and terminate this franchise at any time upon thirty (30) days' notice if Owner shall move its operations under this franchise to any other physical location than that under which he commenced operation under this franchise. (d) This agreement shall terminate automatically if the Owner shall at any time sell or liquidate the Store, or if he shall die.

12 In the event this agreement is terminated upon any of the conditions in paragraph 11 hereof, with the single exception of termination by Distributor under sub-paragraph (a) of Paragraph 11 at the end of any full calendar year, the Distributor shall have the option, within one hundred twenty (120)

days from and after the effective date of such termination or notice thereof to Distributor, whichever is later, to purchase the assets of the Owner's store (including the unexpired term of any lease on the premises in which said business may then be conducted at no additional rent) upon the payment of a price to be computed as follows: (a) Merchandise available through the Ben Franklin System at cost or market price, whichever is lower as determined by physical inventory. Any remaining merchandise not identified with the Ben Franklin System shall be purchased at a negotiated price. (b) Fixtures and equipment at original cost, less ten percent (10%) depreciation per annum from the date of purchase, provided, however, that if under this formula fixtures would be depreciated below fifty percent (50%) of original cost, Distributor and Owner or Owner's personal representative, shall agree upon the fair value for such fixtures and equipment which fair value shall not exceed 50% of original cost.

However, it is agreed that if the heirs of the Owner, upon the death of the Owner, shall be qualified and desire to continue the operation of the business under and pursuant to a similar agreement, and shall within one hundred and twenty (120) days after the death of the Owner enter into such an agreement with Distributor for a period of not less than five (5) years, then Distributor shall not have the option to purchase hereunder.

13 For and in consideration of the services to be rendered by Distributor hereunder, Owner agrees to pay the fees specified on Schedule A attached hereto and the Distributor agrees to make available to the Owner a specific allowance or discount as specified on attached Schedule A in the amounts and for the period designated.

14 Any notice required to be given hereunder shall be given in writing and shall be served by depositing the same in the United States Post Office in a sealed envelope, postage prepaid, addressed, in the case of

the Distributor, to the Distributor at _____

_____

and in the case of the Owner, to the Owner at _____

_____,
to be sent by certified mail, and any such notice shall be deemed to have been served at the time the same was deposited in the United States Post Office as aforesaid.

15 This agreement and all rights hereunder apply only to the retail variety operation in the store building in which the Owner commenced business under this franchise, and not to any retail operation in any other store building whatsoever. This agreement shall inure to the benefit of and be binding upon the successors and assigns of the Distributor, but shall be personal to the Owner, and neither this agreement, nor any right or privilege hereunder, shall be assignable or transferable by voluntary or involuntary action of the Owner or by operation of law.

The execution of this instrument by City Products Corporation shall be binding on said Corporation when it is accomplished by the manual signing hereof by a Vice-President and the Secretary or an Assistant Secretary of City Products Corporation; or by affixing hereto, by any mechanical device, of a facsimile signature purporting to be that of a Vice-President of City Products Corporation and the manual signing hereof by the Secretary or an Assistant Secretary of City Products Corporation; or by the affixing hereto, by any mechanical device, of facsimile signatures purporting to be those of a Vice-President and the Secretary or an Assistant Secretary of City Products Corporation and the manual signing hereof in the place below provided by a person duly authorized by the Board of Directors of City Products Corporation.

IN WITNESS WHEREOF, this Franchise has been duly executed, under seal, on the day and year first above written.

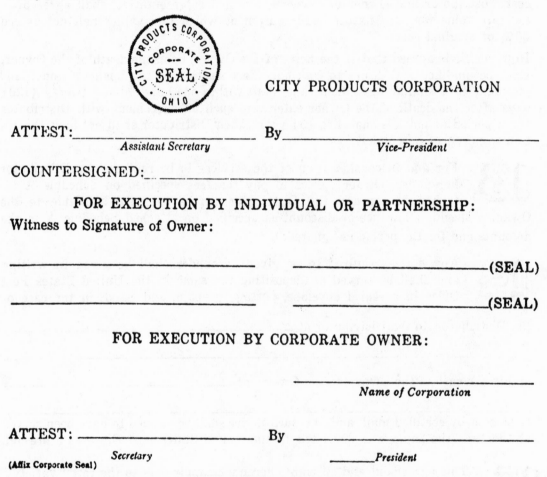

CITY PRODUCTS CORPORATION

ATTEST:_____ By_____
          Assistant Secretary   *Vice-President*

COUNTERSIGNED:_____

FOR EXECUTION BY INDIVIDUAL OR PARTNERSHIP:
Witness to Signature of Owner:

_____   _____(SEAL)

_____   _____(SEAL)

FOR EXECUTION BY CORPORATE OWNER:

_____
                   Name of Corporation

ATTEST: _____ By _____
(Affix Corporate Seal)   *Secretary*   _____*President*

SCHEDULE A

Attached to and by reference made a part of Ben Franklin Franchise Agreement

dated_____ between City Products Corporation

and_____.

 USE OF NAME "BEN FRANKLIN"

(a) Outside sign.

As long as Owner's store shall conform to standard specifications for store front and physical appearance established by Distributor, Owner's store sign shall appear as either:

BEN FRANKLIN

or

5-10 BEN FRANKLIN 5-10

Owner shall at all times disclose his own name and proprietorship by appropriate means approved by Distributor.

Owner shall not change or replace the outside sign without the written approval of the Distributor.

Owner shall maintain, repair or replace outside sign, as deemed adequate for the location, by the Distributor, in the manner and at the time designated by the Distributor.

(b) Interior advertising and displays.

Owner shall display cards, price ticket forms and all other material supplied by the Distributor bearing the name "Ben Franklin Stores."

(c) All other advertising and promotion.

Unless otherwise specifically permitted or prescribed by Distributor in individual instances, Owner shall use all other advertising and promotional material to the same extent and in the same manner as prescribed in subparagraph (a).

RETAIL MERCHANDISING SERVICE TO BE FURNISHED

The retail merchandising service to be furnished by the distributor to the owner currently includes the following:

a. *A Complete Warehouse Service*—one source for all merchandise necessary to operate a store with supplementary factory listings on important lines.

b. *Basic and Seasonal Check Lists* which are also complete merchandise listings and merchandise stock control records . . . with store size classifications on most recommended items.

c. *Detailed Procedures for Operating a Ben Franklin Store*—explanation of field tested methods and systems developed for efficient store operation.

d. *Accounting Manual and Accounting Forms,* comprising a simplified retail accounting system for merchandise and operating records required by variety stores.

e. *Planned Program*—A Monthly Program of Store Management Plans, Promotions, and Displays. Includes standard counter layouts, seasonal features, signs, guidance for sales people—keyed to 6-months promotional calendar.

f. *Sale Plans*—completely coordinated store-wide promotions for major selling seasons. Professional display material, colorful circulars, ad mats included.

g. *Syndicate Merchandise Service*—provides automatic shipments of new goods in trial quantities with reordering information—one of several methods of getting new goods and promotional items to Ben Franklin Stores quickly.

h. *Services of a Retail Operating Man* to explain and interpret all phases of the Ben Franklin program.

i. *Poster Service*—provides chain store type of display material . . . colorful posters, banners, and signs for seasonal events and scheduled promotions—coordinated with Planning Calendar and Planning Profits.

Note: A separate charge will be made for printed forms, supplies, merchandise, and other items furnished to the Owner in paragraphs "d", "f", "g", and "i".

 DISTRIBUTOR STORE COOPERATIVE DISCOUNTS

(a) Distributor will give Owner a special Distributor Store Cooperative Discount, to be payable within ninety (90) days after the end of each calendar year of operation hereunder or upon the date of termination of this franchise (as soon as computation thereof may be made by Distributor), for Owner's purchases (excepting franchise fees or services) during a calendar year, in accordance with the following schedule:

2.0% discount on purchases from Distributor in excess of $10,000 up to $20,000,

2.5% discount on purchases from Distributor in excess of $20,000 up to $35,000,

3.0% discount on purchases from Distributor in excess of $35,000 up to $55,000,

3.5% discount on purchases from Distributor in excess of $55,000 up to $80,000,

4.0% discount on purchases from Distributor in excess of $80,000.

(b) In the event Owner's new store is opened on or before March 31 of a calendar year, credit shall be given on purchases from the Distributor made on or after November 1 of the preceding year.

(c) Should Owner qualify for this franchise by purchasing the assets of an existing store, whether the store is owned by Distributor or not, no Cooperative Discount shall be paid on any purchase of existing assets or previous purchases made by Seller.

PERSONAL SERVICES TO BE FURNISHED

(a) The Distributor's Retail Operating man will call at reasonable intervals to advise the Owner in the professional application of the Ben Franklin program covering operating, merchandising, promotional and record keeping systems. The services of such Retail Operating man will be rendered at such time or times as shall be considered necessary and appropriate in the sole judgment of the Distributor.

(b) Individual consultation may be given either by mail or personally at the offices of the Distributor, on any special problems relating to the operation of the Owner's store on which the Owner desires the advice of the Distributor.

(c) The Distributor maintains a trained staff of Store Layout Specialists, Accounting Specialists, and Lease and Location Specialists, whose services are available to the Owner, upon request, at rates to be mutually agreed upon.

5

For all franchise benefits enumerated in this Schedule or the Franchise Agreement of which it is a part (except any special service provided pursuant to sub-paragraph (c) of this Paragraph 4 of Schedule A and except the separate sub-paragraphs noted in Paragraph 2 of Schedule A), the Owner agrees to pay an annual fee of $, payable in equal monthly installments, during the term of the franchise to which this Schedule A is attached, beginning on the first day of the month nearest the opening day of business or on the first day of the term of this franchise for a store in operation.

EXCLUSIVE FRANCHISE AGREEMENT

GROUTLOCK CORPORATION

A Subsidiary of Stark Ceramics, Inc.

Canton, Ohio 44701

THIS AGREEMENT made in the City of ...., State of .... by and between Groutlock Corporation, ar Ohio corporation organized and existing under the laws of the State of Ohio, with its principal offices located in Canton, Ohio, hereinafter referred to as "COM-PANY", and ....

residing at ....

hereinafter referred to as the "FRANCHISEE", ...

WITNESSETH:

WHEREAS, the COMPANY has developed and protected by patents the GROUTLOCK block and equipment required for manufacture of the GROUTLOCK block; and

WHEREAS, the COMPANY has the exclusive right and power to use the name GROUTLOCK and the Trademarks and logos used in conjunction therewith; and

WHEREAS, the FRANCHISEE desires to make use of the name GROUTLOCK and manufacture and distribute its unique products utilizing the commercial benefits of the name, advertising, promotion and reputation related thereto;

NOW, THEREFORE, in consideration of the sum of One Dollar ($1.00) and other good and valuable consideration, and the covenants herein contained, it is agreed as follows:

1. The COMPANY hereby grants to the FRANCHISEE the exclusive, non-transferable right and license to establish and operate a manufacturing facility and sales agency to be located within the County of .... State of .... and, while this agreement is in force, no other such right and license will be granted to any other FRANCHISEE within the territory as shown in Schedule A hereto.

2. The COMPANY further grants to the FRANCHISEE the following unassignable rights and privileges:

A. Use of the name GROUTLOCK and the GROUTLOCK trademark, logo, signs, etc., in order that the FRANCHISEE may conduct his business under the name of "Groutlock of .... ". However, use of the name GROUTLOCK is not exclusive. FRANCHISEE agrees to cooperate and supply any and all consents and agreements necessary for additional franchisees to operate under the name of GROUTLOCK in the FRANCHISEE'S State of Incorporation, and municipality of operation.

B. To use the COMPANY plan, methods, systems and sales tools in the conduct of the business of GROUTLOCK block manufacture and sales.

C. To purchase from the COMPANY and its authorized sources of supply, all equipment and supplies necessary to produce a GROUTLOCK block wall system or structure and no purchases may be made from other sources without the expressed written permission of the COMPANY, which permission will be given provided standards and qualities are equal or better, as determined by COMPANY. Prices and terms of payment of such equipment and supplies may be varied by COMPANY.

3. The COMPANY shall further provide to the FRANCHISEE:

A. Intensive training in the operation and conduct of his business.

B. Assistance when required in selection of office and showroom space and lease negotiations.

C. Selection and training program for sales and office personnel.

D. Detailed Formal Grand Opening Promotion Kit.

E. Supply of GROUTLOCK Advertising Mats.

F. Supply of GROUTLOCK Direct Mail Materials.

G. Supply of Requisition Forms, Order Forms and Report Forms.

H. Publicity and Promotion Kit.

I. Sales Mate Projector with Documentary Film and Sound Production.

J. Operating Sales Demonstration Kit.

K. GROUTLOCK Confidential Operations Manual.

L. GROUTLOCK Bookkeeping and Tax Records System.

M. Salesmen's Training Course Curriculum.

4. The COMPANY further undertakes to do the following on behalf of the FRANCHISEE:

A. Provide a course of Home Office Training and Field Training with respect to:

1. Manufacturing Methods.
2. Obtaining Prospects.
3. Selling Methods and Procedures.
4. Construction Methods and Procedures.
5. Obtaining Raw Materials.
6. Inventory Control.
7. Employee Recruitment and Training.
8. Sales Management Procedures.
9. Administration of Business.
10. Record Keeping Methods and Procedures.

B. Supply periodic bulletins, reports and memoranda covering trends and developments in all phases of the business.

C. Provide periodic visits to the FRANCHISEE'S location by an executive of the COMPANY and unlimited consultation, advice and information concerning the growth and operation of the FRANCHISEE's business.

D. Organize and sponsor district, regional and national meetings of Franchisees for the dissemination and exchange of ideas, experiences, techniques and developments.

E. Provide assistance as may be deemed necessary by the COMPANY within the provisions of this Agreement.

5. In consideration of all of the foregoing rights and privileges and the issuance of this franchise, FRANCHISEE agrees to pay to COMPANY:

A. A franchise fee of $10,000.00, receipt of which is hereby acknowledged.

B. A royalty fee of 2c for each block manufactured and sold, or 5% of the total gross sales or revenues derived from the sale of blocks manufactured, whichever shall be larger. This royalty payment must be received by the COMPANY no later than the 10th of each month for the sales made during the month immediately preceding.

6. In consideration for the equipment, tools and office furniture to be furnished and sold to FRANCHISEE by COMPANY per Schedule B attached hereto, the FRANCHISEE shall pay $ .... to COMPANY as follows:

A. Within ten days following receipt by the FRANCHISEE of a countersigned copy or this Agreement $ ....

B. Balance upon delivery of equipment $ ....

7. In the event the FRANCHISEE has signed a Lease Agreement with COMPANY for equipment, tools and office furniture dated ...., 19...., FRANCHISEE agrees that said Agreement shall be a prerequisite to this Franchise Agreement and is incorporated by reference with this Agreement. In consideration for the equipment, tools and office furniture to be furnished by COMPANY under such Lease Agreement, FRANCHISEE shall pay an advanced rental of $............ and make succeeding rental payments after delivery of such equipment under the terms of the Lease Agreement. The Lease Agreement is a separate and independent contract, except that this Agreement may be canceled by COMPANY if FRANCHISEE is in default of any obligation under the terms of the Lease Agreement or if that Agreement is terminated by FRANCHISEE.

8. The FRANCHISEE agrees:

A. That he will, at his own cost and expense, make all necessary improvements to his premises for the construction and establishment of his plant, showroom, offices and warehouse facilities in order to meet the minimum standards as set forth in the Confidential Operations Manual. If such premises shall be leased by FRANCHISEE from a third party, such lease shall be submitted to COMPANY for examination. If such lease is not satisfactory to COMPANY, COMPANY shall have the right to terminate this Agreement. Upon approval of such lease by COMPANY, no amendment or assignment or sub-lease shall be made or entered into by FRANCHISEE without the written approval of COMPANY.

B. That he will construct and equip his plant, showroom, offices and warehouse facilities in accordance with a plan and layout provided by COMPANY. Said facilities are to be used exclusively for the manufacture, storage and sale of GROUTLOCK products and services.

9. The FRANCHISEE further agrees:

A. That promptly following completion of the construction and installment of equipment described in paragraph 8.B, and continuing through the remainder of this Agreement, FRANCHISEE shall continuously operate a GROUTLOCK block manufacturing and service facility (except if prevented by Act of God or other cause beyond the control of FRANCHISEE), devoting FRANCHISEE's best and exclusive efforts, skills and diligence to the conduct of the business of manufacturing, selling and distributing GROUTLOCK block products and services, and that he will not manufacture, distribute or sell products competing with, or which could be confused with, GROUTLOCK block products.

B. That he will promote sales and construction activities within his franchised territory and maintain an adequate and properly trained staff.

C. That he will advertise regularly in his territory, in such media as will acquaint the public of his services. The COMPANY has the right to require the FRANCHISEE to expend annually for advertising an amount equal to two per cent (2%) of his gross sales from his Operations; that the advertisements used will be only those supplied by or approved by the COMPANY; that the tear sheets and copies of all paid invoices for advertising will be submitted to the COMPANY immediately after the last day of each month.

D. That he will manufacture a minimum of 200,000 GROUTLOCK blocks during each calendar quarter; provided, however, that such minimum requirement shall not apply to the first ninety (90) days after manufacturing operations begin.

10. It is agreed that all advertising material, promotional material, signs, forms, and all other documents furnished to the FRANCHISEE by the COMPANY shall not be used for any purpose other than to promote the Sale of GROUTLOCK products, nor shall they be copied without prior written permission of the COMPANY.

11. FRANCHISEE further agrees that for the duration of this Agreement, FRANCHISEE will annually furnish to COMPANY, by mail, a copy of Schedule C of FRANCHISEE's individual United States Income Tax Return, or a copy of FRANCHISEE's corporate return, it being understood that such information is necessary for the operation of the Franchise Agreement and will be held confidential by COMPANY.

12. It is agreed that authorized COMPANY personnel shall be permitted to enter upon the premises of FRANCHISEE during regular business hours for the purpose of examining the premises, conferring with the FRANCHISEE and his employees, inspecting and checking products, furniture, fixtures, equipment, operating methods, books and records. The COMPANY shall also have the right and authorization to inspect the installations made by the FRANCHISEE and to require any changes or improvements in such installations in order to have them conform with minimum standards as established by the COMPANY.

13. It is further agreed that FRANCHISEE will promptly advise COMPANY of any developments or improvements made in the method of manufacturing GROUTLOCK block or in methods of application of GROUTLOCK block systems, it being understood that any such development or improvement shall be made available to COMPANY without payment of royalties or fees, and it being further understood that any such developments or improvements made known to COMPANY may be disseminated to all GROUTLOCK block Franchisees without payment of any additional fees or royalties by such Franchisees.

14. The COMPANY and the FRANCHISEE are each independent contractors, and the FRANCHISEE shall not be the agent for the COMPANY in any manner or capacity whatsoever, nor shall either be responsible for the debts, bills or liabilities incurred by the other. The COMPANY's and the FRANCHISEE's interest in each other shall be limited to the purpose set forth herein. The FRANCHISEE shall indemnify and save the COMPANY harmless from or against all claims, demands, costs and expenses in connection with the operation of this Agreement or following therefrom. No partnership, joint venture or relationship of principal and agent is intended.

15. FRANCHISEE further agrees:

A. To procure and maintain in full force and effect a so-called public liability insurance policy or policies protecting FRANCHISEE against any loss, liability or expenses whatsoever from personal injury, death, property damage or otherwise arising or occurring upon or in connection with such premises, or by reason of FRANCHISEE's operation upon, or occupancy of, such premises. Such policy or policies shall be written by a responsible insurance company or companies, satisfactory to COMPANY in an amount not less than $............. The insurance afforded by this policy or policies shall not be limited in any way by reason of insurance maintained by COMPANY. Upon the signing of this Agreement, certificate of insurance showing compliance with the foregoing requirements shall be furnished by FRANCHISEE to COMPANY for approval. Certificates shall state that policy or policies will not be cancelled or altered without ten (10) days prior written notice to COMPANY. Maintenance of such insurance and the performance by FRANCHISEE of the obligation under this paragraph shall not relieve FRANCHISEE of liability under the indemnity agreement set forth in this Agreement.

B. That he shall insure the premises, equipment, furnishings, and fixtures, and any additions thereto, and FRANCHISEE's inventory in accordance with standard fire and extended coverage insurance policies then in effect for similar businesses. FRANCHISEE will make provision for statutory Workmen's Compensation insurance, social security, unemployment insurance, unemployment compensation disability, and will upon request exhibit evidence thereof to the COMPANY.

16. During the term of this Agreement, FRANCHISEE will not, without the consent in writing of COMPANY, mortgage, pledge or otherwise assign as security, or sell, transfer, assign, lease or sublease such premises or any part thereof, or any equipment, furnishings or fixtures located thereon, or any interest which the FRANCHISEE may have in any part thereof.

17. FRANCHISEE shall conduct his business and maintain such premises in strict compliance with all applicable laws, ordinances, regulations, and other requirements of any Federal, State, County, Municipal or other government, and will obtain all necessary permits, licenses or other consents for the operation of his business.

18. Unless previously terminated, as hereinafter provided, this Agreement and the appointment of the FRAN-CHISEE hereunder shall be for an intial term of five (5) years from date hereof, and thereafter this Agreement shall be automatically extended for successive five (5) year terms, provided that the covenants and undertaking assumed by the FRANCHISEE in this Agreement are truly and faithfully performed.

19. COMPANY shall have the option and right to terminate this Agreement by giving ten (10) days written notice to FRANCHISEE by registered mail addressed to FRANCHISEE at his place of business upon the occurrence of any of the following:

A. In the event FRANCHISEE becomes insolvent or is declared bankrupt, or makes an assignment for the benefit of creditors, or in the event that a receiver is appointed or any proceeding is demanded by, for or against FRANCHISEE under any provisions of the Federal Bankruptcy Act or any amendment thereof.

B. In the event FRANCHISEE defaults in the performance of any agreement made hereunder, and such default shall not be remedied to COMPANY's satisfaction within thirty (30) days upon demand.

C. In the event the business of FRANCHISEE is sold, leased or for any reason passes from the actual supervision or control of FRANCHISEE.

D. In the event the FRANCHISEE is a corporation and there is a transfer, sale, exchange or any other disposition of shares of such corporation which results at any time in a change of ownership to a third party of the majority interest of such corporation.

E. In the event that production of GROUTLOCK block produced by the facility is less than 200,000 units during any calendar quarter; provided, however, that such minimum requirement shall not apply to the first ninety (90) days after manufacturing operations begin.

F. In the event that the operation of such business in producing and servicing GROUTLOCK block products and services is not commenced on or before .... , 19.......; provided, however, that this specific right of termination shall not apply if the operation of such business is prevented by act of God or other cause beyond the control of FRANCHISEE.

20. In the event of termination of this Agreement, FRANCHISEE agrees as follows:

A. FRANCHISEE shall surrender all rights and privileges granted under this Agreement and shall cease the use of the trademark in any and all connections, including change of any corporate name using the word "GROUTLOCK".

B. FRANCHISEE will return without delay all material described herein as property of the COMPANY.

C. That COMPANY shall have the option to repurchase from the FRANCHISEE any or all business products and equipment in the possession of the FRANCHISEE at prices paid by the FRANCHISEE less twenty-five per cent (25%), or at its depreciated value according to the books of the FRANCHISEE, whichever is the lesser.

D. Should FRANCHISEE'S premises be leased from a third party, COMPANY shall have the option to sublease such premises. All rights and privileges contained in the original lease shall be transferred to the COMPANY upon exercise of this right.

E. Should FRANCHISEE hold legal title to the premises described herein, COMPANY shall have the option to lease or to buy such premises. FRANCHISEE shall offer to lease and to sell, assign and transfer to COMPANY FRANCHISEE'S entire interest in such premises and all property used in connection therewith. If upon such offer of lease and sale FRANCHISEE and COMPANY are unable to agree as to a purchase price and terms, or to the amount of rents to be paid, a fair price and fair terms or a fair rental amount shall be determined by arbitration as provided by paragraph 23 of this Agreement.

F. The COMPANY shall have the option to retain all rights to the telephone number assigned to the FRANCHISEE, and to such advertising privileges as are concurrent therewith.

21. This Agreement shall be binding upon the respective heirs, assigns, personal representatives and successors of the parties, but no sales, assignment or other transfer may be made without the prior written consent of the COMPANY.

EXCLUSIVE FRANCHISE AGREEMENT

GROUTLOCK CORPORATION

A Subsidiary of
Stark Ceramics, Inc.
Canton, Ohio 44701

© GOES 438

22. This Agreement is divisible, and any provision herein held to be violative of the applicable statutes and varied regulations thereunder of any governmental agency having jurisdiction, such invalidity shall affect the portion in conflict only, and the remaining portions of this Agreement shall remain in effect thereby.

23. This Agreement shall be construed under the laws of the State of Ohio. Any dispute arising out of or concerning this Agreement shall be settled and determined by impartial arbitration in accordance with the rules and regulations then prevailing and in effect of the American Arbitration Association, except that nothing contained therein shall be deemed to deprive the parties of their right to any equitable relief to which they may be otherwise entitled. The decision of the arbitrator shall be binding upon both parties.

24. This Agreement is subject to the approval and confirmation of the COMPANY at its Home Office, and shall not become binding unless and until it is officially countersigned.

25. This instrument contains all of the agreements, representations and conditions made by or between the parties hereto. Neither party shall be liable for any representations made unless set forth herein, and all modifications and amendments hereto must be in writing.

In WITNESS WHEREOF, the parties have signed this Agreement effective the .... day

of ...., 19 ....

WITNESS:

GROUTLOCK CORPORATION

....
                                                 John H. Stewart, Jr., President

FRANCHISEE:

....
Groutlock Selection Manager

FRANCHISE AGREEMENT

EDU-CENTER, INC.

250 West 57 Street
New York, N. Y. 10019

THIS AGREEMENT, MADE IN THE City of ....,
State of ...., by and between EDU-CENTER, INC., with principal
offices located at 250 West 57th Street, New York, N. Y., hereinafter referred to

as the "COMPANY", and ....

....

residing at ....
hereinafter referred to as the "FRANCHISEE".

WHEREAS the COMPANY has obtained from Sight & Sound Education Limited of England the exclusive right and license to promote and develop the use of the Parkes System for touch typing instruction within the United States and Puerto Rico, and

WHEREAS the COMPANY has obtained from Sight & Sound Education Limited of England the exclusive right and license to use and lease instruction machines and apparatus connected therewith, in connection with the system of touch typing referred to above, and

WHEREAS the COMPANY owns and has the exclusive right and power to use the name EDU-CENTER and EDU-CENTERS, and

WHEREAS the COMPANY is desirous of establishing a nationwide group of franchised EDU-CENTERS, utilizing said system and equipment, and

WHEREAS the FRANCHISEE is desirous of establishing a typing center, using the name, system and methods referred to above and to enjoy the commercial benefits related thereto,

NOW, THEREFORE, in consideration of the sum of One Dollar ($1.00) and other good and valuable consideration, and the covenants and conditions herein contained, it is agreed as follows:

1. A. The COMPANY hereby grants to the FRANCHISEE the exclusive right and license to establish and operate an EDU-CENTER to be located within the County of ...., City of ...., State of .... While this agreement is in force, no other such right and license will be granted to any other franchisee within the territory as shown in Schedule A hereto; provided that it is specifically agreed that the COMPANY will have the right to lease Sight & Sound equipment and systems of instruction to commercial, industrial and governmental organizations, and public, private and parochial schools, colleges and universities located within the FRANCHISEE's territory for the exclusive use by these organizations, schools, colleges and universities for the training of their own employees or full time students.

B. The COMPANY will not lease Sight & Sound equipment and systems of instruction to any school or college specializing in typing or secretarial training, which is located in the territory as shown in Schedule A hereto.

2. The COMPANY grants to the FRANCHISEE the following unassignable rights and privileges:

A. Use of the name EDU-CENTER and the EDU-CENTER trademark, logo, signs, etc. in order that the FRANCHISEE may conduct his business under the name of "EDU-CENTER". This privilege is contingent upon compliance with the terms of this Agreement and is limited to the term of this Agreement. However, use of name EDU-CENTER is not exclusive — FRANCHISEE agrees to cooperate and supply any and all consents and agreements necessary for additional franchisees, who may be assigned to operate under the name of EDU-CENTER in the FRANCHISEE's state of incorporation, outside the territory assigned to the FRANCHISEE. While FRANCHISEE shall have the free use of the trademark during the term of this Agreement, is is specifically understood and agreed that FRANCHISEE shall not have the right or privilege of adopting or using EDU-CENTER as part of a corporate name.

B. To use the COMPANY plan, methods, systems, and sales tools in the conduct of its business.

C. To lease from the COMPANY all Sight & Sound equipment pertinent to the operation of an EDU-CENTER, as listed in Schedule B, hereto and under the conditions enumerated in Par. 5 and Schedule C hereto.

3. The COMPANY shall further provide to the FRANCHISEE:

A. An initial supply of the following materials:
- 1000 booklets for Trainee recruitment
- 3 Presentation Books for industrial organization contacts
- 500 "Invitation" letters to mail to corporation executives
- 500 letters to mail to private schools
- Newspaper ad mats for trainee recruitment
- Radio Scripts and tapes for trainee recruitment
- Grand Opening Program
- Publicity kit to help obtain local publicity
- Promotion kit
- 2000 direct mailers for trainee recruitment
- 1000 letterheads
- 1000 envelopes
- 500 business cards
- One Comprehensive Operations Manual
- 5 personnel-use Manuals
- 1000 Trainee Registration forms
- One Record Keeping System
- One month's average supply of control and administrative forms
- All Trainee leads obtained by Home Office originating in the FRANCHISEE's territory.

B. The following services:

• Design plan for layout of Center including recommendations for furniture and equipment.

• Assistance in selection of Center and in lease negotiation.

• Approximately one week training for the FRANCHISEE or his representative in the Home Office.

• Assistance of a Field Executive who will help FRANCHISEE establish operations.

• Hotel accomodations while in New York attending training.

• Supply periodic bulletins, reports, memos, etc. covering trends in developments of all phases of the business, as published by EDU-CENTER.

• Provide periodic visits to the FRANCHISEE's location by an executive of the COMPANY and consultation, advice and information concerning the growth and operation of the FRANCHISEE's business.

• Organize and sponsor, when deemed feasible by the COMPANY, regional and national meetings of the FRANCHISEES for the dissemination and exchange of ideas, experiences, techniques and developments.

4. In consideration of all the foregoing rights and privileges granted hereunder, the material to be furnished hereunder and the undertakings to which the COMPANY has committed itself hereunder, the FRANCHISEE shall make payments to the COMPANY as follows:

A. A fee of $9,500 to be paid as follows:

    1. Initial payment of $6,000, receipt of which is hereby acknowledged.

    2. Payment of $3,500 one week prior to attendance at training center.

5. The FRANCHISEE agrees that he will lease from the Company the equipment referred to in Paragraph 2C and listed in Schedule B hereto at an annual rental of $4,900. payable as follows:

A. First $4,900 payment to be due one week prior to attendance at Training Center.

B. Second payment to be due at the commencement of the twelve month period beginning one year from the date of shipment of the equipment leased hereunder;

C. Each subsequent payment to become due at the commencement of each successive twelve month period thereafter, during the term of the lease.

6. The term for the leasing of the equipment listed in Schedule B hereto shall coincide with the term of this franchise agreement, and shall be renewed automatically with the renewal of this Franchise Agreement as specified in Paragraph 15 hereof. The leasing of said equipment to be subject to such other conditions as set forth in Schedule C.

7. The FRANCHISEE hereby agrees:

A. That he will obtain, with COMPANY's assistance and advice, suitable space for the Center of type and size specified by the COMPANY within 60 days of the effective date of this agreement. That he will furnish said space at his own cost and expense in accordance with specifications laid down by the COMPANY, and mutually agreed upon.

B. That he will use his best efforts to promote the sale of EDU-CENTER typing courses and that he will not offer any other competitive courses, and not be concerned in any way with any competing business or any business which in the opinion of COMPANY would conflict with its interest hereunder.

C. That he will confine his business activities to the territory described in Schedule A hereto.

D. That he will maintain the COMPANY's suggested schedule of tuition prices unless local factors make changes advisable in which case written COMPANY approval must be obtained.

E. That he will operate his business in every respect in accordance with the procedures set forth in the Operating Manual furnished to the FRANCHISEE, including reasonable changes and modifications that might be made from time to time; and that said Operating Manual plus reasonable revisions becomes part of this agreement.

F. That upon commencement of his business activities he will recruit and train with COMPANY guidance a qualified staff in accordance with procedures specified in the Operating Manual.

G. That his books and records will be kept accurately and currently. Quarterly profit and loss statements on report forms provided by the COMPANY shall be forwarded to the COMPANY within thirty days after the expiration of each respective quarterly period. A balance sheet and Profit and Loss statement shall be furnished to the COMPANY as of the end of each fiscal year, no later than 30 days from the end of each such fiscal year.

H. That the FRANCHISEE will not at any time divulge any secrets, information, experience or details of EDU-CENTER, its machines or business methods, to any company, firm or person, in any way whatsoever, and that he will not make or cause to be made any copy or reproduction of any machines or methods of the Center or film, tape, record, print, photograph, or broadcast any material, sound signal or method incorporated in or produced by the machines, and it is hereby expressly agreed that the undertakings of this Paragraph 7H shall remain in force, notwithstanding the termination, for any cause, of this agreement.

I. That the FRANCHISEE will require employees, at time of hiring, to sign a form containing substantially the same agreement as expressed in Paragraph 7H above.

J. That the FRANCHISEE or his employees, salesmen, agents, or representatives will not conduct themselves in any manner that would be detrimental to, or reflect adversely upon, the reputation of the COMPANY.

K. That the FRANCHISEE or his representative will attend the Home Office Training Center for a period of approximately one week.

L. That he will achieve the following minimum standard of gross receipts from tuition:

   1. First twelve (12) month period — $52,500.
   2. Each twelve (12) month period thereafter — $70,000.

M. Visits of EDU-CENTER executives, requested by FRANCHISEE, shall be at FRANCHISEE's expense.

8. In addition to the sums to be paid pursuant to the provisions of Paragraph 4 hereof, the FRANCHISEE shall pay to the COMPANY, simultaneously with the submission of each monthly report form, a royalty based on gross receipts. Such royalty shall be 6% of the gross tuition receipts with a minimum annual royalty of $4200; provided that the FRANCHISEE shall have a three month grace period commencing on the date of shipment of the equipment leased hereunder, so that the minimum royalty for the first year shall be $3150. Such payments and reports are to be made within ten days from the end of each month.

9. It is agreed that the FRANCHISEE will advertise regularly in the territory described in Schedule A hereto, in such media as will most effectively publicize his services. The COMPANY has the right to require the FRANCHISEE to expend for advertising the amount of $1,000 a month or 15% of gross receipts, whichever is greater. The advertisements used will be only those supplied by or approved by the COMPANY; the tear sheets and copies of all paid invoices for advertising will be submitted to the EDU-CENTER Home Office immediately after the last day of each month.

10. It is agreed that the COMPANY will establish a fund to provide national and/or regional advertising and promotion for the benefit of the franchisees. This fund will be administered by the COMPANY as it deems best. The COMPANY will use its best efforts to keep the FRANCHISEE informed as to media schedules and expenditures for such advertising and/or publicity. Money not expended will remain in the fund for future allocation in fulfillment of the purpose of this fund. The FRANCHISEE will pay into this fund 3% of his gross tuition receipts. Payments will be made monthly with the submission of the monthly report form. This payment will not be required during the first 3 months of the FRANCHISEE's operation.

11. It is agreed that all advertising material, promotional material, signs, forms and all other documents furnished to the FRANCHISEE by the COMPANY shall not be used for any purpose other than to promote the services of EDU-CENTER nor shall they be copied without prior written permission of the COMPANY.

12. It is agreed that authorized COMPANY personnel shall be permitted to enter upon the premises of the FRANCHISEE during regular business hours for the purpose of examining the premises, conferring with the FRANCHISEE and his employees, inspecting and checking furniture, fixtures, equipment, operating methods and books and records.

13. The COMPANY and the FRANCHISEE are each independent contractors and the FRANCHISEE shall not be the agent for the COMPANY in any manner or capacity whatsoever, nor shall either be responsible for the debts, bills or liabilities incurred by the other. No partnership, joint venture or relationship of principal and agent is intended. The COMPANY's and the FRANCHISEE's interest in each other shall be limited to the purpose set forth herein.

14. The FRANCHISEE shall indemnify and save the COMPANY harmless from or against all or any loss and/or damages, claims, demands, costs and expenses in connection with the operation of this agreement, and the equipment leased hereunder, or following therefrom.

15. The FRANCHISEE shall obtain and maintain in full force and effect during the term of this agreement, an insurance policy protecting the COMPANY and the FRANCHISEE against all loss, liability or expense whatsoever for personal injury, death, property or equipment damage or otherwise arising or occurring in connection with FRANCHISEE's business or the occupancy of its premises. The COMPANY shall be an additional named insured in such policy. The following limits shall be observed: Workmen's compensation as required by statute; fire insurance for 80% of value per Schedule C; general liability, $200,000 each person and $500,000 each accident. The FRANCHISEE may, at his option obtain any other insurance as he deems necessary or advisable. Within ten days from the opening of the FRANCHISEE's place of business, certificates of insurance will be furnished to the COMPANY. The insurance shall not be terminable without at least ten days' prior notice to the COMPANY.

16. The FRANCHISEE acknowledges that the word "EDU-CENTER" is a valid trade name and service mark owned by the COMPANY and the FRANCHISEE hereby expressly acknowledges the validity of any and all patents and trade marks relating to the machine and related apparatus, and that the COMPANY has granted the use thereof to the FRANCHISEE. The FRANCHISEE will use this name only in the manner and to the extent specifically permitted by this Agreement.

17. This agreement, and the appointment of the FRANCHISEE hereunder, shall be for an initial term of five (5) years commencing upon the delivery of the first machine and thereafter this agreement may be extended automatically for successive one (1) year terms upon payment of $1.00 renewal fee for the grant of such extension, provided that the covenants and undertakings assumed by the FRANCHISEE in this agreement are truly and faithfully performed.

18. Failure to meet the yearly quota shall give the COMPANY at its option, on 30 days' written notice by registered mail addressed to FRANCHISEE at his place of business, the right to terminate this agreement. .

19. If the FRANCHISEE fails to abide by any terms of this agreement or if bankruptcy or insolvency proceedings are commenced by or against the FRANCHISEE or if the FRANCHISEE makes assignment for benefit of creditors, the COMPANY, at its option, shall have the right to cancel this agreement by giving ten (10) day's written notice by registered mail addressed to FRANCHISEE at his place of business as set forth on this agreement. Failure to exercise this option shall not constitute a waiver of the right upon a recurring breach nor shall the cancellation of this agreement for cause constitute a waiver of the right to pursue such other remedies as the COMPANY may have.

20. Upon termination of this agreement, FRANCHISEE agrees as follows:

A. FRANCHISEE shall surrender all rights and privileges granted under this agreement and shall cease the use of the trademark and name EDU-CENTER in any and all connections.

B. FRANCHISEE shall return, without delay, all material described herein as property of the COMPANY.

C. The COMPANY shall have the option to repurchase from the FRANCHISEE any or all material, equipment and furnishings in the possession of the FRANCHISEE, which was purchased from or through the COMPANY at prices paid by the FRANCHISEE less twenty-five percent.

D. The COMPANY shall have the option to sublease the premises described herein and all rights and privileges contained in the original lease, set forth on Schedule D attached hereto, shall be transferred to the COMPANY upon exercise of this right. Said original lease shall contain the landlord's express permission for the COMPANY to sublease the aforesaid premises.

E. The COMPANY shall have the option to retain all rights to the telephone number assigned to the FRANCHISEE, and to such advertising privileges as are concurrent therewith.

21. This agreement shall be binding upon the respective heirs, assigns, personal representatives and successors of the parties, but no sale, assignment or other tranfer of the rights granted hereunder may be made without the prior written consent of the COMPANY.

22. This agreement is divisible, and if any provision herein is held to be violative of the law or unenforceable for any reason such illegality or unenforceability shall affect the portion in conflict only, and the remaining portions of this agreement shall remain in effect.

23. Any controversy or claim arising out of or relating to this agreement, or the breach thereof, shall be settled by arbitration in New York, New York in accordance with the rules then prevailing of the American Arbitration Association and the laws of the State of New York, and judgment upon the award rendered by the arbitrator may be entered in any court having jurisdiction thereof.

24. This agreement is subject to the approval and confirmation of the COMPANY at its home office and shall not become binding unless and until it is officially countersigned.

25. This instrument contains all of the agreements, representations, and conditions by or between the parties hereto. Neither party shall be liable for any representations made unless set forth herein and all modifications and amendments hereto must be in writing.

IN WITNESS WHEREOF, the parties have signed this Agreement effective the ....

day of ...., 196 .

Witness: ....

Witness: ....

FRANCHISEE ....

FRANCHISEE'S ADDRESS ....

....

APPROVED: EDU-CENTER, INC.

By ....

Title .... Date ....

SCHEDULE A

TERRITORY referred to in Paragraph 1, as described below and/or outlined in attached map, which becomes part of this Agreement.

SCHEDULE B

LEASED EQUIPMENT as referred to in Paragraphs 2-C and 5.

ROOM A EQUIPMENT

- 1 Electronic Console
- 1 Electronic Panel
- 1 Reserve Electronic Unit for Console
- 1 Cable (to link Console to Panel)
- 1 Exercise Board
- 6 Tapes (Lessons 1 to 6)
- 6 Reserve Tapes (Lessons 1 to 6)
- 1 Take-up Spool
- 1 Reserve Take-up Spool
- 25 Yards Twinflex Wire (to link Console with alarm bell outside Room A — each tape has built-in-signal at end of tape)

ROOM B EQUIPMENT

- 1 Console consisting of 4 Transmission Decks
- 1 Reserve Transmission Deck for Console
- 1 Main Cable (linking Console to 6 other cables)
- 6 Other Cables, each one having 6 Selector Units
- 36 Head Sets
- 36 Reserve Head Sets
- 150 Ear Pips
- 6 Twin Track Tapes for different speeds
- 6 Reserve Twin Track Tapes for different speeds
- 5 Take-up Spools
- 1 Reserve Take-up Spool
- 260 Exercise Sheets
- 260 Reserve Exercise Sheets

SPARE PARTS

12 Transistors	12 Fuses (mixed)
8 Diodes (Silicon Rectifiers)	6 Lamp Holders
6 Electrolitic Capacitors	3 Indicator Bulbs
2 Tape Replay Heads	3 Volume Control
2 Tape Deck Drive Belts	12 Main Plug & Sockets
2 Operating Arm Coil Springs	12 Jack Sockets
2 Relays	2 Control Switches
3 Space Bar Bulbs (special bulbs)	

FRANCHISE AGREEMENT

EDU-CENTER, INC.

250 West 57 Street
New York, N. Y. 10019

© GOES 435   LITHO U S A

SCHEDULE C

CONDITIONS OF LEASING EQUIPMENT referred to in Paragraph 5, as agreed upon between the COMPANY and FRANCHISEE.

The component parts of the machine and related equipment and apparatus, as listed in Schedule B, are hereinafter collectively referred to as the "machine" or "the machine".

1. The machine shall remain the property of the COMPANY or its lessor and the value of the machine is stipulated and agreed to as $14,700.

2. The COMPANY shall not be liable for any consequential loss arising from breakdown of the machine or from any delay in carrying out repairs.

3. The FRANCHISEE shall not remove (or cause to be removed) the machine from the installation address without authorization of the COMPANY.

4. In the event of termination of the FRANCHISE agreement the FRANCHISEE shall return the machine in working order and good condition to the COMPANY at such location specified by the COMPANY, at his own cost and expense.

5. Installation of the machine will be at the expense of the COMPANY, in accordance with procedures laid down in the operations manual. Local sources at the FRANCHISEE'S location, authorized in advance by the COMPANY, may be utilized for simple maintenance and repair, as specified by the operations manual. Such repairs and maintenance will be at the expense of the FRANCHISEE. The COMPANY shall replace the machine if such replacement should be necessary. Such replacement will not affect the terms of the original leasing agreement herein; provided that if the replaced machine is more than 6 years old, the COMPANY may charge the same rental for the new machine as it is then charging for the rental of new machines. The COMPANY will provide such technical advice and instructions as may be necessary for the guidance of authorized local repair sources.

6. The COMPANY may affix on the machine such plates or other marks indicating that the machine is the property of Sight & Sound Education Limited. The FRANCHISEE shall not remove, obliterate, deface or cover up same.

STORE FRANCHISE AGREEMENT

SIR PIZZA INTERNATIONAL, INC.

701 South Madison Street

Muncie, Indiana

THIS AGREEMENT, dated as of the .... day of .... 19........

made in the City of ...., State of .... by and between SIR PIZZA INTERNATIONAL, INC., a corporation of the State of Indiana, with its principal offices located at 701 South Madison Street, Muncie,

Indiana, hereinafter referred to as the "COMPANY", and ....

....

residing at ....,
hereinafter referred to as the "FRANCHISEE".

WITNESSETH:

    WHEREAS, the COMPANY has developed and operated Pizza Shops with unique format, style and merchandising methods, and

WHEREAS, the COMPANY has registered the name SIR PIZZA, and owns copyrights on the trademark and logos used in conjunction with the SIR PIZZA shops, and

WHEREAS, the FRANCHISEE is desirous of operating a similar retail operation in the city of ...., State of .... to be located at........................ ...., and

WHEREAS, the FRANCHISEE desires to make use of the name SIR PIZZA and to enjoy the commercial benefits of the use of that name, and the benefits of the advertising, promotion and reputation related thereto,

NOW THEREFORE, in consideration of the sum of one dollar ($1.00) and other good and valuable considerations, and the covenants and conditions herein contained, it is agreed as follows:

1. The COMPANY hereby grants to the FRANCHISEE the exclusive right and license to establish and operate a SIR PIZZA Store at the premises above listed, and no other such right and license will be granted to any Franchisee within a radius of .... miles.

2. The FRANCHISEE is further granted the exclusive right and license to sell and promote the sale of any and all merchandise manufactured and/or processed by the SIR PIZZA Commissary in his area.

3. The FRANCHISEE will receive from the COMPANY without additional cost, a DESIGN PLAN for layout of his store, dining room and kitchen, with all of the equipment, furniture and supplies provided by the COMPANY, as listed in Schedule A attached hereto and made a part hereof.

4. The COMPANY shall further provide to the FRANCHISEE:

    A. Complete training in the operation and conduct of his business.
    B. Assistance in site selection and lease negotiation.
    C. Assistance in selection and training of personnel.
    D. Detailed Formal Grand Opening Promotion Kit.
    E. Supply of SIR PIZZA Advertising Mats.
    F. Supply of Menus and Interior Signs.
    G. Supply of Requisition Forms, Order Forms, Guest Checks, etc.
    H. Publicity and Promotions Kit.
    I. Store exterior Identification Materials.
    J. Exterior distinctive lighted sign. (Leased.)
    K. SIR PIZZA Confidential Operations Manual.
    L. SIR PIZZA Bookkeeping and Tax Records System.

5. The FRANCHISEE will receive from the SIR PIZZA Commissary in his area, sufficient food supplies and other necessary supplies, to meet his needs. These items as shown on Schedule B, attached hereto and made a part hereof will be delivered on a regularly scheduled basis, and will be invoiced in accordance with the current price list.

6. The FRANCHISEE will receive a cooperative advertising allowance from the SIR PIZZA Commissary in his area, under the terms and conditions as listed in the Sir Pizza CO-OPERATIVE ADVERTISING PROGRAM.

7. The FRANCHISEE shall purchase and maintain adequate inventory of all items as listed in Schedule B.

8. The FRANCHISEE shall not sell or offer for sale any items which are not supplied by the SIR PIZZA Commissary, except those specifically approved by the COMPANY.

9. The FRANCHISEE shall purchase and display for sale such additional new items as the COMPANY shall prescribe from time to time.

10. The FRANCHISEE hereby agrees:

    A. That he will use his best efforts to promote the success of his SIR PIZZA Shop.

    B. That he will maintain the suggested schedule of retail prices.

    C. That he will achieve and maintain the following minimum standards of gross dollar volume:

        First six month period $

        Succeeding Quarterly Periods $

11. In consideration of all of the foregoing rights and privileges granted hereunder, the material and equipment to be furnished hereunder and the undertakings to which the COMPANY has committed itself hereunder, the FRANCHISEE shall make payments to the COMPANY as follows:

    A. An initial investment fee of $, to be paid as follows:

        1) Initial payment of $, receipt of which is hereby acknowledged.

        2) Payment of $, upon acceptance of the FRANCHISEE by the COMPANY. Such acceptance shall be signified by the delivery of a countersigned copy of this Agreement to the FRANCHISEE.

        3) Balance of $, upon notification to the Franchisee by the COMPANY of the date of the commencement of his home office training, such notification to be at least one week before training begins, either in writing or by telegram to the FRANCHISEE'S address as hereinbefore set forth.

12. The FRANCHISEE agrees to pay to the COMPANY a sum equal to 2.8% of his monthly gross dollar volume, said sum to be paid by the 10th of each month for the month immediately preceding.

13. The FRANCHISEE agrees that he will, at his own cost and expense, make all necessary improvement to his leased premises, in order to meet the minimum standards as set forth in the Confidential Operations Manual. Further, the FRANCHISEE agrees to secure and maintain in full force and effect, liability insurance in an amount and kind reasonably satisfactory to COMPANY, and to indemnify and save COMPANY harmless from the claims or demands of any person, persons, firms, or corporations for products liability and for accident or misadventures in connection with FRANCHISEE'S operation.

14. The FRANCHISEE further agrees that he will advertise regularly in his territory, in such media as will acquaint the public of his services. The COMPANY has the right to require the FRANCHISEE to expend annually for advertising an amount equal to three per cent (3%) of his Gross Sales; that the advertisements used will be only those supplied by or approved by the COMPANY; that the tear sheets and copies of all paid invoices for advertising will be submitted to the SIR PIZZA Commissary immediately after the last day of each month.

15. It is agreed that all advertising material, promotional material, signs, forms and all other documents furnished to the FRANCHISEE by the COMPANY shall not be used for any purpose other than to promote the sale of SIR PIZZA products, nor shall they be copied without prior written permission of the COMPANY.

16. It is agreed that authorized COMPANY personnel shall be permitted to enter upon the premises of the FRANCHISEE during regular business hours for the purpose of examining the premises, conferring with the FRANCHISEE and his employees, inspecting and checking products, furniture, fixtures, equipment, operating methods and books and records.

17. The COMPANY and the FRANCHISEE are each independent contractors and the FRANCHISEE shall not be the agent for the COMPANY in any manner or capacity whatsoever, nor shall either be responsible for the debts, bills or liabilities incurred by the other. The COMPANY'S and the FRANCHISEE'S interest in each other shall be limited to the purpose set forth herein.

18. Unless previously terminated, as hereinafter provided, this Agreement and the appointment of the FRANCHISEE hereunder, shall be for an initial term of five (5) years from date hereof, and thereafter this Agreement shall be automatically extended for successive five (5) year terms, provided that the covenants and undertakings assumed by the FRANCHISEE in this Agreement are truly and faithfully performed.

19. Failure to meet quota, or failure of the FRANCHISEE to abide by any of the terms of this Agreement, or if the FRANCHISEE is declared insolvent, bankrupt or makes assignment for benefit of creditors, the COMPANY, at its option, shall have the right to cancel this Agreement by giving ten (10) days written notice by registered mail addressed to FRANCHISEE at his place of business. Failure to exercise this option shall not constitute a waiver of the right upon a recurring breach nor shall the cancellation of this Agreement for cause constitute a waiver of the right to pursue such other remedies as the COMPANY may have.

20. In event of termination of the Agreement, FRANCHISEE agrees as follows:

A. FRANCHISEE shall surrender all rights and privileges granted under this Agreement and shall cease the use of the trademark and name SIR PIZZA in any and all connections.

B. FRANCHISEE will return, without delay, all material described herein as property of the COMPANY.

C. The COMPANY shall have the option to repurchase from the FRANCHISEE any or all COMPANY products and equipment in the possession of the FRANCHISEE at prices paid by the FRANCHISEE less twenty-five percent (25%).

D. The COMPANY shall have the option to sub-lease the premises described herein and all rights and privileges contained in the original lease shall be transferred to the COMPANY upon exercise of this right.

E. The COMPANY shall have the option to retain all rights to the telephone number assigned to the FRANCHISEE, and to such advertising privileges as are concurrent therewith.

21. This Agreement shall be binding upon the respective heirs, assigns, personal representatives and successors of the parties, but no sale, assignment or other transfer may be made without the prior written consent of the COMPANY.

22. This Agreement is divisable, and any provision herein held to be violative of the applicable statutes and valid regulations thereunder of any governmental agency having jurisdiction, such invalidity shall affect the portion in conflict only, and the remaining portions of this Agreement shall remain in effect thereby.

23. This Agreement shall be construed under the laws of the State of INDIANA. Any dispute arising out of or concerning this Agreement shall be settled and determined by impartial arbitration by the American Arbitration Association in accordance with the rules and regulations then prevailing and in effect, except that nothing herein contained shall be deemed to deprive the parties of their right to any equitable relief to which they may be otherwise entitled. The decision of the Arbitration Association shall be binding upon both parties.

24. This Agreement is subject to the approval and confirmation of the COMPANY at its home office and shall not become binding unless and until it is officially countersigned.

25. This instrument contains all of the agreements, representations and conditions made by or between the parties hereto. Neither party shall be liable for any representations made unless set forth herein and all modifications and amendments hereto must be in writing.

IN WITNESS WHEREOF the parties have signed this Agreement effective the day and year first above written.

SIR PIZZA INTERNATIONAL, INC.

....
Robert W. Swartz, President

FRANCHISEE:

....

WITNESS:

....
SIR PIZZA Selection Manager

SCHEDULE B

Items to be prepared, warehoused and distributed to the retail stores by the commissary:

Cheese - Pizza
    - Plain Shredded
Garlic Bread
Ham Sandwich - Ham
    - Buns
Hamburger
Onions Sliced
Parmesan Cheese
Pepperoni
Sausage
Spaghetti - Whole
    - Half
Spaghetti Sauce
Salad Bowl - Ham
    - Egg
    - Cheese
    - Crouton
Mustard
Small Dough
Large Dough
Beef Boats
Submarines
Flour
Anchovies
Bar B-Q Sauce
Dill Pickles
Dressings - French
    - Oil & Vinegar
    - 1000 Island
    - Mayonnaise
    - Italian
Green PEPPERS
Red Peppers
Mushrooms
Tomato Paste
Waverly Wafers
Salt
Pepper
Granulated Garlic
Hot Pepper Pods
Sugar Packets

Anti-Bac
Garbage Liners
Bags - No. 10 White
    - 133 Maret
    - Small Pizza
    - Large Pizza
    - Beef Boat
Bags - Submarine
Boxes - Small Pizza
    - Large Pizza
    - Spaghetti
Alum. Foil - Rolls
Salad Bowl Plates
Coffee Containers
    - Lids
Dressing Cups
    - Lids
Salad Containers
    - Lids
Matches
Napkins - Printed
Paper Towels
Plastic Forks
Straws
Tooth Picks
Checks - Dining Room
    - Phone
Menu, Carry-Out
Reports - Cash Check out
    - Daily Cash
Salt Packets
Oregano
Italian Seasoning
10" Circles
14" Circles
Souflé Cups #39
Order Blanks
Monthly Reports
Green Towels
Cleaning Soap
Silver Potato Foil

The following Items may be obtained at the local level by the retail store:

Coffee as specified
    by Company
Lettuce
Carrots
Celery
Floor Wax
Toilet Tissue
Other necessary
    Janitorial Supplies

Soft Drinks -
    Pepsi Account
Milk Products
Vinegar
Ammonia
Comet Cleanser
Scouring Pads
Soap - Dish
    - Hand

STORE
FRANCHISE
AGREEMENT

SIR PIZZA
INTERNATIONAL,
INC.

701 South Madison Street
Muncie, Indiana

© GOES 435   LITHO USA

SCHEDULE A

Cash Register (Anchor) - (New)
Two (2) each Blogett 999 Pizza Ovens
Oven Hood
Exhaust Fan
Menu Board
Condiment Pan Holder (Refrigerated)
Walk-in-Cooler Complete
Six Stainless Steel Pans
Ten Stainless Steel Pans
Six Circle Drying Carts
Bag Rack
Board Drying Rack
Two Oven Racks
Three Seltzer Posts
Four Paddles, #5116
Oven Scraper
Oven Brush
Sink (Stainless Steel) - 3-compartment
Circle Holder
Garbage Can
Twelve Pizza Boards - 11"
Twelve Pizza Boards - 13"
Twelve White Pans
Two Dexter Cook Knives
Two Stainless Steel Spoons
Two Flour Squeezets
Two Salt Shakers
One Can Opener - Edlund
Two Can Opener Blades
Two Spatulas - 14"
Two Spatulas - 12"
One Wall Clock
One Mop
Ticket Holder
Two Rubber Spatulas
Six Light Fixtures
One Egg Cutter
One Bucket
Two Brooms
One Fire Extinguisher
One Bread Knife
One Carrot Peeler
One Dust Pan
Cash Allowance of
$300 for construction
of serving counter

COMMISSARY FRANCHISE AGREEMENT

SIR PIZZA INTERNATIONAL, INC.

701 South Madison Street
Muncie, Indiana

THIS AGREEMENT, dated as of the .... day of .... 19 ......,

made in the City of ...., State of .... by and between SIR PIZZA INTERNATIONAL, INC., a corporation of the State of Indiana, with its principal offices located at 701 South Madison Street, Muncie,

Indiana, hereinafter referred to as the "COMPANY", and ....

residing at ....,
hereinafter referred to as the "FRANCHISEE".

WITNESSETH:

WHEREAS, the COMPANY owns, and has the exclusive right and power to use the name SIR PIZZA, and the trademarks and logos used in conjunction therewith, and

WHEREAS, the COMPANY has developed and successfully operated Pizza Commissary operations and retail outlets therefor, using unique format, style and merchandising methods, and

WHEREAS, the FRANCHISEE is desirous of operating a similar Commissary and retail operation, to be located in the City of .... , State of .... , and

WHEREAS the FRANCHISEE desires to make use of the name SIR PIZZA and to enjoy the commercial benefits of the use of that name, and the benefits of the advertising, promotion and reputation related thereto, NOW THEREFORE, in consideration of the sum of One Dollar ($1.00) and other good and valuable consideration, and the covenants and conditions herein contained, it is agreed as follows:

1. The COMPANY hereby grants to the FRANCHISEE the exclusive right and license to establish and operate a SIR PIZZA Commissary and Store at the location above listed, and no other such right and license will be granted to any Franchisee within the State of .... within counties as listed in Schedule C, except as listed in paragraph 8 hereto.

2. The COMPANY will provide to the FRANCHISEE, without additional cost a DESIGN PLAN for the layout of his Commissary, Kitchens and Store, and will further provide all of the equipment and furniture and supplies as listed in Schedule A, attached hereto and make a part hereof.

3. The COMPANY grants to the FRANCHISEE the following unassignable rights and privileges:

A. Use of the name "SIR PIZZA" and the SIR PIZZA Trademark, logo, signs, etc., in order that the FRANCHISEE may conduct his business under the name of "SIR PIZZA of .... ". This privilege is conditioned upon compliance with the terms of this Agreement, and is limited to the period of compliance.

B. To use the COMPANY'S plan, methods and systems for conducting the business of food processing and food sales, and serving as the wholesale distribution center for all of the items as listed in Schedule B, attached hereto and make a part hereof, to the chain of SIR PIZZA Store Franchisees located within the aforementioned market area.

C. To purchase from the COMPANY and/or its' authorized sources of supply, all equipment, food supplies, paper goods, spices and condiments, etc., whether for use by the Commissary or for resale to the Store Franchisees, and no purchases may be made from other sources without the express written permission of the COMPANY.

4. The COMPANY shall further provide to the FRANCHISEE:

A. Complete training in the operation and conduct of his business.
B. Assistance in site selection and lease negotiation.
C. Assistance in selection and training of personnel.
D. Detailed Formal Grand Opening Promotion Kit.

E. Supply of SIR PIZZA Advertising Mats.

F. Supply of Menus and Interior Signs.

G. Supply of Requisition Forms, Order Forms, Guest Checks, etc.

H. Publicity and Promotions Kit.

I. Store exterior identification Materials.

J. Exterior distinctive lighted sign.

K. SIR PIZZA Confidential Operations Manual

L. SIR PIZZA Bookkeeping and Tax Records System.

5. The COMPANY further undertakes to do the following on behalf of the FRANCHISEE:

A. Expend all reasonable effort, in order to establish a number of operating, successful SIR PIZZA Store Franchises within the FRANCHISEE'S Market area.

B. Provide thorough home office and field training with respect to product knowledge, food processing procedures, purchasing, inventory control, administration, financing and record keeping. Initial home office training program will consist of at least one week in the Muncie, Indiana Commissary and Store, with room and board at the expense of the COMPANY.

C. Supply periodic bulletins, reports memos, etc., covering trends and developments in all phases of the business.

D. Provide periodic visits to the FRANCHISEE'S location by an executive of the COMPANY and unlimited consultation, advice and information concerning the growth and operation of the FRANCHISEE'S Business.

E. Organize and sponsor district, regional and national meetings of the Franchisees for the dissemination and exchange of ideas, experiences, techniques and developments.

F. Provide assistance as may be deemed necessary and consistent with the provisions of this Agreement.

6. In consideration of all of the foregoing rights and privileges granted hereunder, the material and equipment to be furnished hereunder and the undertakings to which the COMPANY has committed itself hereunder, the FRANCHISEE shall make payments to the COMPANY as follows:

A. An initial investment fee of $, to be paid as follows:

 1) Initial payment of $, receipt of which is hereby acknowledged.

 2) Payment of $, upon acceptance of the FRANCHISEE by the COMPANY. Such acceptance shall be signified by the delivery of a countersigned copy of this Agreement to the FRANCHISEE.

3) Balance of $_____, upon notification to the FRANCHISEE by the COMPANY of the date of the commencement of his home office training, such notification to be at least one week before training begins, either in writing or by telegram to the FRANCHISEE'S address as hereinbefore set forth.

B. In addition, FRANCHISEE shall, within fifteen (15) days after the end of each calendar month during the term of this Agreement, commencing with the calendar month in which operations begin at the Franchised Business, pay to the COMPANY two percent (2%) of the gross billings of his Commissary operations during the preceding month, plus 2.8% of the monthly gross sales volume attributable to his Store operations during the preceding month.

7. The FRANCHISEE will supply to all of the Store Franchisees within his market area, all of the equipment, food supplies, paper goods, etc., in accordance with the current price lists of the COMPANY. Deliveries will be made in accordance with an approved delivery schedule, and diligent effort will be made by the FRANCHISEE to maintain said delivery schedules.

8. The FRANCHISEE hereby agrees, that when a minimum of fifteen (15) Store Franchises have been established within his market area, he will either:

A. Take such steps as are necessary to increase his processing and service capabilities, or

B. Establish additional Commissary facilities at another location within his market area, subject to all terms and conditions of this agreement.

If the acquisition of additional Store Franchisees exceeds the ability of the FRANCHISEE to properly service them in accordance with the procedures as detailed in the SIR PIZZA Confidential Operations Manual, relative to minimum delivery and inventory requirements, the COMPANY will have the right and authority to appoint additional Commissary Franchisees, in order to assure such service, and the FRANCHISEE will execute all documents necessary for such appointment and subsequent operations.

9. The FRANCHISEE will establish a Co-Operative Advertising Reserve Fund, depositing therein monthly an amount equal to one (1%) per cent of the gross purchases by the Store Franchisees said fund to be disbursed in accordance with the SIR PIZZA Co-Operative Advertising Program.

10. The FRANCHISEE agrees that he will, at his own cost and expense, make all necessary improvements to his leased premises, in order to meet the minimum standards as set forth in the Confidential Operations Manual.

11. The FRANCHISEE further agrees that he will advertise regularly in his territory, in such media as will acquaint the public of his services. The COMPANY has the right to require the FRANCHISEE to expend annually for advertisements an amount equal to three per cent (3%) of his Gross Sales from his Store Operations; that the advertisements used will be only those supplied by or approved by the COMPANY; that the tear sheets and copies of all paid invoices for advertising will be submitted to the COMPANY immediately after the last day of each month.

12. It is agreed that all advertising material, promotional material, signs, forms and all other documents furnished to the FRANCHISEE by the COMPANY shall not be used for any purpose other than to promote the sale of SIR PIZZA products, nor shall they be copied without prior written permission of the COMPANY.

13. It is agreed that authorized COMPANY personnel shall be permitted to enter upon the premises of the FRANCHISEE during regular business hours for the purpose of examining the premises, conferring with the FRANCHISEE and his employees, inspecting and checking products, furniture, fixtures, equipment, operating methods and books and records.

14. The COMPANY and the FRANCHISEE are each independent contractors and the FRANCHISEE shall not be the agent for the COMPANY in any manner or capacity whatsoever, nor shall either be responsible for the debts, bills or liabilities incurred by the other. The COMPANY'S and the FRANCHISEE'S interest in each other shall be limited to the purpose set forth herein. Further, the FRANCHISEE agrees to secure and maintain in full force and effect liability insurance in an amount and kind reasonably satisfactory to COMPANY, and to indemnify and save COMPANY harmless from the claims or demands of any person, persons, firms, or corporations for products liability and for accident or misadventures in connection with FRANCHISEE'S operation.

15. Unless previously terminated, as hereinafter provided, this Agreement and the appointment of the FRANCHISEE hereunder, shall be for an initial term of five (5) years from date hereof, and thereafter this Agreement shall be automatically extended for successive five (5) year terms, provided that the covenants and undertakings assumed by the FRANCHISEE in this Agreement are truly and faithfully performed.

16. Failure of the FRANCHISEE to abide by any of the terms of this Agreement, or if the FRANCHISEE is declared insolvent, bankrupt or makes assignment for benefit of creditors, the COMPANY, at its option, shall have the right to cancel this Agreement by giving ten (10) days written notice by registered mail addressed to FRANCHISEE at his place of business. Failure to exercise this option shall not constitute a waiver of the right upon a recurring breach nor shall the cancellation of this Agreement for cause constitute a waiver of the right to pursue such other remedies as the COMPANY may have.

17. In event of termination of the Agreement, FRANCHISEE agrees as follows:

A. FRANCHISEE shall surrender all rights and privileges granted under this agreement and shall cease the use of the trademark and name SIR PIZZA in any and all connections.

B. FRANCHISEE will return, without delay, all material described herein as property of the COMPANY.

C. The COMPANY shall have the option to repurchase from the FRANCHISEE any or all COMPANY products and equipment in the possession of the FRANCHISEE at prices paid by the FRANCHISEE less twenty-five percent (25%).

D. The COMPANY shall have the option to sub-lease the premises described herein and all rights and privileges contained in the original lease shall be transferred to the COMPANY upon exercise of this right.

E. The COMPANY shall have the option to retain all rights to the telephone number assigned to the FRANCHISEE, and to such advertising privileges as are concurrent therewith.

18. This Agreement shall be binding upon the respective heirs, assigns, personal representatives and successors of the parties, but no sale, assignment or other transfer may be made without the prior written consent of the COMPANY.

19. This Agreement is divisable, and any provision herein held to be violative of the applicable statutes and valid regulations thereunder of any governmental agency having jurisdiction, such invalidity shall affect the portion in conflict only, and the remaining portions of this Agreement shall remain in effect thereby.

20. This Agreement shall be construed under the laws of the State of INDIANA. Any dispute arising out of or concerning this Agreement shall be settled and determined by impartial arbitration by the American Arbitration Association in accordance with the rules and regulations then prevailing and in effect, except that nothing contained shall be deemed to deprive the parties of their right to any equitable relief to which they may be otherwise entitled. The decision of the Arbitration Association shall be binding upon both parties.

21. This Agreement is subject to the approval and confirmation of the COMPANY at its home office and shall not become binding unless and until it is officially countersigned.

22. This instrument contains all of the agreements, representations and conditions made by or between the parties hereto. Neither party shall be liable for any representations made unless set forth herein and all modifications and amendments hereto must be in writing.

IN WITNESS WHEREOF the parties have signed this Agreement effective the day and year first above written.

SIR PIZZA INTERNATIONAL, INC.

....
Robert W. Swartz, President

FRANCHISEE:

WITNESS:

....
SIR PIZZA Selection Manager

SCHEDULE B

Items to be prepared, warehoused and distributed to the retail stores by the commissary:

Cheese - Pizza
     - Plain Shredded
Garlic Bread
Ham Sandwich - Ham
          - Buns
Hamburger
Onions Sliced
Parmesan Cheese
Pepperoni
Sausage
Spaghetti - Whole
     - Half
Spaghetti Sauce
Salad Bowl - Ham
     - Egg
     - Cheese
     - Crouton
Mustard
Small Dough
Large Dough
Beef Boats
Submarines
Flour
Anchovies
Bar B-Q Sauce
Dill Pickles
Dressings - French
     - Oil & Vinegar
     - 1000 Island
     - Mayonnaise
     - Italian
Green PEPPERS
Red Peppers
Mushrooms
Tomato Paste
Waverly Wafers
Salt
Pepper
Granulated Garlic
Hot Pepper Pods
Sugar Packets

Anti-Bac
Garbage Liners
Bags - No. 10 White
     - 133 Maret
     - Small Pizza
     - Large Pizza
     - Beef Boat
Bags - Submarine
Boxes - Small Pizza
     - Large Pizza
     - Spaghetti
Alum. Foil - Rolls
Salad Bowl Plates
Coffee Containers
     - Lids
Dressing Cups
     - Lids
Salad Containers
     - Lids
Matches
Napkins - Printed
Paper Towels
Plastic Forks
Straws
Tooth Picks
Checks - Dining Room
     - Phone
Menu, Carry-Out
Reports - Cash Check out
     - Daily Cash
Salt Packets
Oregano
Italian Seasoning
10" Circles
14" Circles
Souflé Cups #39
Order Blanks
Monthly Reports
Green Towels
Cleaning Soap
Silver Potato Foil

The following Items may be obtained at the local level by the retail store:

Coffee as specified
   by Company
Lettuce
Carrots
Celery
Floor Wax
Toilet Tissue
Other necessary
   Janitorial Supplies

Soft Drinks -
   Pepsi Account
Milk Products
Vinegar
Ammonia
Comet Cleanser
Scouring Pads
Soap - Dish
   - Hand

COMMISSARY FRANCHISE AGREEMENT

SIR PIZZA INTERNATIONAL, INC.

701 South Madison Street
Muncie, Indiana

© GOES 439   LITHO U S A

SCHEDULE A

Koch Clean Cutter
Globe Automatic Slicer
Sheeter
Mixer - Leland
Walk-in-Cooler
    Two each 1½ HP Compressors
    Walk-in Door
    Service Doors
    Construction Allowance up to $1000.
Stove
Duchess Dough Cutter
Scales - Three each
Proofing-room Heater
Work Tables (Stainless Steel)
Two Cook Pans - Sausage
Chinese Strainer
Two Large Cook Pots - Spaghetti
Colander
Twelve White Pans
Two Boning Knives
Six Rubber Spatulas
Two Large Serving Spoons
One Large Open Spoon
Three Paring Knives
One Carving Knife
Two Metal Scoops
Measuring Cups
Measuring Spoons
Carrot Peeler
Strainer
GM Refrigerated Truck
Two Decals for Truck
Strainer Roller
Meat Fork
Butter Brush
Foil Cutter
Two Utility Knives
Gas Fired Kettle
Paddle for Kettle
Two Loading Carts
Six Plastic Buckets
Exhaust Fan - (Proofing Room)
Exhaust Fan
Twelve 14" x 20" Trays
Dust Pan
Stainless Steel Scullery Sink

DINING ROOM EQUIPMENT

Nine (9) Booths
Four (4) Tables
Sixteen (16) Chairs
Silverware & Trays
China
Serving Trays
Salt & Pepper Shakers

Glasses - Two (2) sizes
Coat Racks
SIR PIZZA Ash Trays
Tea Pots
Glass Racks
Pizza Serving Trays
Dish Drainer
Water Fountain
Coffee Maker - (Bunn)
Cash Register (Anchor) - (New)
Two (2) each Blogett 999 Pizza Ovens
Oven Hood
Exhaust Fan
Menu Board
Condiment Pan Holder (Refrigerated)
Six Stainless Steel Pans
Ten Stainless Steel Pans
Six Circle Drying Carts
Bag Rack
Board Drying Rack
Two Oven Racks
Three Seltzer Posts
Four Paddles, #5116
Oven Scraper
Oven Brush
Sink (Stainless Steel) - 3-compartment
Circle Holder
Garbage Can
Twelve Pizza Boards - 11"
Twelve Pizza Boards - 13"
Twelve White Pans
Two Dexter Cook Knives
Two Stainless Steel Spoons
Two Flour Squeezets
Two Salt Shakers
One Can Opener - Edlund
Two Can Opener Blades
Two Spatulas - 14"
Two Spatulas - 12"
One Wall Clock
One Mop
Ticket Holder
Two Rubber Spatulas
Six Light Fixtures
One Egg Cutter
One Bucket
Two Brooms
One Fire Extinguisher
One Bread Knife
One Carrot Peeler
One Dust Pan
Cash Allowance of
$300 for construction
of serving counter

GENERAL BUSINESS SERVICES FRANCHISE AGREEMENT

APPOINTMENT OF AREA DIRECTOR

THIS AGREEMENT, made as of the ....day of ...., 19 ...., by and between GENERAL BUSINESS SERVICES, Inc., a Maryland corporation, with its principal office and place of business at 7401 Wisconsin Avenue, Washington, D.C. 20014 (hereinafter referred

to as the "Company") and _____ ,

residing at _____

(hereinafter referred to as the "Area Director");

WITNESSETH:

WHEREAS, the Company is in the business of selling annual Subscriptions to its standard "General Business Services" and of providing such services through franchised distributors who purchase such Subscriptions for resale to Subscribers; and

WHEREAS,
is desirous of being appointed by the Company as one of such distributors to be known as an "Area Director";

NOW, THEREFORE, in consideration of the mutual promises and covenants herein contained, the parties hereto mutually agree as follows:

1. Appointment

The Company hereby appoints the Area Director as the exclusive and sole distributor for the territory described in Addendum No. 1 hereto (hereinafter referred to as the "Territory") for a period two (2) years from the date of this Agreement.

The Area Director, providing he has fulfilled the conditions of this appointment, shall be reappointed for succeeding two (2) year periods upon payment of a fee of Ten Dollars ($10.00) for each renewal.

2. *Payment*

mm Upon the execution of this Agreement the Area Director will pay to the Company the sum of Five Thousand Five Hundred Dollars ($5,500.00).

3. *Training and Assistance*

(a) The Company will maintain a Training Institute for the training of Area Directors and their Associates. The Company will pay all of the expenses, including transportation, related to the Area Director's attendance at a Training Institute.

(b) The Company will also furnish, without charge, at least two (2) days of field training for the Area Director.

(c) During the term of this Agreement, the Company will also furnish to the Area Director, without charge periodic followup assistance and instruction as the Company deems necessary or appropriate to assist the Area Director in developing his business. The Area Director will participate and cause any Associate of his to participate in all training programs, seminars, and field training as provided by the Company.

4. *Subscriber Materials and Operating Supplies*

The Company will furnish the Area Director, without charge, after full payment and upon completion of the Area Director's Training Institute course, all of the materials set forth in Addenda Nos. 2 and 4, hereto.

5. *Preparation of Income Tax Returns*

The Area Director will not be responsible for, now will he prepare, income tax returns. The income tax service rendered the Subscriber shall be the sole responsibility of the Company.

6. *Trust Fund*

The Company shall set aside the sum of Five Dollars ($5.00) out of the sale price of each standard subscription to General Business Services sold to the Area Director (exclusive of the original inventory of Subscriber services furnished pursuant to Paragraph 4 above) and shall deposit the same with a bank of its selection in a separate trust account, until the first of the following events occurs:

(a) The amount of said deposits reaches a total of Five Thousand Five Hundred Dollars ($5,500.00), at which time the Company will withdraw that amount from said trust account and pay it over to the Area Director.

(b) Five (5) years from date of this Agreement, at which time the Company will withdraw from said trust account and pay over to the Area Director the then total of such deposits unless the Area Director requests the Company to continue making such deposits until a total of Five Thousand Five Hundred Dollars ($5,500.00) has been deposited. In the event such extension is requested, the Company will continue to make such deposits until a total of Five Thousand Five Hundred Dollars ($5,500.00) has been deposited, at which time the Company will withdraw from said trust account and pay over to the Area Director said sum of Five Thousand Five Hundred ($5,500.00) Dollars.

Said trust account shall be at all times under the complete control of the Company. In the event of termination, the Company will be entitled to withdraw and retain all amounts deposited. The Company shall be entitled to all interest earned thereon (and may withdraw the same periodically) and shall pay all expenses in connection therewith.

The provision for refund of the purchase price by setting aside Five Dollars ($5.00) on each General Business Services Subscription purchased shall not be included in any renewal of this Agreement if the minimum purchase requirements listed in Paragraph 10 have not been met.

7. *Insurance*

The Company will provide group life insurance coverage for the Area Director in the face amount of Ten Thousand Dollars ($10,000.00) and will pay the premium costs thereof for the first six (6) months of coverage. Effective date of this insurance is to be the date of this Agreement.

8. *Trade Name Rights*

The Area Director, for the term of this agreement, has the right to use and unless otherwise instructed by the _____ Company will use the trade name "General Business Services." The Area Director agrees to register with appropriate governmental authorities and to obtain a telephone listing as "General Business Services" in the Territory.

9. *Associates*

The Area Director will cause any Associate appointed by him to execute a standard Associate Agreement with a copy being forwarded immediately to the Company for acknowledgment and approval.

The Area Director, at his sole and complete expense, will require the Associate Director to attend, as soon after his appointment as is convenient to the Company, a one (1) week training session at the Company's Training Institute.

The Area Director will not permit other persons to sell General Business Services subscriptions in his territory unless they are properly appointed Associates who have attended the Training Institute.

10. *Minimum Purchase Requirements*

Commencing with the seventh (7th) calendar month following attendance at the Training Institute, the Area Director will purchase from the Company at least the following quantities of General Business Services subscriptions for both new and renewal Subscribers:

First two (2) calendar quarters .... 10 per quarter
Next four (4) calendar quarters .... 15 per quarter

Minimum purchase requirements per calendar quarter under renewals of this Agreement will be as follows:

Third Year.............................. 20 per quarter
Fourth Year .... 25 per quarter
Fifth Year .... 30 per quarter
Sixth Year .... 35 per quarter
ALL subsequent years .... 150 per year

The purchase price of the subscriptions will be established from time to time by the Company. A thirty (30) day advance notice will be given the Area Director in the event of a change of purchase price. The price list currently in force is attached as Addendum #3 hereto. All orders by the Area Director shall be on forms furnished by the Company, and all orders will be shipped freight prepaid.

Purchases during any one (1) of the periods specified above in excess of the minimum for that period may be credited against the minimum specified for any subsequent period.

11. *Registration Cards*

The Area Director will complete and return to the Company within seven (7) days after installing a General Business Services subscription the numbered Registration Card furnished with each System. This Registration Card remains the property of the Company, and failure to return as required is a violation of this Agreement.

12. *Advertising and Promotion*

The Area Director will obtain the Company's prior written approval of any advertising copy, promotional material, or other written or printed material used by him in promoting sales.

13. *Restrictions*

The Area Director shall not, within the territory or in any place within forty (40) miles of the outside boundary of the territory, at any time during the continuance of this Agreement, or for a period of five (5) years after the termination of this Agreement (regardless of the cause of such termination), divert any employees of GBS away from GBS, or directly or indirectly as principal, agent, employee or otherwise, engage in or be concerned with or interested in any business in competition with the Company. Further, the Area Director shall not, at any time during the continuance of this Agreement (except in pursuit of his responsibilities under this Agreement), or any time thereafter, divulge or use for his own purpose any confidential or business information relating to the business affairs of the Company.

The Area Director covenants and agrees that neither he, nor his successor or assigns, will have the right after termination of this Agreement to use the name "General Business Services"; "GBS"; or similar name which may confuse or tend to confuse the general public. The Area Director further covenants and agrees that violation of this restriction will result in stipulated damages against him in the amount of Five Thousand Dollars ($5,000.00), in addition to other rights and remedies available to the Company.

14. *Sale*

The Area Director may at any time sell his rights under this Agreement provided:

(a) The purchaser is approved by the Company in writing, which approval shall not be unreasonably withheld. This approval will be considered effective upon the execution by the purchaser and a Company officer of the standard Area Director Agreement then being issued by the Company to all new Area Directors.

(b) Prior to the execution of a standard Agreement with the new Area Director for the Territory, the Company will be paid the sum of Two Thousand Seven Hundred Fifty Dollars ($2,750.00) as reimbursement for providing the new Area Director field training, transportation, Institute training and insurance, as described above, and the operating supplies listed in Addendum #4.

(c) It is further agreed the Company will be paid One Thousand Eight Hundred Fifty Dollars ($1,850.00) as reimbursement for providing the new Area Director with the Subscriber Materials listed in Addendum #2. Any Subscriber Materials returned by the terminating Area Director in usable condition will reduce this charge on a pro-rata basis.

15. Termination

Except for purposes of resale described above, this Agreement may be terminated only by the Area Director or by the Company as provided below.

(a) The Area Director may terminate this Agreement at any time by not requesting renewal, or by notifying the Company in writing of his desire to cancel this Agreement and by surrendering to the Company any items supplied or sold to him by the Company and still in his possession.

(b) The Company may terminate this Agreement by notifying the Area Director in writing of such termination, but only if the Area Director has violated a provision of this Agreement and has been notified in writing of such default, and has failed to remedy such default within thirty (30) days of the giving of such notice.

16. Estate

This Agreement shall be considered as a property right of the Area Director to be included in his estate upon his death provided that:

(a) The Company is notified by the Executor within thirty (30) days of the name of the person responsible for fulfilling the obligations of this Agreement.

(b) The person so named must have attended a Company Training Institute or be willing to attend within ninety (90) days after the death of an Area Director.

Failure to continue operations as provided above will be considered an automatic request for termination under Paragraph 15 (a) above.

17. Waiver

Failure of either party at any time to require performance by the other party of any provision hereof shall not be deemed a continuing waiver of that provision or a waiver of any other provision of this Agreement whether or not of the same or similar nature.

18. International Creditors Alliance

The Company stipulates that it has entered into an agreement with International Creditors Alliance, Inc., establishing its right to grant to the Area Director exclusive selling rights for International Creditors Alliance's copyrighted "MagicWrite" collection system. The Area Director may at his option elect to accept this grant by entering into an Area Director Agreement with International Creditors Alliance, Inc.. This Area Director Agreement provides, among other things, that the selling rights extend to the same territory as shown in Addendum and that the Area Director will pay $505.00 for the initial inventory and supplies

19. Modification

This Agreement contains all the agreements, understandings, representations, conditions, warranties, and covenants by and between the parties hereto Neither party shall be liable for any representation made unless expressly set forth herein, and this Agreement may not be modified or amended except in writing signed by both of the parties hereto.

IN WITNESS WHEREOF, the parties have caused this Agreement to be executed as of the day and year first above written.

AREA DIRECTOR

GENERAL BUSINESS SERVICES, INC.

By ....

....

ADDENDUM #1 – TERRITORY

ADDENDUM #2 — SUBSCRIBER MATERIALS

31 Standard General Business Services Subscriptions
3 Partnership Service Kits
3 Corporation Service Kits

ADDENDUM #3 — GENERAL BUSINESS SERVICES PRICE LIST

	Area Director Cost	Suggested Subscriber Cost
Sole Proprietor Subscription	$ 50.00	$160.00
Partnership Subscription	100.00	250.00
Corporation Subscription	100.00	250.00

ADDENDUM #4 — OPERATING AND ADVERTISING SUPPLIES

Operating

1 Operations Manual
1 Service Attache Case
500 Business Cards imprinted
250 Letterheads & envelopes imprinted
1 Address stamp
200 Address labels
1 Daily work planner
5 Subscriber Information Record Pads
2 Purchase Order Pads
800 Prospect cards
250 Speed messages imprinted
25 Subscriber Change of Address
25 Cancellation Cards
50 Tip Record Cards
50 Repair Sales Record #5100
50 Job Cost Record #5705
50 Sales by Employees #5102
50 Sales & Income #5803
50 Payroll Sheet #6502
50 Payroll Sheet #6503
50 Analysis Sheet #5802
50 Income by Unit #5101
50 Service Station Purchases #5700
50 Cost of Goods Sold #5900

Advertising

1500 Direct Mail pieces
50 Everyman's Income Tax Booklet
1 Business Analysis Interview Pad
10 Subscriber Presentation folders
100 Extra Profits folders
50 Business Counseling Foldouts
50 Tax Service Foldouts
50 Wall St. Journal reprints
50 Bar Management reprints
50 Rental Equipment Register reprint
25 Opinion Leader cards
1 Lobby Exhibit
     with
100 Reply Cards #2015
1 Set Subscriber Testimonial letters

8.

WHICH TYPE OF FRANCHISE SHOULD YOU SELECT?

The Sales-Type Franchise

Many different sales-type franchises are available—applicable to all types of products and all types of sales approaches, such as homes, industry, offices, and institutions.

For this category of franchise, the franchisee usually operates in one or both of the following ways:

. . . As sales manager—recruiting and managing a sales staff from his office.

. . . As salesman, doing his own selling.

Many prospective franchisees like the challenge of a sales-type franchise. They can give full vent to their capacities and energies . . . and their earnings potential is practically unlimited. It is pleasant "outside" work, putting them in constant, congenial contact with varied types of people. To this franchisee, being confined to a store or shop would prove too dull and unchallenging and utilize only a portion of his capacities.

Another aspect of the sales-type franchise is that there is a minimum of expense and overhead. In many instances, the franchisee can operate from his home (usually his wife assists); in other instances an office may be required (with minimum equipment and refurbishing expenses). In most instances he can move into an office "as is" with minimum lease and rent—commencing his operation almost immediately.

In your case, to determine your qualifications for a sales-type franchise you should assess your own personality or your basic "likes" and basic "desires." For example:

- Do you have an "outgoing" personality?

- Do you enjoy meeting people at all levels?

- Have you had sales experience, of any type, in your previous activities?

- Are you basically optimistic?

- Are you articulate—able to clearly and concisely present the benefits of your product or service?

- Are you persistent—so that you will adhere constantly to each day's schedule, not letting yourself become diverted or discouraged?

- Are you self-motivated—so that you can generate enthusiasm for what you are doing and *show it?* To the extent that *you* are enthusiastic, your prospect will react favorably.

- Are you a good "self-manager"—so that you will plan each day and work your plan each day—to the same extent as if you were not self-employed and were working for a third party?

- Are you a good "manager" of people—so that you can recruit, train, manage and motivate other salesmen?

If the answer is "yes" to all the above, then you should do a superb job as a sales-type franchisee. In many instances your net income can be quite substantial—often exceeding many other types of franchises—in view of your minimum expenses.

Service-Type Franchises—When to Select

Service franchises are often very profitable since the overhead is usually comparatively low, and the profit margin high. Inventory is usually minimal. A "continuity" of customer patronage is gradually established, achieving consistent earnings.

Generally speaking, many service-type franchises require the following:

. . . A desire to "work with the hands" . . . and a willingness to wear work clothes and "get soiled."

Included are such franchises as:

- automatic transmissions
- lawn-care services
- sewer cleaning
- auto repair
- appliance repair
- furniture and carpet cleaning

Thorough training by the franchisor indoctrinates the franchisee in all aspects of the work, so that prior experience is, generally, not needed. However, mechanical aptitude is often helpful and desirable for a service-type franchise.

Store-Type Franchises—When to Select

The varieties of store-type franchises are extensive. They vary from foods to books, to hardware.

Unlike other types of franchises, these factors are pertinent to a store-type franchise:

- Selection of a proper site
- Comparatively large investment (to construct building, lease or buy land, and equipment structure)
- Financing
- Extensive inventory and inventory control
- Personnel (needed in most store-type franchises . . . although some store-type franchises are of the "Mom and Pop" variety.
- Comparatively large overhead and a high Break-Even point
- Expensive signs
- Need for local permits and licenses
- Need for comparatively large rental security—in some instances three months or more

On the basis of the above, the franchisee entering into a store-type franchise generally requires substantial monies—often $25,000 and up. He also needs a "cushion" of approximately $10,000 to "tide him over" until he passes the Break-Even point and achieves profits.

9.

HOW TO SELECT A PROPER LOCATION FOR YOUR FRANCHISED BUSINESS

In this chapter the matter of physical location and its importance will be considered. Location is of extreme importance and cannot be over-emphasized. No matter how good the potential of your business, it can flounder and fail and never even "get on its feet," if your location is poorly selected. This applies to both product and service types of franchise.

In selecting a location, there are a great many points you must consider:

(1) Is the particular business *self-generating?* Will this type of business attract people to its location and not necessarily depend on the location to attract customers? Examples of this type of business are: drive-in theatres, discount houses, food supermarkets, beauty parlors, and "big-name" stores (Sears, Montgomery Ward, K-Mart, J.C. Penney and such). Franchised automotive stores are another example of the *self-generating* type of business.

(2) Does the business depend on *transient trade*? Examples of this type of business are: gasoline stations, drive-in restaurants, auto repair shops, florists, liquor stores.

(3) Is it a business that demands trade compatibility? In other words, should it be located near or among related businesses, where "togetherness" is a virtue and each shop helps attract business for the other? In New York City, for instance, one section of Grand Street is devoted, almost exclusively, to wedding gown shops. There are other sections devoted, almost exclusively, to furniture and home furnishing stores. In Los Angeles there is a "Restaurant Row."

In selecting your location, bear in mind that the more remote your location and the lower your rent, the more you have to spend in advertising to draw customers to your place of business. Hence you may be paying a good-location rental without necessarily enjoying good-location benefits.

Also bear in mind that the expense of a location should be measured in terms of the ratio of rental to sales, rather than in terms of dollars cost per month. A low-rent location may prove very costly if the customers are scarce; a high-rent location may prove inexpensive indeed if the flow of customers keeps your cash register constantly ringing. Below is a suggested *Table of Rent Averages* for varied businesses, based on estimated gross volume of sales. It is not claimed that these percentages are current, accurate or have applicability to diverse types of operations within a specific field. However, these averages may nevertheless be valuable when used as general guidelines around which the specific facts pertaining to one's own particular business and desired location can be molded.

Type of Business	Percent
Apparel, Children's & Infants'	5.00
Apparel, Men's and Women's	2.35
Apparel, Men's Specialty	4.50
Apparel, Women's Specialty	4.90
Appliance Stores	2.60
Automobile Parts	2.29
Automotive, Miscellaneous	1.52
Bakeries	4.55
Barber & Beauty Shops	6.45
Car Dealers, New	.70
Car Dealers, Used	1.05
Confectionary Stores	2.91
Contractors, Building	.55
Contractors, Specialty	.76
Dairies	.55
Drug Stores	2.75
Feed, Fuel, Ice Dealers	.75
Florists	2.50
Food Stores, Specialty	4.00
Furniture Stores	5.10
Garages	4.60
Gift & Novelty Shops	6.20
Grocery Stores, Combination	1.25
Hardware Stores	2.30
Jewelry Stores	3.85
Laundry Plants	4.15

Laundry & Cleaning Agencies	5.45
Liquor Stores	3.10
Lumber & Building Materials	.65
Machine Shops	2.25
Meat Markets	4.55
Motels	7.30
Music Stores	3.50
Nursery & Garden Supplies	1.65
Paint, Glass & Wallpaper Stores	3.70
Photographic Studio & Supply Shops	4.15
Plumbing & Heating Equipment	1.05
Repair Services	3.45
Restaurants	4.20
Service Stations	2.55
Shoe Stores	4.75
Sporting Goods	2.90
Taverns	4.70
TV Radio Sales & Service	2.05
Upholsterers	2.45
Variety Stores	5.30

Statistics of the minimum amount of population normally needed to support a specific business can be helpful in the analysis of your location decision.

Type of Business	Minimum Population
Grocery Store	500
Restaurant	800
Drug Store	1,200
Bakery	2,500
Hardware	2,700
Shoe Store	3,400
Jewelry	5,000
Florist	6,500
Appliances	5,000
Book Store	5,000
Athletic Goods	8,500
Toys	3,000
Photographic Supply	5,000

Purchasing power of the area is, of course, another important consideration. The success of your business—and your anticipated sales volume—can be estimated with surprising accuracy by carefully assessing the economic status of the community. It is wise to be conservative in appraising the sales volume you believe an area will produce. The following factors should be carefully checked:

1. Volume of retail trade of the district.

2. The number of telephone subscribers.

3. Number, age, and make of cars owned.

4. Number of bank depositors and volume of deposits.

5. Census reports of rents.

6. School and utility figures.

7. A study of wealth produced in the area.

In considering a location, be sure also to investigate *Taxes and Insurance Rates.* Remember that local taxes add to your cost of doing business—as do certain licenses and fees imposed by communities. An otherwise attractive location might be inadvisable because of excessive taxes, fees, and insurance rates.

Transportation Facilities, too, are very important. The condition of railroads and highways can bear heavily on your operations.

Before deciding on your actual site, there are a few rather simple, but generally reliable, ways of "sizing up" the location you are considering.

(a) Have a talk with the local postman. He is usually a fountain of information about conditions (pro and con) in the area he serves.

(b) Mail a postpaid return questionnaire to a sampling of residents in the area concerning their desire and need for your product or service.

(c) Have a "chat" with your competitors (either openly or incognito) as to how they are doing.

(d) Interview local merchants for a general idea as to business and business conditions.

(e) Talk to the local banker; also to the local Chamber of Commerce.

Now, in search for a location, be ever mindful of possible "dead spots." Traditionally, there are certain spots that shoppers just don't like to pass. These include lumber yards, coal companies, vacant lots, and strictly residential areas where no other businesses exist. Other spots that people generally seek to avoid are: parks, police stations, public utilities, offices, churches and libraries. These tend to stem the flow of traffic rather than encourage it.

Once you have decided that all factors are favorable, it is wise to seek a long-term lease. A one- or two-year lease is a mistake, if no provisions are made for renewal.

Checklist for Guidance in Selecting an Area

(For each of the points below record an answer in the first column and then make a check mark in the rating column showing how it reflects your appraisal of the answer in the first column.)

Points upon which area is rated	(Check, yes or no, numerical or other answer)	Rating			
		Excellent	Good	Fair	Poor
A. Competition:					
Number of stores of same kind........					
Sales of stores of same kind...........					
Drawing power of the market					
Number of blocks					
Number of chains of all kinds.........					
New...					
Well-established........................					

Check List for Guidance in Selecting an Area (cont.)

Points upon which area is rated	(Check, yes or no, numerical or other answer)	Rating			
		Excel-lent	Good	Fair	Poor
Number of chains of same kind of store					
New					
Well-established					
B. Population:					
Total population in area					
Total families in area					
Trend of population: growing, stationary, or declining					
Character of population:					
Native born					
Mixed					
Chiefly foreign					
Occupation of population:					
Laborers					
Clerks					
Executives					
Retired					
Age of population:					
Old					
Middle-aged					
Young					
Buying power:					
Average rent of homes					
Average taxes of homes					
Per capita income					
Number of telephones					
Number of automobiles					
C. Zoning ordinances:					
Restrictions on type of store contemplated					

Check List for Guidance in Selecting an Area (cont.)

Points upon which area is rated	(Check, yes or no, numerical or other answer)	Rating			
		Excel-lent	Good	Fair	Poor
D. Physical factors:					
Parking					
Transportation facilities					
Natural barriers — hills, bridges, etc.					
Unpleasant factors such as:					
Cemetary....................................					
Industries					
Vacant buildings (percent of occupied buildings)..................					
Others					

10.

HOW TO ACHIEVE THE PROPER START IN YOUR FRANCHISED BUSINESS

There is a tide in the affairs of men, which, taken at the flood, leads on to fortune; omitted, all the voyage of their life is bound in shallows and in miseries; and we must take the current when it serves, or lose our ventures.

—Shakespeare

The most critical phase of your new franchise operation is the very beginning. The first ninety days can make the difference between success and failure.

The stage is set during this initial, crucial period. It's the momentum you establish at the very outset that can set the pattern for your entire new career. That is why it is most important that you start with determination, with energy, and enthusiasm, and not be "sidetracked" by meaningless procedures that will interfere with the realistic and proper organization of your new franchise operation.

Bear in mind that what you do and how you do it, in the beginning, can be most effective in putting you on the "high road" to success. Your energies and efforts should be directed onto the following paths, immediately:

(1) Familiarize yourself fully with your operation.

(2) Familiarize yourself with your community.

(3) Devise a workable operating plan and set it into motion.

Familiarizing Yourself with Your Operation:

If you have newly purchased a franchise, no doubt you have just completed your home-office schooling. You have been briefed with a vast miscellany of facts and your head may be "crammed full" of undigested information. Now that you are back home, it is important that you review the entire situation in perspective . . . that you go through a leisurely period of analysis, so that you can completely assimilate and comprehend the facts which have been made available.

This is not the work of a day, a week, or even a month. The "digestive" process is slow. You master a little information at a time. As you get into the practical work of your operation, most of the facts will come back to you and you will comprehend them more clearly as each problem arises and requires solution.

The field-training, as given you by the Home Office, is of vital importance. You are now on the "firing line." Generally, you are in the company of a Home Office expert. It is to your advantage to observe all his procedures closely and to make careful notes, so that you can refer to them once he leaves and you are thrown on your own resources. If you have not learned and properly absorbed your field-training, you may find yourself doing things the wrong way indefinitely and wrongly blaming the Home Office for failure that you might well have avoided.

Generally the franchisor's Home Office will provide a comprehensive Franchisee Operations Manual. This usually is divided into pertinent chapters, such as "Knowing Your Product," "Most Effective Sales Methods," "Administering Your Office," "Communicating With The Home Office," "Hiring Salesmen To Help You," etc. You should make this book your "Bible" since it repeats, re-emphasizes and sets before you, permanently, the information received during your Home Office schooling. Certainly you would be wise to refer to it often.

Familiarizing Yourself with Your Community:

From the day you receive an exclusive franchise in your area, you are "wed" to the economy of your community. This is your territory, your "hunting grounds" for prospective business.

Now, it is vital that you take immediate steps to "get to know" and become "known" in your community. It is essential that you set out at once to create a favorable image while you develop an ever-widening circle of friends and acquaintances. Thus, you "set the stage" for constantly increasing sales and the opportunity for bigger and bigger profits.

Here is how this is done:

(1) *Contact Influential Community Leaders.* Seek out and cultivate important people and institutions in your area. Make friends of people who influence other people and who are in a position to assist you, advise you and help you establish that so-important "image" . . . and who can give you enthusiastic references and recommendations.

Such influential contacts would include:

- President of the Chamber of Commerce

- Local banks and bank officials

- Editors of local papers

- Better Business Bureau

- Educational leaders

- Community industrial leaders

- Civic and political leaders

- Community clubs (e.g., Kiwanis, Lions, Rotary, Eagles, Elks, etc.)

- Leaders of church groups and organizations

Make as many such contacts as you can and do it promptly. Acquaint these people with your operation and with the product or service you are offering. Make your field sound as interesting as possible, enlist their cooperation and solicit their referrals. You will be agreeably surprised at the extent to which these community good-will contacts "pay off."

(2) *Be a Joiner.* Join as many clubs in the community as you can. This will bring you into direct social contact with important people who represent a cross section of your community groups.

(3) *Arrange for Publicity.* Seek to place articles in local papers and news sheets which will publicize your business and get people acquainted with your operation. Start out with about three such articles. The first should contain your picture and a notice stating that you are now the "Blank Co." franchisee for your particular area. The second should inform readers about your "grand opening." The third should give interesting and unusual "human interest" sidelights about your franchise operation, such as unusual prospects

you have met and interesting problems you have solved. Ask your Home Office for sample news stories to guide you.

(4) *Send Out Mailings.* These mailings should go to prospects in your area and to lists which are appropriate for your product or service. If your product appeals to home owners, you might want to consider "occupant" mailings. Such mailings should invite residents to your "grand opening;" if the franchise comprises a store, shop, or showroom, it should notify them of your service and offer some special "first-customer" inducement. Your Home Office may have a direct mail program in which you can participate.

(5) *Organize a "Tip" Club.* It has been our experience that a wealth of prospect leads can be obtained from various salesmen in the community, no matter what type of product or service they are selling. A "Tip" Club serves to bring together a group of such salesmen (approximately 15 in number is recommended) to meet at specific times and dates, usually at a restaurant where leisurely and congenial get-togethers can be held. During these sessions "tips" are exchanged. Each member will endeavor to provide at least five prospect tips for other members. You will find it quite simple to organize such "tip" clubs. Most salesmen appreciate the opportunity for such an exchange. For example, a towel company serviceman was able to give a "tip" about an office that needed an adding machine. An office equipment salesman gave a "tip" about a firm in need of a record-keeping system. A water-softener salesman was able to offer "leads" on homes needing carpet cleaning. Other instances include a printing salesman who gave some wonderful leads to an advertising agency representative . . . while an air-conditioning salesman presented some fine leads to a storm window salesman.

You will find that once you get your operation "off the ground" in the proper way, your Home Office will be happy to give you all the assistance possible, to maintain a profitable momentum. Be sure to bear in mind that those first 90 days of your franchise operation may well predict the success or failure of your venture. Within those 90 days you can so "invigorate" your project as to assure its continued success.

Devise a Good, Workable Plan

Every business should have a plan. If you are a franchisee in a service business, you should plan to make a fixed number of contacts each day and a fixed number of re-contacts. Once you set up this schedule, stick to it steadfastly and do not permit yourself to deviate.

Also, you should have a territorial plan. Map out the streets (and prospects) in your community. Cover a section of your community each day, massing together prospects in a given area, in order not to waste valuable time and to make every moment of your "contact" time count to the utmost.

Also, you should have a promotional plan. Establish a schedule for the placement of advertising . . . and a schedule for direct mail advertising. Plan your budget and schedule yourself for at least three months ahead. In this way, your promotions will not "bog down," and you will proceed automatically, thereby assuring yourself of maximum effectiveness and success in your program.

11.

MARKETING AND THE FRANCHISEE

Generally speaking, two categories of marketing information are essential for most franchise operations. The first is the marketing facts you should know about your selected territory *prior* to your acquisition of your franchise. The second category is the marketing facts you should know about your territory *after* you have acquired your franchise . . . to help you achieve maximum sales.

Marketing Facts Prior to Franchise Acquisition

Your general objectives are to assess those factors that help you determine the "worthwhileness" of your prospective franchise in your area. For example:

- Does your territory have the potential of giving you ample patronage for your particular product or service, assuring you sufficient income?

- Do you have adequate territory—based on this marketing evaluation—to help you attain your earnings goal?

- Does your territory have proper composition so that you are not excluded from adjoining patronage, potential areas that are really part of your greater marketing area?

The normal franchise territory is one that gives you a complete "trading area." The usual measurement of a trading area is that territory covered by the local newspaper (the heaviest concentration of their circulation).

Certain vital statistics about your territory are essential, in order to properly "pinpoint" its potential. Each area—no matter where it is—usually has such statistics available. These include:

- population per square mile

- population increase or decrease within the past 5 and 10 years

- number of residences

- number of apartment dwellers

- age categories (under 5 years, 21 years and over, 65 years and over, etc.)

- births and marriages

- number and size of families

- family income

- education factors and school enrollment

- number of unemployed

- population expenditures (ownership of electrical appliances, TV sets, telephones, automobiles, etc.)

The above-listed data conveys valuable information about your territory and you. This includes: potential prosperity factors, general buying habits and purchase potential. This data is available from many, varied, local sources, state government sources and independent commercial sources.

Community Sources

Almost every area can provide extensive data about itself.

Included are:

- City government statistical publications

- Chamber of Commerce statistical information

- Department of Housing statistics

- Bureau of Vital Statistics

State Government Sources

Most states publish statistical data pertinent to the various localities in the state. These may be obtained by writing to your state government—to the Department of Publications or Department of Commerce.

Independent Data Sources

- Rand McNally and Company

- American Map Company

- Dun and Bradstreet

- McGraw-Hill Publications

- Editor and Publisher—Market Data Directory

- Hammond Maps

- R. L. Polk Company

- Sales Management (magazines and directories)

Facts You Should Know After You Have Acquired the Franchise

Now you are in your own territory complete with your "spanking new" franchise business. What should be your next step?

Your next step commences with thorough research and territorial analysis. Equip yourself with a clear, large map of your area that provides a detailed division of all segments. Also, equip yourself with local statistical booklets or directories.

Here is the information that you would want to obtain:

- Wealth status of varied sections of your area, giving you a "barometer" of purchasing power and potential customers

- Ethnic factors (to the extent that this data is applicable to your business)

- Population concentration—enabling concentrated sales contacts

- Industry concentration

- Main avenues and arteries accommodating maximum traffic flow

- Competitors—how close are they to you? What promotions do they use? What new usable ideas do they have?

- Housing—where are residences concentrated? What new "developments" are being constructed?

- Schools and churches

- Theatres and other centers of entertainment and recreation

- Shopping centers—where are they? How do they compete with or supplement your business?

- Teen-agers—numbers, areas of greatest concentration, buying habits

- Agricultural sections

Next question: now that you have accumulated the above information, what can you do with it? How can it be transformed into dollars and cents?

Here are a few illustrations:

1. *Wealth status:* This data shows you where to "pinpoint" your promotions. Is your product or service purchasable by people in the higher-income bracket? medium? low?

2. *Ethnic factors:* A careful study could point out possible product preferences, enable "tie-ins" with various holidays and festivals, and the sponsoring of specific ethnic events.

3. *Population concentration:* This information will help you plan your mailings and your sales contacts.

4. *Industry concentration:* This data will help you sell your products to industry. You'll be able to sell to various types of personnel, pinpointing your promotions to each plant so that you can achieve a desirable degree of personalization. You'll be able to insert handbills in autos while they're parked in industry parking lots, or even perform services for these cars.

5. *Main avenues and arteries:* This information will tell you where your advertising and promotion can be seen by most people.

6. *Housing:* Are you selling central air conditioning? Burglar alarms? Water conditioners? Normally you'd contact residences and you want to know where they are, to plan your sales contacts. Are you selling closed-circuit television or a building-maintenance service? You'd want to contact

owners of high-rise buildings. These are just a few examples of how housing data can be used.

7. *Schools:* You may want to advertise in the school papers . . . to pass out handbills to students . . . to sponsor school events . . . or to personalize your products around a particular school.

8. *Churches:* In addition to religious activities, a church comprises many members and committees, who buy many things . . . or are interested in selling things for you, in connection with their fund-raising or party-plan programs.

9. *Theatres and other recreation centers:* Nearby theatres and other recreation centers bring "customer flow" to your products or services. In addition, there are many possible "tie-ins" with the recreation or entertainment center itself—program advertising, premium or brochure distribution, etc.

10. *Shopping centers:* Can you benefit from the volume traffic that shopping centers attract?

11. *Teen-agers:* Does your product appeal in any way to teen-agers? Knowing where they are enables you to concentrate and personalize your promotions.

12. *Agricultural sections:* Are there farms and farmers in your area? Their needs are specialized. Determine how you can best reach them and sell them your products.

As a franchisee, knowing your market gives you the proper start, keeps you in proper momentum towards building a successful, enduring local business operation.

12.

TESTED IDEAS FOR PROMOTING BUSINESS IN YOUR FRANCHISED AREA

Now that you have selected your franchise and have set up an office or structure in your designated area, your next task—and your prime objective—is to attract business in a continuing flow.

Your franchisor will help you to a certain extent. He will supply you with his proven procedures, recommended ads, recommended direct mail pieces and other pertinent promotional tools. Once you have all of the above, use them as prescribed by the franchisor.

Fundamentally, however, it is up to *you* to do the major job. You are there, "on the spot." You are in constant contact with your customers on a local person-to-person level. Thus, you develop the sensitivity that alerts you to the varied nuances of your particular territory: What are the things that make people respond? What are the things that obstruct response?

You can depend on the franchisor's assistance to only a partial extent. It is "up to you" to familiarize yourself with all possible promotional approaches and tools—both those supplied to you by your Home Office and those resulting from your own experiences—so that you can implement your program with precision . . . using the things that will work best for *you* in *your* area.

The objective of this and the following chapters is to acquaint you with the types of promotions that have proven successful for other franchisees, so that you can judge what may be most effective for you. After presenting seven brief case histories of how small businesses increased sales and twenty-one tested sales-building ideas, this chapter shows you how to search for customers, how to use "tip" clubs, how to stage contests and special promotions, how to take advantage of publicity, how to use the telephone to sell and how to create effective advertising ideas.

Specifically, these subjects comprise:

(a) Case Histories of "How 7 Small Businesses Obtained More Sales"

(b) 20 Tested Sales-Building Ideas

(c) Prospecting for Customers in Your Franchise area

(d) "Tip Clubs"—How They Help Franchisees Obtain Increased Sales

(e) 36 Contests and Promotions

(f) Tested Publicity Ideas for the Franchisee

(g) Using the Telephone to Sell

(h) How to Create Effective Advertising Ideas

Case Histories of How 7 Small Businesses Obtained More Sales

Firm "A"—RANG DOORBELLS to get more trade. He organized a "Home Service" department, using a selection of items sold directly to homes. This personalized service helped to build a substantial "plus" patronage. Eventually he hired a group of salesmen, on a commission basis, to make contacts.

Firm "B"—DRAMATIZED his truck by painting it prominently all-white and lettering on it a list of all his services. Thus it became a mobile "billboard" advertising him wherever it went. This was so successful that he prevailed upon his friends (for a small fee) to carry his cartop billboards.

One hardware store franchise went still further. To promote his ladders, he attached an actual aluminum ladder to the roof of his car. An advertising message was contained on each rung. His ladder sales increased 40%.

Firm "C"—Benefited from PERSONALS COLUMN ADVERTISEMENTS. This is an inexpensive type of advertising, inserted in classified columns of newspapers under "Personals." It has an informality that attracts attention . . . gets better-than-usual results. For example: (if you're a beauty salon), "Mary—Remember that permanent you admired. I had it done at (your name) Beauty Salon. Wonderful people . . . wonderful service . . . and wonderful price!'' Or: (if you're a service firm), "Vexed by a TV set that 'acts up'? See us for quick, reliable repairs. Phone (your number).''

Firm "D"—Arranged a local BANK EXHIBIT. They displayed his products in their window along with a placard listing his name and address. This publicized his store and products—and helped attract added trade. Most banks are glad to cooperate with local merchant depositors.

Firm "E"—ENLISTED AID OF NEIGHBORHOOD STORES (non-competitive) to insert signs in their windows advertising his work. This is particularly effective for service-type businesses. They received a small commission on all referrals obtained. (A brochure which they distributed contained a "key number" that identified the referral store.)

Firm "F"—ORGANIZED A "HOSTESS" PLAN to exhibit and sell the product. Parties were run in various homes in the neighborhood, with tea and cookies served, where items were displayed. The hostess received a small commission on all sales made. Each visitor was given a chance to run her own party (thus one party generated another).

Firm "G"—MADE A LIST OF SUPPLIERS from whom he purchased things regularly—24 in all. He reasoned that since he patronized them, they would want to patronize him . . . or refer prospects to him. His contacts "paid off" in greatly increased business. This list included:

Grocer	Electrician
Doctor	Men's Apparel
Newsstand	Dairy
Gas Station	Dentist
Landlord	Tobacco Store
Insurance Agent	Appliance Shop
Hardware	Bank
Optician	Radio & TV Shop
Women's Apparel	Liquor Store
Bakery	Jeweler
Drugstore	Car Dealer
Fuel Supplies	Dry Cleaner

20 Tested Sales—Building Ideas

As a franchisee, your most important quest is to get more business. Few franchised operations (or any other type of business, for that matter) can afford to sit back and wait for business to come to them. It's necessary to plan attractive campaigns that will publicize you . . . which will reach out and bring prospects to you.

We are listing below a number of ways such campaigns have been successful for franchisees, located in various parts of the country and representing practically every type of business. In most instances these constitute pretested procedures. It's suggested that you keep this list handy. Use it as a check-off list for constant referral.

1. FUND-RAISING PROMOTIONS: Most clubs (business and social), charitable organizations, church groups, etc. sponsor fund-raising programs. These are usually related to a "pet" charity project, a pre-established club financial goal, a building improvement program or a myriad of other factors. You can assist their project and at the same time produce community good will, valuable publicity, and the cooperation of the many members by having them act as "quasi-salesmen" for your services or products. Contact the secretary of the respective organizations. Offer a commission to the club (applicable to their earning fund) for all member referrals or member purchases. In some instances, franchisees have received permission to conduct talks on their services before the complete member group. In other instances, franchisees have publicized their services via audio-film presentations. This "fund-raising" approach has proven constantly successful.

2. REFERRALS: There's a "gold mine" of new business awaiting you among your present customers. It's there—it just requires the asking. Make it a habit to ask each customer for at least five referrals to friends, relatives and associates. Offer a gift for their efforts and another (more substantial) gift for "sold" referrals. You'll find this is a highly effective, yet extremely inexpensive, form of business-getting. It gives you a personalized "tie-in" with the prospect. In most instances, "the referred-to" person is easiest to sell.

3. "CAPITALIZE" ON CURRENT JOBS: Every job performed represents a valuable opportunity to get additional work in the same area. While servicing a customer on any block, knock on doors of all other homes on that block. Your approach is: "Good afternoon, Mr. Smith. While we are servicing your neighbor Mr. Blank down the street, we are in a position to extend the same service to you at similarly low cost . . . ." This is a personalized form of approach that can increase your trade potential substantially. If you happen to be in working coveralls at the time, do not let this deter you. This conveys an informality that often aids your sales approach.

4. DIRECT MAIL: Most effective direct mail is that which conveys a specific "get acquainted" offer. Above all, use your direct mail as a "door-opener." Follow it up with phone calls or personal visits. You'll find that

mailings normally achieve a minimum response. Your "follow-up" contacts will help to move the prospect from hesitation to buying action. Hence, one of the strongest benefits of direct mail is that it offers an excuse for such "follow-up" action.

5. OPEN HOUSE: Most people like to be invited out, especially to a festive occasion. Send mailings to prospects, in your area, inviting them to an "open house" at your place. Offer refreshments and music (perhaps a door prize). Use the occasion to exhibit your products. You'll find that this plan—providing a warm, informal prospect approach—can bring traffic into your place, thereby improving sales growth.

6. COMMUNITY "TIE-INS": An Indiana franchisee contacted other (non-competitive) businesses in his locality. He arranged to set up displays of his product in their stores (or, at the least, a sign publicizing his product or services). A "pocket" was attached to the sign containing literature plus a business reply postcard. The cooperating storekeeper received a designated commission on all sales generated through his store. Thus, the franchisee has dozens of effective "sub-locations" engaged in selling on his behalf.

7. MAIL ORDER: You can greatly multiply your potential through a well-planned mail order program. Solicit direct-by-mail orders from prospects in your area, either through letters, catalogs or newspaper ads. It has been estimated that over two billion dollars of business is done via mail order. As a franchisee you'll find this to be a profitable adjunct to your business.

8. GROUP DEMONSTRATIONS: Try to sell your services before groups. Thus, you can make many sales via a single demonstration. Groups to contact are: trade associations, conventions, various community clubs, and business groups. An Illinois franchisee, selling a record-keeping system, covered all trade and professional association meetings. He arranged to make group demonstrations and achieved as many as 20 orders with a single sales pitch.

9. WELCOME NEWCOMERS: Make it a habit to compile name lists of "newcomers" in your area. Send them a letter welcoming them into your community. Offer something free (or a special discount) as a "get acquainted" feature.

10. HOME DEMONSTRATIONS: Macy's Department Store in New York City increased their business in draperies substantially by offering to bring swatches to the home, as a "shop-at-home" service. The same procedure has proved successful for many other types of organizations selling many types of products or services. How about your own business—does it

lend itself to home demonstration? If so, you'll find that you can increase your business to a substantial extent.

11. NEWSPAPER ADS: Regular newspaper ad insertion is a cardinal rule for most businesses. General ads (with no specific offerings) rarely pay off. It's advisable to tie-in your ad with a specific offer (one that has attractive appeal). If possible, incorporate a coupon offer in your ad.

12. TELEPHONE DIRECTORY ADVERTISING: By inserting ads in the telephone directories of all the surrounding cities of your locality, you can greatly increase your trading area range, especially if your products or services are not readily available in those other areas.

13. HANDBILLS: Distribute handbills around your area at regular intervals. Get them into homes and offices—insert them under the windshields of parked cars. Include an attractive special offer.

14. DISTRIBUTE PRODUCT SAMPLES: Do you have s store franchise pertaining to foods? A donut franchisee stationed an attractive girl outside his store offering "bite-sized" samples of donuts to passers-by. A pizza shop offered samples of pizza . . . etc.

15. "HAPPY DOLLARS" PROMOTION: A Nebraska furniture store publicized a "Happy Dollars" sales event. During this event, one "Happy Dollar" would be given free for any ten dollars in purchases. At a designated time, an auction sale was conducted whereby customers could bid with these "Happy Dollars" for various items featured.

16. YOUR AUTO: Are you realizing the full business value of your auto or truck? Since it is constantly in transit, it can become a valuable "mobile billboard." A donut shop erected a huge facsimile donut on the roof of the car. Other franchisees have found it effective to attach or paint signs on their cars or trucks listing their services.

17. USE OF OUTSIDE SALESMEN: You can expand the prospect potential of your business by using the services of outside salesmen who sell "door-to-door." If the use of outside salesmen fits in with your own operation, use the method to multiply your sales. Equip them with a presentation book which dramatizes and documents the benefits derived from your products or services.

18. PERSONALIZE YOUR WINDOWS: Take candid photos of passers-by. Attach these photos to your windows. Offer a prize to those who can identify their photos. This will help to draw traffic to your window displays.

19. REMEMBER BIRTHDAYS: A birthday is a highly personal matter with most people. They appreciate having their birthdays remembered. Utilize this fact in your business by maintaining birth-date records of your customers. When this event arrives, send them a "good wishes" letter plus an offer of a birthday gift which they can obtain by bringing the letter to your place of business.

20. CUSTOMER COMMENTS: An Indiana restaurant franchisee had his customers write their comments about his food on a sheet of paper. He then combined all these comments about his food and had them photostatically "blown-up." He displayed this sign outside the door with a caption "WHAT OUR CUSTOMERS THINK OF US." This attracted a great deal of attention since most people like to "eavesdrop" on handwriting. In addition, the handwriting engenders a feeling of "believability."

Prospecting for Customers for Your Franchise Operation

Prospecting for customers in your franchise area is just like prospecting for gold. It requires plenty of "digging." Moreover, it requires "digging" with the right tools—at the right place and at the right time.

Whether you are selling a product or a service, the extent to which you prosper is governed by the extent to which you prospect. And that isn't a matter of quantity but of quality and continuity, as well.

Your prospecting program, to be successful, must be planned carefully. You must determine in advance:

1. Whom you want to reach.

2. What is the best way to reach them.

3. How to organize your program for maximum results and minimum waste of time and effort.

In this connection it is important to keep an alphabetical file of lists used, as well as a date file that tells you when the various lists and people should be "followed up."

As to whom you wish to reach, this might seem rather elementary. You can say to yourself, "Since I know my product, I should certainly know my prospects." For example, someone in the jewelry handicrafts line might well say, "My prospects, of course, are women." Then again, someone selling Finnish-type sauna baths might answer, "My prospects are homes." Or someone in the toy business might say, "Children."

Of course, in the broad sense each would be right. However, the categories are too general and are tantamount to "flock shooting," rather than shooting at a particular target. It is important to aim individually at the various components of your market, rather than to scatter your fire indiscriminately. The difference between concentration and "hit or miss" can be the difference between success and failure. Concentrating your fire on one segment at a time can, in the overall picture, multiply your results many times.

It is highly essential to take a microscopic view of your market and to ask yourself, "What specific attributes do our products have that will make them desirable for select groups and encourage their wider use?" For example, to take one of the businesses mentioned previously, let us analyze the market for the jewelry handicrafts field and try to determine precise groups which would be logical prospects:

- Junior achievement groups
- Geriatric groups
- Women's clubs
- Earning fund programs
- Industrial firms (employee handicraft classes)
- Party plan promotions
- Hospital rehabilitation groups

Now let us do the same with the sauna-bath field and see precisely where that market lies:

- Hotels
- Motels
- Health clubs
- Hospitals
- Gymnasiums
- Massage parlors
- Individual homes

Next let's examine the market for toys and instead of finding merely "children" we find:

- Industrial firms seeking children's premiums to attract business for their own products
- Earning fund programs
- Mail order businesses
- Private kindergartens and schools

Now let us leave the subject of who to reach and go on to the best ways to reach them. We find our means of contact are: (a) the mails, (b) the telephone, and (c) publication ads. We shall now pursue each of these, as follows:

BY MAIL: The first step is to get prospect lists. These are obtainable through mailing list brokers, city directories, trade directories, reverse telephone directories, referral names. The various types of mailings you can use include: postcards, self-mailers, letters, brochures.

BY TELEPHONE: This is a highly personalized and particularly effective approach. All mail contacts should be followed up by phone (or personal visits). In this way, you achieve maximum utilization of your mailing lists. In your telephone "pitch," you should refer to the offer that was sent by mail. Such telephone or personal follow-ups have been known to increase a 2% mailing response to as high as 30% or 40% conversion to sales.

PUBLICATION ADVERTISING: Newspaper ads help you to "pinpoint" the specific geographic areas you desire to reach. Magazine ads, in most instances, enable you to reach specific trades or business audiences. The ad should be so designed as to actively produce sales . . . in many cases a coupon will prove especially effective.

Finally, as to organizing your "prospecting" program, it is essential to keep a chart of your potential market along the lines outlined below, which, in effect, is a "checklist" of the prospects you want to reach:

Men _____ Women _____ Children _____ Age Level _____

Type of business _____

Occupational Level:

_____ Executive _____ Sub-executive _____ Business

_____ Students _____ Professional _____ Laborers _____ Housewives

Economic Level:

_____ Wealthy _____ Middle Income _____ Low Income

Cultural Level:

_____ College Education _____ High School _____ Grammar School

A list of this type can provide exceptional benefits in planning your "prospecting." It will help identify exactly who your prospect is . . . so that you can plan your approaches, in the most effective manner, to the maximum number of individuals or businesses who are prospects for your products or services.

"Tip Clubs"—How They Help Franchisees Obtain Increased Sales

Since franchised businesses are involved with making sales, the franchisee is vitally concerned with the answers to these basic questions: (a) Where can I find prospects? (b) Where can I find them at a minimum cost to me? (c) How can I assure myself of a constant flow of such prospects?

There have been many answers to these questions, many of them successful ones. One highly effective formula for obtaining non-cost prospect leads, on a continuing basis, has been achieved by "Tip Clubs"—a unique type of organization that is becoming more and more popular among franchisees throughout the country.

Properly conducted "Tip Clubs" can help to increase sales as many as 10, 20 or more times (depending on the number and activity of members of each club).

What are "Tip Clubs?" They are not lavish country club "set-ups." Normally a "Tip Club" is organized by a franchisee in an area as a means of increasing his sales.

Simply stated, the franchisee makes contact with 10 or more salesmen in his area. They can be salesmen representing practically any product or service in the community, provided that they are non-competitive with each other.

They form a local "Tip Club" for their mutual good to receive and give prospect leads to each other on a reciprocal basis.

The basis of such an association is that each sales person contacting any prospect for sales is usually conversant with that prospect's needs above and beyond his own products or services. He "tips off" a member of his group—who does provide such products or services—relative to such a prospect need.

It's amazing how many such "tips" are obtained, almost on a daily basis and how many sales result.

Often "Tip Clubs" go even further than the mere supplying of information between members. With the proper spirit of cooperation, "Tip Club" members can often make the approach necessary to enable another member to set up a profitable interview and demonstration.

For instance, you may be selling grocery products . . . and John Jones, a member of your "Tip Club," sells store fixtures. John may be called in to supply fixtures for a new grocery store. While talking to his customer, John asks what brands of products he expects to handle and mentions that he has a friend who sells wholesale groceries whom he can recommend in terms of product quality and service. If the grocer seems interested, John will tell him that he'll have you get in touch with him. On the other hand, you may have a customer who is planning a store alteration. So, when you get an opportunity to discuss his plans with him, you will mention John Jones as a reliable person who may have the best answers to his fixture problems.

It's logical, isn't it, that this cooperation between members of a "Tip Club" can multiply the sales potential of each member by a good many times?

To get your own "Tip Club" started, use this three-point formula:

1. SELL YOURSELF. Become convinced in your own mind that a "Tip Club" can be a highly effective sales-generator for you and other members.

2. SELL ONE OTHER . . . or maybe two. They will each sell one or two other non-competitive salesmen . . . and they will sell still others. The first thing you know, your club will mushroom like a "chain" letter.

3. PLAN YOUR FIRST MEETING. Set a specific date, not more than a week ahead, to get your first meeting going. Run it like a club . . . maintaining meeting schedules and keeping it always on a business-like basis.

Described below are suggested procedures to follow:

First, it's important that your membership consist of the right kinds of business people (salesmen constitute an ideal grouping). They should be non-competitive to each other but they should call on the same general types of prospects. For instance, if you sell to retail stores, a typical list of your membership might include: bread salesman, insurance salesman, coffee salesman, cigarette vending machine salesman, real estate salesman, commercial laundry salesman, a moving and storage salesman, a general contractor.

This list can be greatly enlarged, if desired, with other types of salesmen who contact businessmen. Care should be taken, however, to limit membership to people who are strictly "outside" salesmen . . . do not enroll "deskmen," telephone salesmen, or inside-the-store salesmen. The "Tip Club" is most successful in the small business market where all decisions and all purchases are made by one boss.

Regularly scheduled meetings should be held, preferably on Monday because it is the beginning of the week and, thus, the salesman who receives a tip can incorporate it in his plans for that week . . . or for immediate action. Luncheon meetings are better than evening meetings because the salesmen attending have their minds on business instead of their desire to get home.

Each meeting lasts about an hour and a half. During the meal, the secretary calls the membership roll, a brief discussion of old and new business takes place, and then the president asks for tips.

Each member, in rotation around the table, rises and gives his "tips." It is vitally important that quiet be maintained while "tips" are being given. Questions regarding "tips" should be held until the end of the meeting.

The "Tip Club" should have a certain amount of formality as far as its organization is concerned. It should have officers, committees, and rules. Each member should realize fully that he is a part of a "select" group which has been formed for mutual benefit. It is essential that each member fully realizes his responsibility to the other members, for it is upon this sense of responsibility that the success of the "Tip Club" depends.

Since "Tip Clubs" are organized for business and not social purposes, a certain amount of discipline must be maintained. Luncheon meetings are held for serious purposes and maximum attention must be required when each member is giving out his "tips." Hence, it is a good idea to establish a "fine" system, with sums of 25¢ or more levied upon members who cannot control themselves while "tips" are being given. Lateness or absence from meetings are also offenses, punishable by fines.

Since the clubs have been organized for mutual benefit and since absences and lateness are disadvantageous to others in terms of the offender's inability to give the "tips" expected of him, these offenses are also punishable by fines of 25¢ or more. Furthermore, excessive absenses, being a manifestation of the fact that a man has other things he considers more important than the "Tip Club," should result in that individual's being dropped from the club since, in most cases, it has been found that shortly after a "Tip Club" is formed, there is a substantial waiting list of interested salesmen. Often this waiting list is larger than the membership of the organization itself.

Because of the nature of the "Tip Club," it is imperative that a code of ethics be established and impressed upon the membership. This code acts as protection against competition from outsiders or against possible resentment by a member's customer that the member may have given out his name as a "tip" to a competitor. A useful set of club ethics includes the following:

1. Tips are strictly confidential. No member will mention a "tip" he may have heard in the club on the outside.

2. No salesman competitive to any of the members can attend a meeting.

3. The meeting must always be held out of earshot of non-members.

4. No comments will be made by anyone during the "tip" presentation.

5. Each member must guarantee his product and service to the satisfaction of the club membership, to insure against resentment, by a customer, against whomever may have given out his name as a "tip."

Numerous accessories or innovations are possible within a "Tip Club" to make it an even more effective instrument than just as a meeting place for "tip-giving." Some "Tip Clubs" print their own business cards which include the names of all salesmen who are members and their businesses. When a member calls on a new place of business, he leaves the card and personally guarantees the service that "Tip Club" salesmen give. He states that the club as a whole endorses each of its members and the products or sevices which he offers.

A practice which can help greatly to increase the effectiveness of the club is for its members to maintain contact with each other on the outside. Thus, a mid-week phone call from one member to another can assure immediate action on a "tip" which otherwise would have to wait until the following meeting.

It's a good idea to charge slightly more for a "Tip Club" meal than its actual cost to the club. For instance, a club in California pays $5.00 for the meal but charges its members $7.00. The $2.00 difference is, in effect, the club dues, and at the end of the year it is lumped with the money collected from fines to form a fund from which the "Tip Club's" annual social function is paid.

An idea as unique as that of the "Tip Club" and as simple to organize and operate, is rare in the annals of salesmanship. What better way could be found to increase the individual's sales potential than to augment his own efforts with those of a large group of other individuals with his interests at heart?

MARKETING PLANS
THAT ACHIEVE
INCREASED SALES

Question:
HOW TO COVER THE OTHER 95% OF YOUR MARKET --AT MINIMAL COST!

CATALOG CORNERS

Expands: SALES OUTLETS
UNIT CAPACITY

LOCAL INDUSTRY TIE-INS

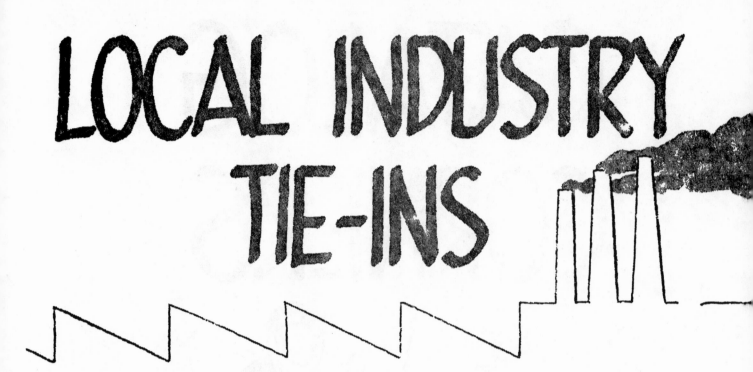

- FOOD COMMISSARY
- SAME-DAY AUTO SERVICES
- PERSONNEL DISCOUNTS

PARTY PLANS

One current plan totaling $100-million in sales

LOCAL MERCHANT CO-OPERATION

Displays on Store Counters

Special Offer

TAKE ONE

Provide Selling Space on No-Rent Basis

FUND-RAISING GROUPS

100's of community's most influential people sell for you!

13.

TESTED IDEAS FOR PROMOTING BUSINESS IN YOUR FRANCHISED AREA (Continued)
36 CONTESTS AND PROMOTIONAL IDEAS

The ideas listed below are applicable to most types of franchised businesses. They have been proven in actual franchise operations and found to be attention-getting and sales-producing.

Refer to them for use in your business. In many instances, the idea may not specifically apply to your operation, nevertheless, it can be of invaluable assistance as a stimulator of your thoughts towards related or supplementary ideas more specifically applicable to you.

Seasonal Promotions

A. January

1. After Christmas sales
2. Safety campaign slogans for New Year's ads
3. Gift certificates to new members of community
4. Large calendar display in store showing coming events during coming weeks and months

B. February

5. Displays centered about Boy Scout Week
6. Valentine's Day promotion

March

7. Lucky bill sweepstakes for St. Patrick's Day
   (A particular denomination of bills is given out for change during the month. Holders of lucky bills are awarded prizes.)

D. April

8. "Mad Hat" Contest
   (Employees design hats from merchandise—event is played up big—judging is staged in store—wide publicity usually follows an unusual stunt.)

E. May

9. Promotion built around baseball season

F. June

10. Father's Day promotion

G. July

11. Fourth of July promotion
    [Non-exploding firecrackers with name of establishment printed on barrel and "Our (product) is not a dud."]

H. August

12. Big Top Theme
    (Stock a big tent with fine buys and refreshments.)

I. September

13. Back-to-school promotion
    (Have a contest for children.)

J. October

14. Halloween promotion
    (Picture of happy ghost laden with merchandise—apple-bobbing contests—costume contest—prizes of gift certificates.)

K. November

15. Thanksgiving—live turkey contest
16. Christmas
    (Have sneak preview of holiday goods and a special night for male Christmas shoppers.)

L. December

17. Christmas and New Year promotions
(Check store housekeeping cleanliness. Check lighting. Don't skimp on special services. Store decorations. Tie-in window display with store interior.)

Other Sales-Boosting Promotions and Contests

18. *WHEEL OF FORTUNE:* At varying hours of the day, the large spin-wheel is revolved. Those with brochure (or other designated item) bearing this number win a prize.

19 *CRAZY AUCTION PROMOTION.* For example, start bid high . . . and work down to ridiculously low price bids.

20. *POSTCARD PROMOTION.* The postcard (with your ad) contains a chance number on it . . . good for a certain designated prize when brought to store.

21. *BALLOON PROMOTIONS.* The store is dressed up with balloons. Free balloons are given to the kiddies and your newspaper ad has the theme centered around balloons.

22. *FOOD OPERATION PROMOTIONS.* There are many effective, appealing promotional opportunities—World Food Fair, Meat 'N Taters, Let Them Have Steak, etc.

23. *TRADING COUPONS*

24. *WISHING WELL.* For customer drawings

25. *MYSTERY GIFT PACK PROMOTION*

26. *PLATTER PROMOTIONS.* For increasing teenage record trade.

27. *GIANT SPOTLIGHT PROMOTION.* "Follow the lights" promotion to giant spotlight stationed in front of your shop.

28. *STORE ANNIVERSARY PROMOTIONS.* Prizes can be offered to oldest person, youngest person, person coming longest distance, largest family attending, newest bride and groom, etc.

29. *ART SHOW.* Sponsor an art show. Exhibit the best entries in your establishment and price them for sale. Try to obtain entries from prominent people.

30. *WESTERN WEEK.* Decorate store and personnel in western motif, play western music, have reward posters, western money, etc.

31. *GROUP PARTICIPATION PROMOTION.* Have everyone donate squares for the "biggest blanket in the world" or have people donate string and cord for a huge string ball.

32. *NAME CONTEST.* For an unusual pet. Keep the animal on display in the store for a week or two. Winner of the best name gets the pet.

33. *GUESSING GAMES.* The following have worked successfully: how many coffee beans in a bathtub? . . . how many bottle caps in a small car? . . . identifying well-known townsfolk from baby pictures.

34. *MISCELLANEOUS CONTESTS.* Run contests for the customer with: the most freckles, biggest ears, biggest feet, fastest gun draw, best smile, funniest face, etc.

35. *MARATHON CONTESTS.* Anything that will move continuously will attract customers. Much local newspaper publicity will be generated. Run marathons for rope skipping, dancing, knitting, gum chewing, chess playing, anything novel.

36. *TREASURE HUNT.* Such as Cinderalla's glass slipper, the oldest citizen in town, etc.

35 Tested Publicity Ideas

There's a "gold mine" of publicity awaiting practically every franchisee. It's just a matter of "digging."

As a franchisee—no matter what type of franchise you have—it's important that you build up a "personality image" . . . both for yourself and your establishment. It is equally important that this "image" be given maximum exposure to prospects in your trading area.

Just starting your operation? Then it's wise to commence building an image right from the outset. Long-established? It's to be hoped that you have already created such an image. However, there's no time like the present to begin.

How does one go about this? How is a proper image created and then how is "exposure" achieved? The answer is (1) through advertising, and (2) through publicity.

Advertising is always effective. Generally, the Home Office supplies the franchisee with pre-tested advertising and promotional aids, specifically designed to achieve maximum results.

However, advertising, no matter how effective, can only do part of the job. First, because the advertising budget of the typical franchisee must be limited (an average of 2% of gross revenues for most small businesses). Secondly, because advertising is frankly commercial and needs to be supplemented with a more subtle public relations program.

Publicity is the catalyst of your advertising program which strengthens and documents the validity of your claims . . . helps to create a favorable "image" and causes prospective customers to prefer your services to those of competitors.

Thousands of lines of free publicity in varied local publications are available to the average franchisee. He must, however, take steps to ask for it!

By local publications we mean newspapers, shopping guides, radio or TV stations, and magazines appealing to specific trades, industrial house organs, amusement guides, and general-interest magazines.

Now, chances are that you are saying to yourself, "How does all of this help me? Publicity means writing. I'm not a writer, nor can I afford to hire a publicity writer, so how can I get free write-ups in publications?" The answer is that you don't need any writing ability. Most newspapers and other publications are looking for newsworthy items, just as much as you are looking for publicity. The test is "What is there about you, your organization, your type of business, or your personnel, that can be considered newsworthy?

Although your inclination might be to say "Nothing," the truth is, that, if you give the matter some thought, you will most likely find that there are dozens of potential news items—and possibly, several feature-length articles—that could be written about you and your organization. Consider just a few write-up opportunities which can be applied, generally, to most franchised establishments:

1) YOUR BUSINESS: What are the "human interest" aspects of your business? What special interest angle is there to your own venture? What are some of the human interest aspects of your customers?

Ask yourself these questions and see if you don't produce some interesting answers. Meanwhile, here are a few of the ideas that got one franchised doughnut firm "into print" quite a number of times. Among them were (a) the numbers of doughnuts consumed, each month, in this store;

(b) the "romance" of doughnuts . . . how the doughnut was "born". . . the background of the hole in the doughnut; (c) the proprietorship: the unusual background of the proprietor . . . the unrelated field from which he came . . . why he finds the doughnut business fascinating.

2) YOUR COMMUNITY PARTICIPATION: As a franchised dealer, it is to your advantage to participate in community activities and to become a "joiner" of various community organizations; also, to become a sponsor of various activities, such as Little League baseball, Boy Scout outings, art shows, etc. Participating in such events lends itself to news write-ups.

3) YOUR ESTABLISHMENT: Unique displays, exciting counter arrangements, unusual advertising . . . all these can be incorporated into newsworthy write-ups.

For example: the automotive store (or gas station) that exhibited antique autos . . . the apparel shop that displayed apparel of 50 years ago . . . the ice-cream store that displayed unusual local hobbies . . . the handicrafts store that displayed a collection of unusual stamps and coins.

4) "TIE-IN" WITH TIMELY EVENTS: As an example, a prominent lawn-maintenance company tied in with a "Keep Our Community Beautiful" program by emphasizing the importance of beautiful lawns. A pharmaceutical franchisee publicized his firm while performing a public service, when he got a write-up on "14 Ways to Avoid the Flu," during a local flu epidemic. An automotive parts franchisee also benefited both himself and the public, when he spotlighted 4th of July accident predictions with a publicity story on "Automotive Parts that Make the Difference Between Life and Death." A franchised slenderizing salon tied in with physical fitness publicity, by preparing a write-up on "25 Ways to Physical Fitness."

Make a list of all publicity ideas you consider suitable for your particular business. Write up all the data in rough form and don't concern yourself with the fine points of writing. Your local newspaper is more interested in substance than in form. After all, they have their own writers who simply need to be fed ideas.

With any news story you suggest to your local paper, it benefits both you and the newspaper to supply some suitable photos. Pictures are always acceptable—they liven up a story and help to get it more attention.

Try to achieve the widest possible circulation for your news stories. Send your completed stories or story suggestions to as many newspapers as possible in your trading area. After they have been published, further enhance their value by enlarging them and displaying them in the most prominent spot available in your establishment.

These suggestions for gaining publicity should serve you well in getting you and your organization better known in your community—which, in turn, should produce increased business. Take advantage of every possibility for publicity. Get yourself "read about." Get yourself "talked about" favorably . . . and you'll get more customers and more sales.

Using the Telephone to Sell

As owner of a business, naturally you are greatly interested in increasing your sales. You want to use every available means of increasing your sales figures. One of the most effective ways is through use of the telephone—which, strange to say, is a widely neglected technique.

The telephone is relatively inexpensive. Even at today's increased rates, the average local phone call is still a business bargain.

By telephone you can achieve a personal contact that can only be surpassed by an actual visit. The telephone brings about a person-to-person relationship difficult to duplicate in any other way (except personal contact) by putting you in vocal contact with your prospect.

Of course, for maximum effectiveness, it is essential that you get properly organized. First thing to do is to make a list of the prospects you want to call. It is also wise to prepare, in writing, a specimen telephone conversation and to time yourself, so that your initial "pitch" does not exceed an attention span of one minute.

As with a personal visit, your personality becomes an all-important factor over the telephone. Your prospective sale can be made possible, or impossible, based on the mental picture registered on your prospect's mind by what you say and how you say it. It's not only the words that count but the tone of your voice which can attract or repel. A telephone company campaign of years ago was based on the theme that "It's the voice with the smile that wins." It's still true.

In your telephone sales talk, try to summarize the advantages of your proposition in one or two sentences. Whatever you do, don't make yourself appear to be delivering an "oration" to a faceless individual. Speak in conversational phrases and in a conversational tone. Envision the person with whom you are speaking as a typical prospect and adopt an attitude, as though you were sitting alongside this person and talking to him. As in talking "face to face," allow pauses in your telephone talk, so that your prospect has an opportunity to say something or ask a question, when one is appropriate.

Telephone calls are highly effective when "tied in" with your direct mail program. There are several ways in which this can be done: (1) as a follow-up to your letter; (2) as an announcement that a letter will be forthcoming. In either case, the telephone helps to support your mailing and give emphasis to it. It adds a personal note that can't help but improve the results of your mailing.

For best results, it is important to be properly organized and to adhere to a planned program. You should arrange to make a specific number of calls each day. Planning ten calls a day, for example, could be your minimum. You should also equip yourself with a chart, listing all the names you plan to call, accompanied by personal notes about each prospect on this list, plus adequate space for notations as to the results of your calls. There should also be space to indicate "call backs" along with the date and circumstances of each such "call back."

Your chart, should look about like this (shown here in reduced size):

Date	Name	Address	Phone No.	Personality Comments	Results of Call	Date to Call Back	Results of Call-Back

Your selling-by-telephone can be divided as follows:

(1) Prospecting for new accounts

(2) Reviving inactive accounts

(3) Improving relations with active accounts and thus obtaining additional orders.

NEW ACCOUNT prospects should be compiled from name lists available from varied sources. It is considered good "prospecting" practice to test different list types until you have established which lists comprise your most productive customer potential, after which you concentrate your attention on those prospects.

INACTIVE ACCOUNTS can often be revived through a telephone call having a strong personal "touch." Such calls make customers feel that you really value their patronage and that you have a personal interest in them. You may be surprised at the results. Recent test telephone campaigns, of this type, have succeeded in reviving nearly 35% of inactive accounts.

ACTIVE ACCOUNTS, solicited by telephone, can prove particularly productive. A phone call now and then indicates that you appreciate their business and it reminds them about another order they've been thinking of placing with you. It also gives you an opportunity to bring new products and services to their attention, as well as information as to new uses for your product, improvements and pending price changes.

Bear in mind that certain hours of the day are better than others for making telephone calls. This, by the way, depends upon whom you are calling. For example:

(a) Homes should be phoned in the afternoon if you wish to speak with the housewife; in the evening if you wish to speak with the husband.

(b) Stores should be phoned in the morning or mid-afternoon; never during their busy noon hours.

(c) Builders should be contacted before 9:00 a.m.

(d) Other service agencies should be contacted early in the morning in order to catch them before they start on their day's work.

There is also magic, in the announcement, "Long distance calling!" Quite a few firms make effective use of a special service and rate offered by the telephone company. This service enables them to reserve time for making an unlimited number of long distance calls into any given area, with the operator prefacing each call with the aforementioned "Long distance calling!" However, instead of paying so much per call, bills are based on a flat over-all, monthly fee. The telephone company also helps by supplying telephone directories for those areas to which calls will be placed.

The spoken word—over the telephone—can be highly persuasive and most effective. If you don't take advantage of it, you're missing a really good "bet!"

Case Histories of How the Telephone Was Used to Build Sales

Firm A—in the Infra-Red Industrial Heating field—uses the phone to arrange appointments, prior to the salesman's call. This helps to "pave the way" for the salesman to achieve actual appointments, prior to his visit.

Firm B—in the Typewriter Sales and Service Field—contacted all past customers on their list, asking whether the typewriters they purchased needed servicing. This good-will type of phone contact was appreciated . . . impressed customers with the reliability of the organization, and led to a good percentage of orders for new typewriters.

Firm C—in Closed Circuit Television Field—used the telephone to conduct conference "sales charts" among their franchisees. Each franchisee was urged to make 10 phone calls the next day to inactive customers and report back (also by phone) as to results achieved.

Firm D—in the Kitchen Cabinets Field—used the phone to notify housewives and apartment owners of an "Open House" to be conducted in their showrooms.

Firm E—owner of a "drive-in" hamburger "stand" franchise— successfully used the phone to announce (1) the grand opening; (2) special discounts for family patronage; (3) the appearance of celebrities at their "stand" on a specific date; (4) special "take-home" gifts for the children.

Firm F—in the Formal Wear Rental Field—successfully used the phone to contact fraternities in colleges . . . informing them of the advantages of their formal wear rental. Similarly, they also telephone caterers and political organizations. The telephone has proven a big factor in their business.

Firm G—in the Sauna Baths Field—regularly uses the phone after each sauna installation, to inquire of the customer how they liked their "first Sauna Bath treatment?". . . and, also, whether the installation was satisfactory and the workmen courteous?

Firm H—in the Record-Keeping and Tax Preparation field—phoned small businesses in the area to inform them of a special "How To Save On Your Taxes" booklet that was available at no charge (this constituted a "door-opener" for the franchisee's follow-up visit).

Firm I—is a franchisee engaged in selling "fun" items such as tricks and games, pre-packaged, on store racks. To help rack sales, residents of the area were telephoned and informed of the availability of these racks in their neighborhood store.

Firm J—in the Industrial Soaps Field—"leases" long-distance telephone lines, on a per-monthly charge basis. Their 10 salesmen contact all industrial firms and institutions in the radius of the phone connection . . . selling to them on a "money back if not satisfied basis." This has proven so effective, that the firm tripled its business in one year and is now doing a volume of nearly $400,000 annually, throughout the country. A new locality is "saturated" by phone regularly—an average of once a week.

Firm K—a Rug-Cleaning Franchisee—re-contacts customers, once every three months, by phone to see whether another cleaning job is desired. It is effective in reminding customers of his work and in stimulating a continued "flow" of new business.

Firm L—in the Credit and Collection Field—uses the phone very effectively to contact all past and present customers, asking for referrals to their business friends. He receives on the average three referrals per call.

Firm M—in the Lawn-Care Field—phones all residents of a

neighborhood in which they have just completed a lawn-care job. The telephone approach is: "We have just landscaped the lawn of your neighbor Mr. Jones. While we are in the neighborhood, we can also take care of your lawn at special prices."

Simple Formula for Quickly Producing Good Advertising Ideas

As has been stated previously, most franchisors provide franchisees with "tailored-to-order" advertisements, that have pre-proven effectiveness. Nevertheless, the franchisee still bears the responsibility of planning his own supplementary advertisements . . . keyed to his specific community, specific business and customer requirements.

Let's say that as a franchisee with a store-type franchise, you plan an advertisement to promote your business . . . one that will help you get increased sales for your products or services.

The advertisement may be one of many types: newspaper or magazine advertisements, sales-helps, window and counter displays, direct mail, or neighborhood "throw-aways."

From the moment you grapple with the task, you find yourself confronted with various problems, each a big one. For example: What merchandise offer should you feature? What headline should you use? What layout and illustration should you select to dramatize your message?

You'll do either of two things at this point. You'll decide (a) the task is too "tough" for you or (b) it takes too much time from your regular work. In either event you'll probably push the work aside for "some other time" (which rarely arrives).

Your advertising plans have gone "pffffft"!

Or, continuing with the project, you find that the idea is slow in coming. Somehow, no matter how you fight against it, you tend to think about irrelevant things rather than the sought-after idea. Eventually, in desperation, you may seize upon some half-acceptable idea—one that proves inadequate for your needs. One franchisee expressed it this way: "I know that constant advertising is vital to my business. Yet I do only a small part of my needed advertising because it takes me so long to think up acceptable advertising ideas."

"If only," he added wistfully, "there was some 'magic genie' who could be summoned to give us the advertising ideas we need, as and when we need them!"

There is not, of course, such a "genie." There is, however, an "assured" method for producing advertising ideas. The method is to "organize" the mind, banishing unrelated thought and permitting concentration on the desired idea only. It requires adherence to the following steps:

(1) Know, specifically, what kind of idea you seek.
(2) Organize all available merchandizing facts on the subject.
(3) Employ "thought-stimulators" to achieve the final idea.

To demonstrate: Let's say you're planning an advertisement for your local newspaper—one that will promote some feature of your products or services. You begin with Step Number One of the procedures given above.

(1) **Know What Kind of Idea You Seek:** Jot down on a sheet of paper all the facts about your products or services that you consider good "sales points" e.g., convenience, durability, appearance, operation, safety, delivery, taste, varied services, or uses. Collect all the facts you can. Examine the advertisements of your competitors, to make sure that no mention-worthy features have been omitted.

(2) **Organize Your Merchandising Facts:** Go over all the sales points you have jotted down. Which do you consider MOST IMPORTANT of them all? Is it lower price (for example—a special sale of your products?); is it reliability (for example—a one-year replacement guarantee?); is it anything else you have, or can do, that attracts attention and "scoops" your competitor?

Having selected your outstanding point, write it down. If, for example, you have selected "lower price" as your featured point, you'll jot down: "Show my prospects how they can get REAL SAVINGS by buying my products."

Now, you have reduced your problem to a single sentence. You have one subject and one subject only to think about. Your mind is thus spared the waste-motion of irrelevant thought or of "hop-skipping" from subject to subject. You are now ready for Step Number Three (the most important step).

(3) **Use thought-stimulators to "Achieve the Final Idea":** What are "stimulators?" Any words and pictures that, when glanced at, serve to excite your imagination and to "fire" your mind with a number of ideas pertinent to your advertising project.

The things that stir imagination differ with different people, hence the "stimulators" you accumulate may be vastly different from those collected by the next person. In time, as you practice using these "stimulators," you can gauge, quickly, which words and pictures are most effective.

Let's say, for example, that the first thing you see in your "thought-stimulator" file is a picture of a magician. (Recall, now, that you are seeking some idea to dramatize the "lower price" feature of your products).

You associate the two thoughts—"magic" . . . "lower prices." Quickly you have a headline idea: "Like Magic—Prices Come Tumbling Down" (during this sale at your store). You'll include an illustration of a magician (top hat, cape and all) waving his wand over a symbolic sketch of "tumbling" prices.

Perhaps you're featuring a number of items for this sale. To "tie-in" the other copy "blocks" with your headline you'll insert smaller sketches of, say, a magician's hat and wand before each offering.

Because the "thought-stimulator" happened to be a magician doesn't, by any means, imply that your idea must embody a sketch of a magician. The thought of "magic" may give you secondary ideas for "slanting" your copy—for example—a magical carpet, or a magic genie.

Not only secondary but also tertiary ideas may suggest themselves from this "stimulator." You think of other words like "magic" and recall "fabulous." How to symbolize the word "fabulous?" You think of, say, Paul Bunyan—the fabulous, mythical woodsman who did such superhuman things and told such "tall" tales and Presto! You have a novel idea for a Paul Bunyan sale of your merchandise. Your headline reads: "Values so fabulously large as to defy the imagination of a Paul Bunyan!" You'll include a sketch of a huge Paul Bunyan (wood-axe in hand). Your copy will be in "exaggerated" style, reminiscent of the mighty woodsman.

This may lead to accessory ideas: Perhaps miniature Paul Bunyan axes given free to those patronizing your sale. Perhaps prizes to those writing "tallest tales a la Paul Bunyan" about the benefits of your merchandise or services—the winner being acclaimed the Paul Bunyan of your city. Perhaps premium booklets containing various Paul Bunyan stories "tied-in" with merchandising facts about your products.

All this . . . from glancing at one "stimulator" of a magician!

Looking further through your "stimulator file" you see a picture of, say, machinery gears. An idea! Your headline reads: "Geared To Give You Lowest Prices." Your illustration comprises a couple of engaged gears. In one gear you place an illustration symbolizing your business (picture of your store or factory, of your trade-mark, or of some representative products). In the other gear you insert a sketch that symbolizes "savings" (e.g., money bags, shattered prices, etc.).

Many other ideas will suggest themselves as you search your "stimulator file." Below are presented additional "stimulators" and a brief discussion of ideas that may be developed from them. Listed are primary ideas only; like the "magician" stimulator, however, they are capable of secondary and tertiary ideas applicable to your advertising project.

CHAIN LINKS—Suggested Headline: "This Sale . . . Links You to Best Buys." Suggested illustration: Two chain links—picture of your establishment in one link and symbolical sketch of customer or of "savings" in other link.

TAPE MEASURE—Suggested Headline: "Prices Tailored to Your Purse . . . Products Tailored to Your Every Need." Suggested illustration: A tailor's tape measure shown "rambling" through your headline.

SCHOOL SLATE—Suggested Headline: "A-B-Cs of Good Value —Stock up ALL Your Needs During This Great Sale." Suggested illustration: Hand with ruler pointing at large blackboard on which the message is handwritten.

INVITATION CARD—Suggested Headline: "You're invited . . . to receive ($50) Savings (by purchasing your products)." Suggested illustration: Typical invitation card bearing script lettering typical of invitations.

We could go on and on—but you have the idea! As you see, these "stimulators"—even though they are entirely unrelated to your business— quickly supply you with dozens of specific ideas, applicable to your advertising project. Merely select the one that fits your needs best.

Where do you get these stimulators? Most everywhere—through examination of the advertisements of others, through research on subjects applicable to your business, through observation and through newspaper items. Clip them out, or jot them down, when you see them. In a short time you'll have an adequate quantity.

You recall that, in the past, most of your best ideas came through experiences—talking to friends, seeing a movie, traveling, reading, or feeling some deep emotion. Your imagination was aroused, your brain went to work.

Normally, we do not have the opportunity to accumulate all the experiences we need. Certainly we can't always leave our place of business to absorb new experiences whenever we want an idea. Hence, the effectiveness of this "stimulator file," giving you a quantity of experiences in vest-pocket form, at your beck-and-call, at the exact moment you need them!

DIRECT-TO-HOME SALES

Achieves: Demonstrations
Relaxed Viewership

BANKS

PROVIDE:

- Lobby Displays
- Window Displays
- Introductions
- Add-on Business (e.g.: record-keeping, taxes)

MAIL ORDER

Multiplies Your Market--As Far as DESIRED

14.

HOW TO ANSWER COMMON SALES OBJECTIONS

Every franchisee seeking to sell his product or service encounters "objections" from his prospective customer. To the extent that he can anticipate and answer these objections properly and believably, will his sales increase and his franchised business prosper.

In discussing the subject of "objections," there is one cardinal rule to remember: don't be afraid to talk back to your prospect! Answering objections adequately only increases your customer's respect for you. Your answers indicate confidence in yourself and confidence in, and knowledge of, your product. A constructive answer, therefore, puts you one step closer to making your sale.

Study the list of objections below. Many of them are probably the same ones you meet every day in your own "selling." Check the usual answers against those given below. You may develop new ideas that will help you in making your own answers more effective.

Finally, as a constructive exercise in salesmanship, without looking at the answers, write down all of the objections you can think of and, next to them, write down your answers. Check this list over, continually, until it becomes a part of yourself and soon you'll be handling objections with ease.

1. **It Costs Too Much:** I agree that it sounds like a lot of money in dollars and cents. But over a one-year period, my product can help you save at least twice its cost, by reducing your operating expense. Hence, it doesn't cost—it pays!

2. Your Price Is Too High: Our price is higher than many inferior, competitive, products; actually you save money by buying from us. You pay only 10% more for a product that will give you 100% more service and satisfaction.

3. We Tried It . . . It Didn't Do The Job: My customers constantly praise the job it does. I feel there must have been some misunderstanding. For example . . . was it used correctly? I'll be glad to demonstrate its proper use—right in your own shop.

4. Our Present Equipment Is Satisfactory: I'm sure you've obtained excellent service from your present equipment. But until you try ours, you'll never know what you've missed in better performance and increased savings. Our equipment makes the difference between being "satisfied" and being "enthusiastic." We're so sure you'll want it that we're willing to put it in "on approval."

5. I'm Over My Budget Now: All the more reason why you should buy now! At the end of the year my product can produce savings that will help bring your budget "into line."

6. I Can't Affort To Gamble On A New Product: I don't want you to gamble, Mr. Customer. All I ask is that you use our product for a week. Try it yourself. In fact, I'll even come to your plant and show you how to use it. At the end of the week, either you send us your check . . . or, if the product is not satisfactory, return it to us.

7. I Haven't Got Time To Listen To Your Story: Could you spare us the time if I paid you $5.00 a minute? My story takes just that—5 minutes—and $25 per week will be the savings that I'll demonstrate to you through the use of my equipment.

8. I'm Using A Competitive Product That's Satisfactory: Satisfaction is a matter of degree, Mr. Customer. A Ford car satisfies a lot of people. On the other hand, who will deny the superior qualities and greater satisfaction of a Rolls Royce? All I ask is an opportunity to demonstrate how you can get increased satisfaction by using my product.

9. I Have A Closer Source Of Supply: You'll find our service just as quick . . . perhaps quicker. We can always ship "rush" orders by air. Our deliveries are often faster than local deliveries. As proof, here's a list of customers in this area who find our service to be outstandingly helpful to them.

10. We've Been Dealing With Our Present Supplier For 30 Years:

Fine . . . but it's often wise to have a second supplier as a "back-up." It gives you a basis of comparison . . . and security against an interruption of supply.

11. **I'll Refer Your Story To The "Powers-That-Be." They'll Have To Make The Decision:** Mr. Customer, I'm sure you'll give my story an adequate presentation; however, questions often arise on details that can only be answered by someone who is thoroughly familiar with our proposition . . . someone from within our Company who knows our policies. Our product has such great benefits for your firm that I would hate to feel that they might be lost to you because of some small misunderstanding on questions that I could answer easily, if I could be present. I'd appreciate an opportunity of attending the meeting with your executives . . . to help you, just in case any questions arise.

12. **I Can't Get The Boss's Okay:** I'm glad to know you tried. That means you're "sold" on my proposition and all you need is a little help to present all the facts properly. I can do that for you if you'll introduce me.

13. **We Can Get A Better Deal From Your Competitor:** Would you mind outlining exactly what the deal is that he has offered you? In that way, perhaps I can help clarify your thinking about the advantages of each proposition.

14. **We Buy Only From Established Firms:** I understand your point, Mr. Customer. However, may I point out that while we are a relatively new organization, the management of our company is composed of people with long experience . . . some of the most successful and highly reputed individuals in the industry.

15. **Your Competitor Offers A Better Guarantee:** Our firm has been in business for 25 years. I'm sure that you'll agree that this would not be true if we were not able to back up our product 100 percent. I have yet to find a customer who felt that we did not fully guarantee the products purchased from us.

16. **Come And See Us Again . . . After You've Been In Business For A Year:** Mr. Customer . . . present indications are that within a year the cost of our product (or service) will be considerably higher. Our service can be useful to you this year, as well as in future years. So why not take advantage of today's low price?

17. **I Can Buy Cheaper Elsewhere:** I have no doubt of that, Sir. But can you be sure you're getting the same value for your money? Our firm has a long-standing reputation for fine product quality. Further, as you know, we

stand foursquare behind your purchase. On a substantial expenditure of this type, I think you'll agree that quality and guarantee should be two of your most important considerations.

18. **Your Competitor's Bid Was Lower:** I'm surprised at that, Mr. Customer. Of course, I'd like to be certain that both of us were calculating on identical specifications. In our business there are so many details that often, upon comparing estimates, we find that two widely different figures occur on the same job because of a misunderstanding of the specific requirements. To assure that you can expect the same quality of workmanship you'd have gotten from us, may I see our competitor's estimate and specifications?

19. **I'm Overstocked On Similar Products Now:** The fact that you're overstocked proves the need for our product . . . and, it proves the other products aren't "similar." For our product is consistently "selling" and the possibility of your being overstocked is remote.

20. **I'm Overstocked With Your Products:** That's unusual. Our merchandise generally goes fast. Tell you what . . . if you'll buy more now, so you can handle a possible rush of orders, I'll supply you with promotional materials (ads and displays) that have proved helpful in moving our stock for other merchants. Jones & Co. sold $_____, using the promotions.

21. **I Still Have Most Of Your Last Order:** Fine . . . then let me help build you a sales-stimulating display. While we're at it, we can tell what items may need fill-ins.

22. **I Don't Like Your Firm . . . Had An Unpleasant Experience:** I'm sorry to hear that, Mr. Customer. Would you mind explaining what happened? If you were offended in any way, I'm sure my firm would like to know . . . so that they can make restitution. I'm sure they would already have done so if they had been aware that a problem existed. I can assure you of my complete cooperation in setting things right.

23. **Your Competitor Gives Better Service After Purchase:** I haven't run into any complaint about our service. I assure you, Sir . . . that I am completely responsible for the handling of your account. You can contact me at any time, between my visits to you, and rely upon my complete cooperation to give you any service you may possibly need in connection with your purchases.

24. **We Don't Use Enough Of Your Product To Warrant Buying The New Model:** If that is true, then I must be at fault . . . for not making clear to you the many ways in which our product is designed to help your firm cut

costs and increase profits. I should like to make this clear to you, in even more emphatic terms, by demonstrating our new product, and its spectacular cost-saving, and profit-building features.

25. **I Understand Jones & Co. Had A Bad Experience With Your Product:** I'm sure misunderstandings occur in your business occasionally, too. Also, there are generally two sides to every question. Frankly, I know nothing of Jones & Co.'s difficulty. If you want, however, I'll get the details from our plant and give them to you on my next visit. Meanwhile, let me show you how our product can give your firm a truly wonderful experience.

26. **See Me Again, When I Return From A Vacation:** I realize how busy you are, getting away for your trip. But wouldn't you enjoy it more even if you went away feeling ''Boy, did I just put a good deal over for our Organization''. And you will . . . when you hear what I have to offer you.

27. **Using Your Equipment Would Necessitate An Expensive Alteration Of Our Methods. The Additional Cost is Not Warranted by Your Product's Benefits:** If you will permit me, I'll show you how long it will take the increased production (which our product assures) to completely amortize the cost of its purchase plus your added procedures costs.

28. **Your Product Doesn't Fit In With This Year's Program:** My product, Mr. Customer, is specifically designed to help you make more money. That's the very reason you are in business. If making money fits in with your program this year . . . or any year . . . our product fits in with your program.

29. **The Quality Difference Doesn't Justify The Additional Cost:** That may appear true on the surface. However, considering the added years of service our product quality assures . . . the higher trade-in value that's yours, at any time . . . together with the prestige of using our equipment, the cost difference is more than justified. It's like a meal at the Waldorf-Astoria as against one in the corner ''beanery.''

30. **Your Credit Policy Is Too Rough:** Our terms are pretty standard with the rest of the industry. Fundamentally, they represent the most that can be given to you in order to assure you foremost quality. Which would you prefer—a few days extra credit or 50% added product value?

31. **Your Competitor's Product Must Be Better. It's Used More Widely:** I'll agree that my competitor's product has far more distribution than ours. That is because it is ''mass-produced,'' designed as an all-purpose product. Our philosophy is just a little different. We feel that the best results are obtained with a product specifically designed to do a certain job well . . . par-

ticularly when the job is an important one. Therefore, our product is designed according to rigid standards, specifically to give you the best possible results obtainable.

32. I'll Have To Get Additional Bids: I'm glad you're going to do that, Sir. That way you'll be able to appreciate better the many factors that go into producing our product. However, be sure your other bids meet the identical specifications. Our price is as low as you'll find for the same quality. So beware of lower bids. In the long run, what is "cheapest" may often prove most costly, and our work is guaranteed.

33. I'll Buy It On One Condition: That I Have Exclusive Rights: I want to help you sell our product in any way I can. Have you considered, Mr. Customer, that demand actually rises in proportion to the number of outlets? The more outlets most products have, the more advertising and publicity the product gets. And demand generally rises to a greater proportional amount for all the outlets.

34. I Haven't Had Any Calls For Your Product: You can't expect many calls if the public doesn't know you handle the product. Display it and promote it and you'll get plenty. I would like to make an analysis of your operation to help create demand. Let me explain what other dealers have done to increase sales of our product.

35. Business Is Bad. I Don't Want To Buy: It seems to be bad with everybody but us. We're selling bigger orders every day. Maybe what you need is a real "live" line that will attract customers . . . a line that has the right kind of promotion behind it . . . like ours does.

36. Your Company I Too Small To Give Us The Service We Require: Our size means better service for you. In a large company a customer might become just a number on a ledger sheet. With us, you're "one of the family" . . . a valued member in whom we have a personal interest. You'll get the best results from the best possible attention.

37. Can I Return The Merchandise I Don't Sell? That's The Only Way I'll Buy It: Mr. Customer . . . you know as well as I do that selling on consignment is the easiest way to go into bankruptcy. You wouldn't want to do business with a firm whose position is that insecure. The first thing you know, you might want to return merchandise and have nowhere to return it to.Our product is planned to "move" from you to your customers . . . not from you back to us.

38. I'm Not Interested: What—not interested in making $100? That's what you'll save in a year by using our product. (OR) Not interested in adding a half hour's extra spare time to each day? That's how much our product saves you.

39. I Don't Want To Deal With So Many Separate Suppliers: I know how you feel. But your customers like to shop in places where they get the fullest selection from which to choose.

40. Your Product's Quality Is Too Good For My Trade: Better-class merchandise can help build customers' confidence in your store and help stimulate business. It can help to improve your trade . . . in addition to enhancing esteem for your establishment.

41. I'll Buy When Your Price Goes Lower: I don't predict the future but I can say that with the great demand we're getting there's a good chance prices will rise. (OR) That may be quite a long way off—you must make sales in the meantime. You'll need stock to tide you over.

15.

35 WAYS TO MAKE PEOPLE WANT TO DO BUSINESS WITH YOU

Positive Methods That Are Used By The
Most Successful Marketing Men To Build
Up Your Image In The Minds Of Your Customers

Every businessman needs and wants business . . . the more the better. Naturally, as a franchisee, you want as much business as you can get in your area.

Obviously, the need for your product or service and its desirability are of great importance. Perhaps even more important is that intangible commodity known as YOU!

First of all, unless YOU act to let people know of the product or service you have to offer, that product or service certainly will not get up and sell itself. To carry that still further, the way you impress your customers . . . the kind of image you create and portray . . . can well make the difference between a prospective customer buying from you instead of from a competitor—or the difference between eager, constant, repeat business and a casual, occasional sale.

This elusive, "hard-to-pinpoint" and almost indefinable "something"—the YOU of YOUR business— is just about "topmost" among your assets and represents an amount of goodwill practically beyond measure and virtually impossible to evaluate.

Indeed, the image you build for yourself, in your community, is all-important and should always be kept in mind. To aid you in this respect, there are outlined thirty-five different ideas. These ideas are applicable to,and practical for, any franchise venture and apply regardless of whether you operate a store with products for sale or are an outside salesman selling insurance. If you study these ideas and put them to use, you will find that they help to make each new customer a repeat customer and that they will put your business on a sound, healthy basis and establish an ever-increasing momentum:

(1) Remember Names and Faces. You yourself know how you like to have people stop you on the street and show recognition with a friendly "Hello, Mr.-------." You are pleased and perhaps a little flattered at this display of personal recognition. Your customers will be similarly pleased, and flattered, by such recognition and greeting on your part. You will find that this simple friendliness and attention will help get additional orders.

(2) Be a Joiner. Socializing and mingling with people, in itself, is fun. In addition, it's good business to join various clubs and organizations in your community and get to be known.

(3) Be a Good Listener. Act interested when people want to talk to you. If they feel they can "get your ear" you'll find that you'll "get their business."

(4) Play Up the "You" Appeal. When explaining your product or service, be sure to emphasize the benefits in the light of your prospect's interests . . . how it can best help and serve him.

(5) Be Helpful. Your helpfulness will be reciprocated in the added business you get. As an example, we know of a salesman who ingratiated himself by clipping news items he considered of importance and interest to his prospects and turning these items over to them.

(6) Give Service. Show a little extra interest through special attention and personalized service. This extra interest will pay off in extra business.

(7) Demonstrate Your Integrity. Let people know that you keep your word. Live up to promises made. You'll find that you don't have to force sales . . . that your reputation for honest dealing will spread quickly by word of mouth and will result in considerable repeat and referred business.

(8) Be Consistent . . . in the prices you quote and in the claims you make. Don't tell one customer one thing and another customer something else. People compare notes and such inconsistencies will do damage to your image.

(9) Be Creative. Keep thinking up new "angles" and new benefits your customers can derive through your product or service. Think of your customers' special problems and how your product or service can help in relation to them.

(10) Be Systematic. Pre-arrange the coverage of your territory from day to day and plan your contacts in order to cover the maximum number of prospects.

(11) Be Self-Motivating. Don't allow occasional adversities get you down. View yourself in proper perspective and set your business course with conviction and determination.

(12) Be Affirmative, Not Negative. Don't go about knocking competitors. Emphasize the "positive"—what can you do, not what others, or competitive products, cannot do.

(13) Be Thoughtful and Considerate. A follow-up thank you note . . . a birthday remembrance . . . an occasional friendly phone call . . . are just good public relations. Thoughtfulness of this kind will not only bring you business but will give you personal satisfaction.

(14) Be Alert. Keep "on the watch" for new ideas and developments in your field . . . and think of how they can be turned to your customer's advantage.

(15) Be Neat. Maintain neatness in dress and in your presentation. Nothing can be more discouraging or distracting to your prospect than furled-up and soiled pages carelessly included in your presentation material.

(16) Be Patient. Remember that your prospects don't know your product or service as well as you do. What you consider elementary may appear complex to them. Develop your sales "pitch" in "stages"—with valid "reasons why" . . . to be absorbed and digested a little at a time.

(17) Be Logical. Appeal to your prospect's intelligence. Make your approach believable and avoid evasive answers to your prospect's questions.

(18) Be Specific. Avoid generalities. Wherever possible, give specific figures . . . and supply documentation to prove your point.

(19) Be Authoritative. "Read up" on all the instruction material furnished by your Company. Familiarize yourself, thoroughly, with your Company's product and sales methods. In this way you can speak with confidence and gain the respect and loyalty of your customers.

(20) Show Humility. As stated in Point 19, answer all questions with authority. When you haven't got the answer, admit it frankly, rather than "bull" your way through. In such cases, merely say, "This I do not know—but we have highly-paid experts in our Company, and I'll be glad to consult them for the answer."

(21) Be Generous. If you are selling a service, small attentions like treating the prospect to a lunch or a cocktail will be appreciated and will "pay off."

(22) Be Punctual. Keep appointments on time. Not to do so may be regarded as an insult by your prospect and an indication that you consider your time is worth more than his.

(23) Display Good Manners. This may certainly seem elementary, yet it is of vital importance in building a proper "image." Little things like asking permission to smoke . . . being considerate of the prospect's time . . . apologizing for outside interruptions . . . help establish you as a person with whom it's nice to do business.

(24) Be Original. Don't allow yourself to become dull or monotonous with the same, unchanged sales talk and approaches. Keep analyzing yourself and keep thinking how you can improve your approach and procedures.

(25) Be Cheerful. Maintain a cheery demeanor. Dejection communicates itself and dampens both your sales efforts and your prospect's interest. Keep your chin up and keep your troubles out of your sales efforts.

(26) Be a Graceful Loser. Even if you don't get the order, show the same amount of cordiality as you did at the onset of your sales effort and don't display any irritation. Your prospect will continue as a prospect and chances are you'll have "better luck the next time."

(27) Respect Time. Time is valuable—especially your time. Don't waste it. Keep your sales "pitch" and visits as brief as possible. Your prospect will respect you for it.

(28) Don't Be a Lecturer. Don't deliver your sales pitch as a monologue. Make it conversational and invite your prospect's participation. Encourage your prospect to ask questions as you go along . . . and answer those questions patiently.

(29) Be an "Anticipator." Before seeing your prospect, anticipate the personal factors, the problems . . . the questions that may arise. Through

this form of anticipation, you can bypass and make "short shrift" of the negatives and can concentrate on the "positives."

(30) Be a Note Taker. Jot down the results of your visit with the prospect as soon as possible and be sure your notes don't get lost. Being able to refer to your notes will help assure correct "follow-through."

(31) Be Friendly, But Not Over-Familiar. Friendship begets friendship. But a prospect feels annoyed by familiarity and resentment can ruin the sale.

(32) Get Fun Out of Your Work. Learn to enjoy your work and your prospects will enjoy doing business with you, rather than with your competitor.

(33) Display Self-Respect. Put yourself on an equal level with your prospect. Be polite but not obsequious.

(34) Be Forthright. Answer each of your prospect's questions "on the bull's eye." Don't give inadequate half-answers. When your prospect sees that you are not trying to avoid any issues, he will respect you and he will respect your product or service.

(35) Exercise Polite Persistence. Don't let a turn-down deter you from trying again. A "polite" renewal of your sales effort, after a "polite" waiting period, won't offend and may well turn a prospect into a customer.

16.

SELL CREATIVELY—
MULTIPLY YOUR PROFITS!

Practically every type of franchise business requires "selling"—whether it's a hamburger "drive-in," or a product or service selling for thousands of dollars. To the extent that the franchisee succeeds as a salesman will his sales and profits increase.

"Creative Selling" can enhance selling results and achieve immediate profits for the franchisee. In many instances, it can spell the difference between a highly successful operation or a bare-subsistence one.

What is Creative Selling?

Let's explain it this way. There are two types of salesmen! One asks the prospect whether he can use the product. The second shows the prospect how he can use the product and why he must buy it!

The first type of salesman is, actually, a "peddler" . . . the second is a "creative sales technician." A related comparison is that of a hunter shooting "pot-shot" at his game, as against one using aim and lead.

Why the difference between the two? Simply this:

If asked whether they want a thing, few people do—their instinct is to say "no." If shown why they need something, most people do—their instinct is to say "yes."

Contained in the above formula is a potential of $5,000 to $10,000 (or more), per year, in added earnings for the franchise.

Creative selling comprises more than merely demonstrating a product or service and its uses. It requires investing the product with "excitement," and "drama"—with "living, breathing" BENEFITS. These aspects make the prospect look beyond the product itself, to his own welfare . . . to how this product can do something to "better his life"—starting right now!

Jed Burton was a famous creative salesman. His product was a very, very ordinary one . . . a wrench. Practically everyone had a wrench, few felt they needed one. Hundreds—perhaps thousands—of salesmen competed with him to sell wrenches.

What made Jed different? Before he started to sell, he sat down to think: how could he "stop" prospects to listen to him. What could he say or do that would "get across" the wrench benefits, as quickly and dramatically as possible? Suddenly—he had it! He used this approach: "I'm here to sell you 1,000 tools for the price of one . . . . "

The fantastic bargain-value of this offer stopped the prospect. Jed received an audience—in fact, every prospect he saw gave him a receptive hearing. He could now get into his selling talk, explaining how the wrench he sold was capable of "1,000 uses."

Within this one simple approach, Jed compressed these selling benefits: First, he "stopped" the prospect to listen. Second, he "grabbed" the prospect's interest. Third, Jed "dramatized" the benefits of his products—all the things it could do for the prospect. Needless to say, Jed's sales soared. Just one single sentence—and his income jumped to 15 times what it had been.

Another example: Bob Henderson sold typewriters. This, you'll agree, is also a very ordinary product. He, too, recognized that he'd make few sales just asking people if they wanted a typewriter. He had to "dramatize" some benefit that his typewriter would give them . . . do for them . . . something that the prospect had never realized before . . . .

Suddenly—it came to him! He said to the prospect:

"I have something sensational to show you—an actual 'IDEA-MANUFACTURING MACHINE!' "

Every prospect stopped to listen and look. Bob had the relaxed, responsible audience to whom to explain the "smoothness" of the typing . . . enabling easy "idea-manufacturing" . . . how the prospect could type and express so much more with this typewriter than others.

Still another example is a friend of ours, George Cole. George sold subscriptions to a travel magazine. On the surface you'd say this is a tough item to sell—who reads travel magazines? Yet—George earned upwards of $20,000 a year.

His approach ran like this: "How would you like to buy a trip through Europe for only $6.00?"

This stopped people, they listened. He then explained how the current issue takes them on a "fascinating, romantic" trip through Europe—"almost as if they were there in person." The next issue would take them through South America. And so on. All for the subscription price of only $6.00.

It's easy to see why George's income was so high . . . .

Another of our favorite creative selling approaches was that used by Dolph Stonehill. His product was a photo-copying machine to reproduce letters, office forms, and similar material. He analyzed the "benefits"—that the machine saved business firms a great deal of money each year over usual duplicating methods. He then created an approach that would get this across best. He said:

"I have something to show you that will interest you very much—a MONEY—MAKING MACHINE!"

People listened. A money-making machine! . . . this, they had to see! Dolph now found it easy to get into his selling "pitch," demonstrating how the machine actually "made money"—lots of it, for business firms, each year, as a result of savings in operating costs and could do so for the prospect's firm, too.

Then there's John Ferguson. He was selling perfume, door-to-door. Generally, that's all he got to see—the door. In most instances it would "slam" in his face, before he got his selling talk started. He then developed a creative approach. As the door opened, the prospect was greeted by an opened perfume bottle—held close to her nose—the fragrant aroma wafting towards her nostrils. This "stopped" her . . . the door didn't shut. It gave John the few moments he needed to say: "Smells wonderful, doesn't it? . . . and it's remarkably low-priced."

This simple approach converted him from failure to the leading man in his company.

Still another case history is that of John Fodor. He sold a refrigerator that saved customers substantial money. His problem: how to "get across" this savings, swiftly and dramatically? His solution: he carried with him an unsigned check for $25.00 filled in with the prospect's name—which he presented to the prospect. He explained: "If you don't save at least this amount of money . . . I'll sign this check for you . . . ."

Creative selling isn't always symbolized by the first words of an approach. It can take on other forms. However, the goal is always the same: to demonstrate and dramatize how the product will benefit the prospect.

For example, Gene Stern sold creatively by performing a useful service for his prospects. Gene sold industrial lighting, a highly competitive activity. He reasoned: why do people buy lighting from salesmen—rather than from the corner hardware store? Why should they buy it from me?

He recognized that lighting was (a) an expense, not an income—hence he had to justify the expense, to show how it could be an income, (b) that few people have the "technical" knowledge of lighting needed for the various operations of a business establishment.

As a result of this analysis, he transformed himself from a lighting salesman into a "scientific lighting consultant." He equipped himself with a pad of Lighting Survey sheets . . . and an impressive, professional-looking light meter. As his new approach, he offered to take a "scientific" lighting survey of the business firm—exposing lighting inadequacies. He used his light meter to measure foot-candles of light and the survey pad to jot down his findings. He pointed out lighting needs, room-by-room.

He went still further: he showed the prospect a previously-prepared chart, listing actual savings that the prospect would make per year through improved lighting . . . and lower maintenance costs . . . in addition to getting better work from employees and attracting more store traffic. Thus, the lighting now represented a "savings" and "profit" to the prospect rather than an expense!

Needless to say, the prospect was impressed—listened respectfully to Gene's recommendations. The result? Where previously, his sales (when he made them) averaged $10 . . . they now averaged $125! Also, he made sales more frequently.

A similar "survey" approach was used by Howard Holmes, a printing salesman. Few prospects had responded when he had asked whether they needed printing. Practically all responded when he offered to give them a "free, scientific analysis of their office forms . . . and letterheads."

Another firm—selling shrubbery—built up a $30-million-a-year business offering prospects a sketch of how their landscape should look. They sold "beauty" not shrubbery!

SHOWMANSHIP is also a part of creative selling. Fred Torket, an awning salesman carried a Polaroid camera with him—took snapshots of homes with awnings that looked shabby. His approach was to show prospects an actual photo of their home—adjoining the photo of another home (that of a customer) with proper awnings!

How can you become a creative salesman? Here are some of the basic rules:

1. KNOW YOUR PRODUCT—what are its outstanding uses and benefits?

2. KNOW YOUR PROSPECT—what does he want and need . . . that your product can supply?

3. BE CURIOUS—get ideas from all available sources including other salesmen, customer's house organs, trade magazines and newspapers. Keep an "idea bank." Jot down your ideas, file and use them. Review them often—they'll produce many creative ideas.

4. BE A PERFECTIONIST—before seeing the prospect . . . sit down and consider exactly what you're going to say . . . how you're going to say it.

5. EXPECT THE SALE!—creative selling breeds self-confidence. You're sure that prospect needs what you have . . . feel, in your mind, that he WILL and MUST purchase it. He generally will.

6. STUDY YOUR MARKETS—where can you find new markets for your products . . . new uses for them?

Bring out the full strength of your creative talents! They're your greatest selling asset!

17.

FINANCING YOUR BUSINESS

Getting Financing For Your Business

Being "under-capitalized" is one of the main reasons for business failure. Often, the entrepreneur believes he has enough capital, and is astounded when—in midstream—unforeseen expenses cause him to "run dry" and to forfeit a business that otherwise could have been a good income producer.

In deciding to enter a business, you must first decide:

1. What are the anticipated operating expenses that you must cover until expected cash flow from your new business develops?

2. How much income do you need during this initial period (normally six months) to cover your usual living expenses?

3. The difference between your answers to numbers one and two above and the amount of your available capital indicates the amount of financing that you must seek prior to entry into the business.

Startup expenses usually comprise:

- cost of rented space
- office equipment and furniture
- inventory
- supplies
- renovations
- advertising and promotions
- wages and salaries

Have you decided that you need financing? Seeking a financing source? Normally, there are two broad categories of financing sources, as follows:

. Collateral Financing: based on "iron-clad" security, that you provide, to assure loan repayment: (e.g., home, fixed property, etc.) This type of financing usually carries lowest interest rates.

. Venture Capital Financing: where you may not have such "iron-clad" security . . . and the investor "takes a chance" on you, based on what he projects to be your potential, and the potential of your planned business. This type of financing usually carries highest interest rates . . . and often an "equity interest" in your business.

In approaching a financing source for a loan, you should have a detailed estimated Financial Statement that:

1. projects expenses of your business

2. projects income of your business (usually over a five-year period)

3. Your own "track record"—your background, business ventures you've entered, your accomplishments

4. a personal financial statement.

Thus, you provide a Financial Statement that shows both where you are now and where you intend to be within the next five years, as a result of your new business. The investor judges both in determining your eligibility for a desired loan or investment.

Private Money-Raising Sources:

Many individuals (or investment groups) are often interested in financing potentially feasible businesses. Insert a classified advertisement under "Capital Wanted" in metropolitan newspapers in your area. This method has proven effective, in many instances, in raising capital on both an "absentee investor" basis, and an "active participant" basis.

15 Franchise Financing Ideas:

Most beginning franchisees need additional capital. Generally, the monies they've accumulated with which to enter their own business are somewhat short of actual needs, such as:

• monies needed to cover franchisee fees

- monies needed to cover franchisee fees
- monies needed for property improvements
- monies needed for a Grand Opening program
- monies needed for advertising and promotion
- minimum of 6-months working capital to cover the franchisee's needs until he reaches the "break-even" point.

Established franchisees, too, often need additional financing. For example:

- monies needed for desired business expansion such as added personnel, property improvements or acquisition of a second territory
- monies needed for increased advertising and promotional activity, seasonal financing, inventory expansion

The question, paramount in their minds, is: "Where can I obtain this needed capital—on reasonable terms?"

Currently, money is extremely "tight and expensive." Sources that were formerly loan-responsive have now literally "dried up." Hence, the franchisee has less likelihood for obtaining favorable loans than in the past.

Your prime loan source—generally most accessible to you—is your nearby bank or savings and loan association. Being local, they are acquainted with you and your business, are familiar with your character, integrity and stability. The guide they use for granting a loan is symbolized by "3 C's" . . . Character, Capital and Capacity to Pay.

Most banks, under normal circumstances, will consider making a reasonable loan to you. A bank loan is most advantageous because the interest rate is generally lowest.

You may obtain various types of loans from your local bank, as follows: (1) short-term loans (payable in about 90 days), (2) long-term loans (extending for as long as 10 years).

"Popular" types of bank loans are:

1. STRAIGHT COMMERCIAL LOANS: (usually 30 to 60 days) based on submitting a financial statement. Generally, this loan is used for seasonal financing or inventory expansion.

2. INSTALLMENT LOANS: These are usually long-term loans, repaid on a monthly basis. These loans can be "tailored" to the business needs, for example, heavier repayments during peak months and smaller repayments during "off-season" periods.

3. TERM LOANS: Such loans have maturities of 1 to 10 years and may either be secured or unsecured. Loan repayments may be made on almost any agreed-upon basis—monthly, quarterly, semi-annually, annually. Early repayments are often relatively small, with a large final payment. Although many term loans are backed by collateral . . . the lender ordinarily requires that current assets exceed current liabilities by at least a 2-1 ratio.

4. BILLS OR NOTES RECEIVABLE: Promissory notes are often given for purchase of goods. These notes can usually be discounted—that is, purchased by the bank. Your account is credited with the amount of the note less the discount to due date. The bank will collect from the note makers when it's due.

5. WAREHOUSE RECEIPT LOANS: Under this form of financing, goods are stored in a warehouse and the warehouse receipt is given to the bank as security for a loan to pay off the supplier. As fast as the borrower is able to sell his merchandise he buys back portions of the inventory.

6. EQUIPMENT LOANS: Loans are made to finance the purchase of machinery or equipment. The lender usually retains title until installment payments have been completed.

7. COLLATERAL LOANS: Based on such collateral as chattel mortgages on personal property, real estate mortgages, life insurance (up to cash surrender value), or on stocks and bonds. If your banker says "no," then contact your local Small Business Administration Office. They are geared to expedite loans (that are justifiable) for small businesses. They request, as your first step, that you initiate your loan request via your local bank. If the bank turns you down, SBA will undertake, in many instances, to "share" your loan with the local bank, assuming responsibility for 50% or more. The majority of banks (even those refusing your initial loan request) usually cooperates with SBA sponsored loans. Other "prime" loan sources are the: SMALL BUSINESS INVESTMENT COMPANIES.

SBICs provide capital for small businesses by means of loans, direct stock investment or by purchase of debentures bonds convertible into common stock. This gives you a loan-procurement opportunity formerly available only to larger companies. These SBICs are generally assisted by the Small Business Administration (authorized to buy up to $1,000,000 in debentures of an individual SBIC). Approximately 480 SBICs are now in operation. Financing costs are generally higher than banks but often lower than other outside "private" sources. To obtain names and addresses of SBICs in your area, write to Small Business Administration, Investment Division, Washington 25, D.C., or to National Association of SBICs, 537 Washington Building, Washington 5, D.C.

Other avenues open to you for obtaining funds:

1. Private Capital: Insert an ad in your local newspaper under "Capital Wanted." Through this medium you may attract private investors who regularly consult this column for investment opportunities.

2. Factors: In each community there are factoring firms who make loans to all types of businesses. Their standards are lower than banks', hence they are more inclined to extend to you your desired loan, even though you have been "turned down" by banks or government sources. Factors are recommended only as a "last resort" since their interest rates are often excessive.

3. Veterans Administration Loans: If you are a veteran, either of World War II or the Korean War, you may be eligible to obtain a loan via your local Veterans Administration Office. Write to them to obtain their detailed pamphlet on types of loans offered and the controlling conditions.

4. Insurance Companies: Many insurance companies maintain loan departments as an important adjunct to their business. Their rates (although generally higher than banks) are much lower than that of factors and other loan sources.

5. Commercial Investment Companies: There are many investment companies, privately constituted, that grant loans. You will find them listed in your local telephone directories (Yellow Pages). Their rates are generally on a par with rates of factoring organizations.

6. Leasing Firms: "Leasing" has become more and more prominent in recent years. Almost any type of product or equipment can now be leased. Thus, it acts to:

   . Finance many aspects of your business—e.g. furniture, fixtures, machinery, equipment . . . giving you a period of 3 to 5 years to pay back (via small monthly payments).

   . Finance your customers (particularly if the product cost is comparatively high). You (as the seller) are paid the full amount due, immediately. The customer pays the leasing company monthly—over a period of years.

7. Franchise "Package" Financing: Often, your franchise "package" comprises products or equipment which can be financed, usually to the extent of 60% of the wholesale cost.

8. Floor Plan Financing: These are usually short-term loans applicable

to merchandise in your store (on the floor). For example: boats, autos, appliances, and similar items.

When should you seek a loan? Do not seek a loan if you do not need the money for specific business purposes, otherwise you are paying the "penalty" of high interest rates without obtaining proportionate benefits. Your "rule of thumb" should be: Will this money I am borrowing help me to earn more money, in excess of interest rates incurred?

Do borrow money if it does help you establish yourself in business, quickens your progress and expands your profits. Bear in mind that it's always good "economics" to pay out "2X" dollars if you are able to obtain "10X" dollars in return—and to accelerate your business success.

GOVERNMENT ASSISTANCE PROGRAMS

Office of Minority Business Enterprise

The Office of Minority Business Enterprise (OMBE) was established within the Department of Commerce to be the focal point of the Federal Government's efforts to assist the establishment of new minority enterprises and the expansion of existing ones.

OMBE is responsible for coordinating operations of the Federal Government which may contribute to establishing and strengthening minority enterprise. It promotes and mobilizes the activities and resources of state and local governments, businesses, and other private groups and organizations to further minority business growth; and coordinates such programs of the Federal agencies. The Office also maintains a center for the collection, analysis, and dissemination of information to assist the establishment and operation of minority businesses.

To provide local assistance to prospective and existing minority businessmen, OMBE Operates six regional and twelve field offices. It has also affiliated with private non-profit business development organizations in cities with substantial minority populations. OMBE assists in funding administrative costs of these centers which serve as a central information source on business opportunities and provide management and technical assistance to individual businessmen. A list of OMBE regional and field offices and funded organizations follows.

ATLANTA REGION

Charles McMillan
Regional Director
Office of Minority Business Enterprise
U.S. Department of Commerce
1371 Peachtree St., N.E., Suite 505
Atlanta, Ga. 30309
404/881-5091

Milton J. White, II
Field Officer
Office of Minority Business Enterprise
U.S. Department of Commerce
First American Bank Bldg., Suite 714
Memphis, Tenn. 38103
901/534-3216

Rudy Suarez
Field Officer
Office of Minority Business Enterprise
U.S. Department of Commerce
Ainsley Bldg.
14 N.E. First Ave.
Miami, Fla. 33132
305/350-4721

BUSINESS MANAGEMENT DEVELOPMENT

SOUTHEASTERN ECONOMIC DEVELOPMENT FOUNDATION
2391 Sewell Road, S.W., Suite 1
Atlanta, Ga. 30311
404/755-1613
Harding B. Young, Dir.

BUSINESS RESOURCE CENTERS

CHARLOTTE BUSINESS RESOURCE CENTER
230 S. Tryon St.
Charlotte, N.C. 28202
704/332-8578
Charles Lent, Dir.

LOUISVILLE AREA CHAMBER OF COMMERCE
300 W. Liberty St.
Louisville, Ky. 40202
502/582-2421
Laurence Dellinger, Dir.

MEMPHIS BUSINESS RESOURCE CENTER
1420 Union Ave., Suite 502
Memphis, Tn. 39101
901/525-8481
Clifford Stockton, Dir.

REGIONAL MINORITY PURCHASING COUNCIL
40 Marietta St., N.W., Suite 1204
Atlanta, Ga. 30303
404/522-4764
Arthur Burks, Jr., Exec. Dir.

CONSTRUCTION CONTRACTOR ASSISTANCE CENTERS

**ALABAMA ASSOCIATION OF ACTIVE CONTRAC-
TORS, INC.**
505 17th St., North, Suite 307
Birmingham, Ala. 35203
Jeffery Teamor, Exec. Dir.

**ATLANTA ASSOCIATED CONTRACTORS AND
TRADE COUNCIL**
374 Maynard Terrace, S.E.
Atlanta, Ga. 30316
404/378-6292
Herbert Williams, Dir.

MEMPHIS NATIONAL BUSINESS LEAGUE
1420 Union Ave., Suite 502
Memphis, Tn. 38104
901/726-5492
Lewis Fort, Dir.

**MID-FLORIDA MINORITY CONTRACTORS ASSOCI-
ATION**
1409 Tampa Park Plaza
Tampa, Fla. 33605
813/223-3628
Israel Rawlings, Dir.

MINORITY CONTRACTORS ASSOCIATION, INC.
120-150 N.W. 54th St.
Miami, Fla. 33127
305/754-4541
Earl Carroll, Dir.

**MINORITY DEVELOPMENT AND MANAGEMENT
ASSOCIATION**
P.O. Box 5905
2221 Devine St.
Columbia, S.C. 29205
803/799-8996
Olga Burke, Dir.

**SAVANNAH AREA MINORITY CONTRACTORS AS-
SOCIATION**
630 E. Henry St.
P.O. Box 156
Savannah, Ga. 31401
912/232-2624
Frank Mathis, Dir.

**SEMINOLE EMPLOYMENT ECONOMIC CORPORA-
TION**
2735 Mellonville Rd.
P.O. Box 2076
Sanford, Fla. 32771
305/323-4360
Theodore Hall, Dir.

TENNESSEE-TOMBIGBEE CAC
605 N. 2nd Ave., Suite 301
P.O. Box 587
Columbus, Ms. 39701
601/328-3251
Esther Harrison, Proj. Dir.

WARREN REGIONAL PLANNING CORPORATION
P.O. Box 158
Soul City, N.C. 27553
919/456-3111
John Hickman, Dir.

CONTRACTED SUPPORT SERVICES

THE ONYX CORPORATION
101 Marietta Tower, Suite 1802
Atlanta, Ga. 30303
404/681-0600
Thaddeus Olive, Dir.

EXPERIMENT AND DEMONSTRATION

BANKS, FINLEY, THOMAS AND WHITE COMPRE-HENSIVE ACCOUNTING MANAGEMENT PRO-GRAM
250 Citizens Trust Bldg.
75 Piedmont Ave.
Atlanta, Ga. 30303
404/659-7470
Marshall Mitchell, Proj. Dir.

LOCAL BUSINESS DEVELOPMENT ORGANIZATIONS

ALBANY BUSINESS DEVELOPMENT CORPORATION
235 Roosevelt Ave., Suite 251
Albany, Ga. 31701
912/883-1083
Johnny Hamilton, Dir.

ATLANTA BUSINESS LEAGUE
2001 Martin L. King, Jr. Dr., S.W.
Atlanta, Ga. 30310
404/758-8751
Franklin O'Neal, Dir.

BUSINESS SERVICES AND ECONOMIC DEVEL-OPER, INC.
1417 North 4th Ave.
Birmingham, Ala. 35203
205/324-3346
L. Paul Banks, Dir.

CENTRAL SAVANNAH RIVER AREA BUSINESS LEAGUE
1208 Laney-Walker Blvd.
P.O. Box 1283
Augusta, Ga. 30903
404/722-0994
Harvey Johnson, Dir.

CHARLOTTE LOCAL BUSINESS DEVELOPMENT ORGANIZATION, INC.
1 NCNB Bldg., Suite 3625
Charlotte, N.C. 28280
705/334-7691
Thomas Station, Dir.

CHATTANOOGA NATIONAL BUSINESS LEAGUE
1408 McCallie Ave.
Chattanooga, Tn. 37404
615/698-8048
Warren Logan, Dir.

DURHAM BUSINESS AND PROFESSIONAL CHAIN, INC.
511 Grant St.
P.O. Box 1088
Durham, N.C. 27702
919/688-7356
Ralph Hunt, Dir.

INTERRACIAL COUNCIL FOR BUSINESS OPPOR-TUNITIES
40 Marietta St., N.W.
Suite 1201
Atlanta, Ga. 30303
404/577-2570
Charles C. Kelly, Acting Dir.

JACKSON BUSINESS LEAGUE
3403 Delta Dr.
Jackson, Ms. 39204
601/981-1652
Andrew Smith, Dir.

JACKSONVILLE URBAN LEAGUE
225 W. Ashley, Room 201
Jacksonville, Fla. 32202
904/354-6729
William Green, Dir.

LEXINGTON BUSINESS DEVELOPMENT ORGANI-ZATION
153 Walnut St., Suite 208
Lexington, Ky. 40507
502/252-8418
Mae Laine
Senior Business Development Officer

LEXINGTON BUSINESS DEVELOPMENT SERVICE, INC.
317 Yazoo St.
P.O. Box 397
Lexington, Ms. 39095
601/834-3515
Wallace Steptoe, Dir.

LOUISVILLE BUSINESS DEVELOPMENT ORGANI-
ZATION
455 River City Mall
Suite 324
Louisville, Ky.
502/588-4020
Chris Redden

MEMPHIS NATIONAL BUSINESS LEAGUE
384 E. H. Crump Blvd.
Memphis, Tn. 38126
901/774-9625
Leonard Small, Dir.

MID-WEST PIEDMONT AREA BUSINESS DEVELOP-
MENT ORGANIZATION
623 Waughtown St.
Winston-Salem, N.C. 27107
919/784-7970
John Duncan, Dir.

MINORITY ASSISTANCE CORPORATION
27 Cross Country Plaza
P.O. Box 6040
Columbus, Ga. 31907
404/563-7631
Henry Thomas, Dir.

MINORITY DEVELOPMENT AND MANAGEMENT
ASSOCIATION
P.O. Box 5905
2221 Devine St.
Columbia, S.C. 29205
803/799-8996
Olga Burke, Dir.

NASHVILLE PROGRESS ASSOCIATION FOR ECO-
NOMIC DEVELOPMENT
2209 Buchanan St., Suite B-100
Nashville, Tn. 37208
615/254-8849
William Garrett, Dir.

NATIONAL ECONOMIC DEVELOPMENT ASSOCIA-
TION
255 Alhambra Circle, Suite 835
Coral Gables, Fla. 33134
305/444-7196
Antonio Machado, Dir.

NORTHERN ALABAMA BUSINESS DEVELOPMENT
CORPORATION
225 East Holmes Ave.
Huntsville, Ala. 35801
205/533-6306
Hanson Howard, Dir.

PINEBELT DEVELOPMENT ASSOCIATION
3220 10th St., Suites G & H
Gulfport, Ms. 39501
601/868-2434
William Lorch, Dir.

PRAIRIE MINORITY DEVELOPMENT ASSOCIATION
1916 A Highway 82E
Columbus, Ms. 39701
601/327-6050
John Jackson, Dir.

S. ALABAMA BUSINESS DEVELOPMENT OFFICE
OF ONP
951 Government St., Suite 400
Mobile, Ala. 36604
205/433-7429
Blondie Perine, Dir.

SAVANNAH AREA MINORITY CONTRACTORS AS-
SOCIATION
630 E. Henry St.
P.O. Box 156
Savannah, Ga. 31401
912/232-2624
Frank Mathis, Dir.

SEMINOLE EMPLOYMENT ECONOMIC DEVELOP-
MENT CORPORATION
2735 Mellonville Rd.
P.O. Box 2076
Sanford, Fla. 32771
305/323-4360
Theodore Hall, Dir.

SPANISH ECONOMIC DEVELOPMENT
990 S.W. 1st St., Suite 201
Miami, Fla. 33130
305/545-8590
Mario Meneses, Dir.

SUNCOAST BUSINESS DEVELOPMENT CORPORATION
5401 W. Kennedy Blvd., Suite 271
Tampa, Fla. 33609
305/879-8405
Noble Sissle, Dir.

TALBOTTON BUSINESS DEVELOPMENT OFFICE, INC.
P.O. Box 455
Talbotton, Ga. 31827
404/665-8575
Roger Williams, Dir.

THE EASTERN BANK OF CHEROKEE INDIANS
P.O. Box 455
Cherokee, N.C. 28719
704/497-9335
Charles Saunooke, Dir.

TUSKEGEE INSTITUTE BUSINESS DEVELOPMENT CENTER
436 Goldwaite St.
Montgomery, Ala. 36104
205/727-3598
Gregg Jennings, Dir.

URBAN LEAGUE OF GREATER MIAMI
8281 N.E. 2nd Ave.
Miami, Fla. 33138
305/751-1662
Stanford Williamson, Dir.

WARREN REGIONAL PLANNING CORPORATION
P.O. Box 158
Soul City, N.C. 27553
919/456-3111
John Hickman, Dir.

STATE OMBE's

ALABAMA STATE OMBE
3815 Interstate Court
Perry Hill Office Park
Montgomery, Ala. 36109
205/832-5633
Robert Geeter, Dir.

KENTUCKY STATE OMBE
2329 Capitol Plaza Towers
Frankfort, Ky. 40601
502/588-4020
Floyd Taylor, Dir.

MISSISSIPPI STATE OMBE
1505 Walter Sillers State Bldg.
Jackson, Ms. 39205
601/354-6715
Thomas Espy, Dir.

NORTH CAROLINA STATE OMBE
P.O. Box 27687
3800 Barrett Drive
Raleigh, N.C. 27609
919/829-2712
Jerry Dodson, Dir.

TENNESSEE STATE OMBE
510 Gay St., Suite B-1
Nashville, Tn. 37219
615/741-2545
Newton A. Solomon, Dir.

CHICAGO REGION

Daniel V. Lemanski
Regional Director
Office of Minority Business Enterprise
U.S. Department of Commerce
55 E. Monroe St., Suite 1438
Chicago, Ill. 60603
312/353-8375

Field Officer
Office of Minority Business Enterprise
U.S. Department of Commerce
100 Lincoln Bldg.
1367 E. 6th St.
Cleveland, Oh. 44114
216/522-3354

Field Officer
Office of Minority Business Enterprise
U.S. Department of Commerce
2 Gateway Center, Rm. 535
4th & State Ave.
Kansas City, Kan. 66101
816/374-4561

Field Officer
Office of Minority Business Enterprise
U.S. Department of Commerce
210 N. 12th St., Rm. 479
St. Louis, Mo. 63101
314/622-4311

BUSINESS RESOURCE CENTERS

CHICAGO REGIONAL PURCHASING COUNCIL
33 North La Salle St., Suite 1732
Chicago, Ill. 60602
312/263-0105
Alfred Davis, Exec. Dir.

CINCINNATI BUSINESS RESOURCE CENTER
120 West 5th St.
Cincinnati, Oh. 45202
513/721-3300
Robert A. Bowen, Exec. Dir.

GREATER CLEVELAND GROWTH CORPORATION
690 Union Commerce Bldg.
Cleveland, Oh. 44115
216/621-3300
Carole Hoover, Dir.

OMAHA MINORITY PURCHASING COUNCIL
1620 Dodge St., Suite 2100
Omaha, Neb. 68102
402/341-1234
Larry Gomez, Exec. Dir.

ST. LOUIS BUSINESS RESOURCE CENTER
112 North 4th St.
St. Louis, Mo. 63102
314/621-7410
Stephen Clark, Exec. Dir.

TALENT ASSISTANCE PROGRAM
19 South LaSalle
Chicago, Ill. 60604
312/641-6722
William E. Goss, Exec. Dir.

CONSTRUCTION CONTRACTOR ASSISTANCE CENTERS

CHICAGO ECONOMIC DEVELOPMENT CORPORATION CONTRACTORS' DIVISION
1339 South Michigan Ave.
Chicago, Ill. 60616
312/341-1380
Consuelo Williams, Acting Dir.

CLEVELAND CONTRACTORS ASSISTANCE CORPORATION
1101 Euclid Ave.
Cleveland, Oh. 44115
216/696-7650
James H. Walker, Exec. Dir.

METROPOLITAN CONTRACTORS ASSISTANCE CORPORATION
4450 Oakman Blvd.
Detroit, Mich. 48204
313/933-7500
James Gray, Exec. Dir.

MOKAN MINORITY CONTRACTORS ASSOCIATION
3101 Troost Ave.
Kansas City, Mo. 64109
816/531-3000
Alex Harris, Exec. Dir.

CONSULTANT CONTRACTOR PROGRAM

W. V. ROUSE AND COMPANY
820 Davis St.
Evanston, Ill.
312/491-1000
W. V. Rouse, Dir.

LOCAL BUSINESS DEVELOPMENT ORGANIZATIONS

AMERICAN-INDIAN BUSINESS ASSOCIATION OF CHICAGO AND THE MIDWEST
4550 North Hermitage
Chicago, Ill. 60640
312/728-1135
Willard LaMere, Exec. Dir.

BLACK ECONOMIC UNION
2502 Prospect
Kansas City, Mo. 64127
816/924-6181
Curtis K. McClinton, Exec. Dir.

BREADBASKET COMMERCIAL ASSOCIATION
10842 South Michigan Ave.
Chicago, Ill. 60628
312/468-3109
Noah Robinson, Exec. Dir.

CHICAGO ECONOMIC DEVELOPMENT CORPORA-
TION
162 North State St.
Chicago, Ill. 60601
312/368-0011
Frank Brooks, Pres.

DETERMINED YOUNG MEN
3880 Reading Rd.
Cincinnati, Oh. 45229
513/221-0180
Mervin Stenson, Exec. Dir.

EXECUTIVE BUSINESS DEVELOPMENT CORPORA-
TION
595 East Broad St.
Columbus, Oh. 43215
614/221-5729
James Burton, Exec. Dir.

HISPANOS ORGANIZED TO PROMOTE ENTREPRE-
NEURS, INC.
State of Michigan Plaza, Suite M-172
6th Ave.
Detroit, Mich. 48226
313/961-7240
Henry Garcia, Exec. Dir.

INDIANAPOLIS BUSINESS DEVELOPMENT FOUN-
DATION
320 N. Meridian St., Suite 317
Indianapolis, Ind. 46204
317/639-6131
H. M. Taylor, Exec. Dir.

INDIANAPOLIS URBAN LEAGUE BUSINESS CEN-
TER
2421 N. Meridian St.
Indianapolis, Ind. 46208
317/925-6463
Huerta C. Tribble, Dir.

INNER CITY BUSINESS IMPROVEMENT FORUM
3049 East Grand Blvd.
Detroit, Mich. 48202
313/875-4700
Walter McMurtry, Exec. Dir.

INTERRACIAL COUNCIL FOR BUSINESS OPPOR-
TUNITY
4144 Lindell Blvd., Suite 401
St. Louis, Mo. 63108
314/535-6906
Nylon Wilson, Dir.

KANSAS STATE OMBE
406 Jackson
Topeka, Kan. 66603
913/354-7741
Kurt Koles, Exec. Dir.

METROPOLITAN ECONOMIC DEVELOPMENT COR-
PORATION
2021 East Hennepin, Suite 370
Minneapolis, Minn. 55413
612/378-0361
Charles W. Poe, Jr., Pres.

MEXICAN-AMERICAN CHAMBER OF COMMERCE
1 South Wacker Dr., Suite 400
Chicago, Ill. 60606
312/236-2319
Juan Fernandez, Exec. Dir.

MILWAUKEE URBAN LEAGUE
836 N. 12th St., Suite 108
Milwaukee, Wisc. 53206
414/278-7330
Exec. Dir. (Vacant)

MINNESOTA CHIPPEWA TRIBES
P.O. Box 217
Cass Lake, Minn. 56633
218/335-2286
Clint Landgren, Exec. Dir.

MINORITY ECONOMIC DEVELOPERS COUNCIL
10518 Superior Ave.
Cleveland, Oh. 44106
216/229-9494
Wendell Erwin, Dir.

NATIONAL ECONOMIC DEVELOPMENT ASSOCIA-
TION
55 W. Van Buren, Suite 330
Chicago, Ill. 60604
312/353-7130
Gilbert M. Vega, Reg. Vice Pres.

NATIONAL ECONOMIC DEVELOPMENT ASSOCIATION
2 Gateway Center, Suite 130
Kansas City, Kan. 66101
913/342-6663
Andrew Gutierrez, Dir.

NORTHERN ILLINOIS BUSINESS CORPORATION
P.O. Box 706
512 Kent St.
Rockford, Ill. 61102
815/963-0400
Donald Moore, Exec. Dir.

ST. LOUIS MEDA
1408 North Kingshighway
St. Louis, Mo. 63113
314/621-6680
Henrietta Dortch, Acting Dir.

URBAN BUSINESS DEVELOPMENT CENTER
5620 Ames Ave.
Omaha, Neb. 68104
402/455-1500
Alvin Goodwin, Exec. Dir.

VICTORY ECONOMIC AND DEVELOPMENT CORPORATION
623 Rowland Ave., N.E.
Canton, Oh. 44704
216/453-1284
John Lucas, Exec. Dir.

YOUNGSTOWN AREA DEVELOPMENT CORPORATION
1555 Belmont Ave.
Youngstown, Oh. 44504
216/746-5681
J. Ronald Pittman, Exec. Dir.

STATE OMBE's

INDIANA OMBE
9 North Illinois, Rm. 1001
Indianapolis, Ind. 46205
317/633-5442
Tony A. Buford, Exec. Dir.

MICHIGAN OMBE
1200 Sixth Ave.
Detroit, Mich. 48226
313/256-3720
W. C. Williams, Dir.

WISCONSIN OMBE
123 West Washington Ave.
Madison, Wisc. 53702
608/266-3222
Richard Archia, Exec. Dir.

DALLAS REGION

Henry Zuniga
Regional Director
Office of Minority Business Enterprise
U.S. Department of Commerce
1412 Main St., Rm. 1702
Dallas, Tx. 75202
214/749-7581

Jesse Rios
Field Officer
Office of Minority Business Enterprise
U.S. Department of Commerce
Federal Bldg.
727 E. Durango St., Rm. B-412
San Antonio, Tx. 78206
512/225-4816

Victor Casaus
Field Officer
Office of Minority Business Enterprise
U.S. Department of Commerce
National Bldg., Suite 1401
505 Marquette Ave.
Albuquerque, N.M. 87101
505/766-3379

Felton Sneed
Field Officer
Office of Minority Business Enterprise
U.S. Department of Commerce
Federal Bldg., Rm. 901
600 South St.
New Orleans, La. 70130
504/527-2935

BUSINESS RESOURCE CENTERS

DALLAS ALLIANCE FOR MINORITY ENTERPRISE
7701 North Stemmons Freeway, #222
Dallas, Tx. 75247
214/637-5170
T. David Jones, Exec. Dir.

GULF SOUTH MINORITY PURCHASING COUNCIL
Chamber of Commerce Bldg.
301 Camp St., Suite 200
New Orleans, La. 70130
504/561-8269
Dennis A. Duclaux, Exec. Dir.

SAN ANTONIO BUSINESS RESOURCE CENTER
505 East Travis, Suite 301
San Antonio, Tx. 78205
512/224-1708
Carlos Ramirez, Exec. Dir.

CONSTRUCTION CONTRACTOR ASSISTANCE CENTERS

AMALGAMATED BUILDERS AND CONTRACTORS OF LOUISIANA, INC.
348 Baronne St., Suite 620
New Orleans, La. 70112
504/524-4881
Claude Steward, Exec. Dir.

COASTAL BEND MINORITY CONTRACTORS ASSO-CIATION
4916 Bearlane
Corpus Christi, Tx. 78416
512/884-2407
Ruben Lerma, Exec. Dir.

CONTRACTORS INDUSTRIAL EDUCATION ASSIST-ANCE ASSOCIATION
805 West Price Rd., Suite B
Brownsville, Tx. 78520
512/546-2229
Joe Reina, Exec. Dir.

NEW MEXICO CONTRACTORS SERVICE CENTER
115 Palomas Ave., N.E.
Albuquerque, N.M. 87108
505/268-2453
Albert Sanchez, Exec. Dir.

OKLAHOMA CITY MINORITY CONTRACTORS
4111 Lincoln Blvd., Suite 4
Oklahoma City, Oklahoma 73105
559/528-3250
G.M. Dodson, Exec. Dir.

PAN AMERICAN CONTRACTORS SERVICE CENTER
2211 East Missouri St., Suite 243
P.O. Box 3811
El Paso, Tx. 79903
915/545-2758
Joe Onopa, Exec. Dir.

SAN ANTONIO CCAC
505 East Travis, Suite 301
San Antonio, Tx. 78205
512/224-1708
Carlos Ramirez, Exec. Dir.

LOCAL BUSINESS DEVELOPMENT ORGANIZATIONS

ACADIANA BUSINESS DEVELOPMENT ORGANI-ZATION
P.O. Box 3443
Lafayette, La. 70502
318/234-6336
Robert Polk, Exec. Dir.

ALL INDIAN DEVELOPMENT ASSOCIATION
2401 12th St., N.W.
Albuquerque, N.M. 87102
505/243-9773
Joe Baca, Exec. Dir.

AMERICAN G.I. FORUM
805 Texas St.
Fort Worth, Tx. 76102
519/429-3161
Richard Contreras, Exec. Dir.

ARKANSAS BUSINESS DEVELOPMENT CORPORA-TION
Union Bank Bldg., Suite 1055
Little Rock, Ark. 72203
569/376-0703
John Pierce, Exec. Dir.

AUSTIN MINORITY ECONOMIC DEVELOPMENT
    CORPORATION
717 West 6th St.
Austin, Tx. 78704
539/477-6507
Carlos Herrera, Exec. Dir.

AVANTE INTERNATIONAL
830 N.E. Loop 410, Suite 400
San Antonio, Tx. 73209
512/828-6411
Rick Bela, Exec. Dir.

CENTER FOR BUSINESS/SOUTHERN UNIVERSITY
2923 Plank Road
Baton Rouge, La. 70805
505/771-3320
Mitchell Albert, Exec. Dir.

COLORADO ECONOMIC DEVELOPMENT ASSOCIA-
    TION
621 Fox St.
Denver, Colo. 80204
303/573-3919
Ed Lucero, Exec. Dir.

COMMUNITY ASSISTANCE COUNCIL
330 Liberty, 2nd Fl.
Beaumont, Tx. 77701
713/838-6275
Charles R. Banks, Exec. Dir.

CORPORATION IN ACTION FOR MINORITY BUSI-
    NESS AND INDUSTRIAL OPPORTUNITY
First National Bank Tower
Las Cruces, N.M. 88001
505/526-3311
John Urioste, Exec. Dir.

CORPUS CHRISTI ECONOMIC DEVELOPMENT COR-
    PORATION
1801 South Staples, Suite 202
Corpus Christi, Tx. 78404
512/883-3887
Humberto Rivera, Exec. Dir.

DALLAS MEXICAN CHAMBER OF COMMERCE
4343 Maple Ave., Suite 201
Dallas, Tx. 75219
214/522-6790
Julian T. Martinez, Exec. Dir.

DENVER COALITION VENTURE
1129 Cherokee St.
Denver, Colo. 80204
303/623-3766
Roy W. Gentry, Exec. Dir.

EAST TEXAS MINORITY ECONOMIC DEVELOP-
    MENT CORPORATION
305 S. Broadway, Suite 710
Tyler, Tx. 75701
609/595-2676
Charles Stein, Exec. Dir.

INTERRACIAL COUNCIL FOR BUSINESS OPPOR-
    TUNITY
2001 Bryan Tower, Suite 630
Dallas, Tx. 75201
214/741-6719
Leon Gauthier, Exec. Dir.

INTERRACIAL COUNCIL FOR BUSINESS OPPOR-
    TUNITY
605 South Pierce St.
Liberty Bank Bldg., Suite 206
New Orleans, La. 70119
504/488-6651
Lawrence Velasquez, Deputy Director

MEDCU
275 E. 200 South, Suite 101
Salt Lake City, Utah 84111
801/355-1122
Jorge Arce-Larretta, Exec. Dir.

METROPOLITAN HOUSTON DEVELOPMENT CEN-
    TER
3333 Fannin St., Suite 203
Houston, Tx. 77004
529/528-2921
John Donley, Exec. Dir.

MEXICAN AMERICAN CENTER FOR ECONOMIC
    DEVELOPMENT
First National Bank, Suite 309
201 15th & Beaumont
McAllen, Tx. 78501
512/682-1518
Joe Garcia, Exec. Dir.

NATIONAL COUNCIL OF LA RAZA
2403 San Mateo N.E., Suite S-14
Albuquerque, N.M. 87110
505/268-2421
Raymond Lopez, Exec. Dir.

NATIONAL ECONOMIC DEVELOPMENT ASSOCIA-
TION
2030 Fourth St., N.W.
Albuquerque, N.M. 87102
505/766-2868
Anna Muller, Dist. Dir.

NATIONAL ECONOMIC DEVELOPMENT ASSOCIA-
TION
6960 Gateway East
El Paso, Tx. 79915
915/543-7400
Edmond Carrera, Dist. Dir.

NATIONAL ECONOMIC DEVELOPMENT ASSOCIA-
TION
302 East Jackson
Harlingen, Tx. 78550
512/425-2800
Gabe Garcia, Dist. Dir.

NATIONAL ECONOMIC DEVELOPMENT ASSOCIA-
TION
1000 Howard Ave., Suite 1002
New Orleans, La. 70113
504/527-6626
Carlos delaVega, Dist. Dir.

NATIONAL ECONOMIC DEVELOPMENT ASSOCIA-
TION
1222 N. Main Ave., Rm. 815
San Antonio, Tx. 78212
512/224-1618
Simon Castillo, Reg. Dir.

NATIONAL ECONOMIC DEVELOPMENT ASSOCIA-
TION
326 Grant Ave.
Santa Fe, N.M. 87501
505/982-8510
Arturo Ulibarri, Reg. Dir.

NATIONAL INFORMATION RESEARCH AND
ACTION LEAGUE
828 Pierre Ave.
P.O. Box 3856
Shreveport, La. 71103
318/221-4261
Alonzo Hodge, Exec. Dir.

OKLAHOMANS FOR INDIAN OPPORTUNITY
555 Constitution Ave.
Norman, Okla. 73069
559/329-3737
Betty J. Olivas, Proj. Mgr.

PROGRESS ASSOCIATION FOR ECONOMIC DEVEL-
OPMENT
4111 N. Lincoln Blvd., Suite 2
Oklahoma City, Okla. 73105
559/528-7969
Ken R. Talley, Exec. Dir.

SOUTH TEXAS ECONOMIC DEVELOPMENT CORPO-
RATION
P.O. Box 685
520 Matamoras St.
Laredo, Tx. 78040
512/722-7691
Julio Sosa, Exec. Dir.

TULSA URBAN LEAGUE
240 East Apache
Tulsa, Okla. 74106
918/584-2571
Ray Freeman, Proj. Dir.

UPLANDS, INC.
777 Main St.
Durango, Colo. 81301
303/247-2862
Gray Peterson, Exec. Dir.

VENTURE ADVISERS, INC.
2731 Lemmon Ave., East, Suite 240
Dallas, Tx. 75204
214/528-1550
Calvin Stephens, Exec. Dir.

MINORITY BUSINESS AND TRADE ASSOCIATION

SERVICE, EMPLOYMENT, REDEVELOPMENT
2829 W. Northwest Highway
Rhine River Bldg., Suite 159
Dallas, Tx. 75220
214/358-3433
Isaac Olivares, Exec. Dir.

REGIONAL PURCHASING COUNCILS

CITY OF HOUSTON
P.O. Box 1562
Houston, Tx. 77001
529/222-3141
John L. Guess, Exec. Dir.

GULF SOUTH MINORITY PURCHASING COUNCIL
301 Camp St., Suite 200
New Orleans, La. 70130
504/561-8269
Dennis A. Cuclaux, Exec. Dir.

STATE OMBE's

LOUISIANA STATE OMBE
Capital Bldg.
Gov. Ewin Edwards' Office
Baton Rouge, La.
Dan Borne, Contact

SOUTH DAKOTA STATE OMBE
108 East Missouri
Pierre, S.D. 57501
650/224-3578
Dolores Hall, Exec. Dir.

TEXAS STATE OMBE
510 Congress St., Suite 218
Austin, Tx. 78704
539/475-5945
Albert Rodgriquez, Exec. Dir.

SUBCONTRACT

DALLAS BLACK CHAMBER OF COMMERCE
2834 Forest Ave.
Dallas, Tx. 75215
214/428-3114
Russell Foster, Exec. Dir.

NEW YORK REGION

Newton S. Downing
Regional Director
Office of Minority Business Enterprise
U.S. Department of Commerce
Federal Office Bldg.
26 Federal Plaza, Rm. 1307
New York, N.Y. 10007
212/264-3262

Frank Bispham
Project Officer
Office of Minority Business Enterprise
U.S. Department of Commerce
441 Stuart St., 10th Fl.
Boston, Mass. 02116
617/223-5375

BUSINESS MANAGEMENT DEVELOPMENT

BRIDGEPORT ECONOMIC DEVELOPMENT CORPORATION
10 Middle St., Park City Plaza
Bridgeport, Conn. 06604
203/579-0808
Randolfo Caballero, Dir., BRC

LEWIS LATIMER FOUNDATION, INC.
133 Mt. Auburn St.
Cambridge, Mass. 02138
617/491-6120
Robert Royster, Exec. Dir.

PIONEER VALLEY BUSINESS DEVELOPMENT CENTER
31 Elm St., Suite 545
Springfield, Mass. 01103
413/781-7130
Charles Rees, Exec. Dir.

ROCHESTER BUSINESS RESOURCE CENTER
55 St. Paul St.
Rochester, N.Y. 14604
716/546-3695
George E. Heller, Exec. Dir.

BUSINESS RESOURCE CENTER

VOLUNTEER URBAN CONSULTING GROUP
300 East 42nd St.
New York, N.Y. 10017

212/687-7420
Brooke Mahoney, Exec. Dir.

CITY OMBE

NEW YORK CITY OFFICE OF ECONOMIC DEVEL-
OPMENT
225 Broadway
New York, N.Y. 10007
212/566-0238
Samuel Hudnell, Exec. Dir.

CONSTRUCTION CONTRACTOR
ASSISTANCE CENTERS

BLACK PEOPLE'S UNITY MOVEMENT ECONOMIC
DEVELOPMENT CORPORATION
622 Cooper St.
Camden, N.J. 08103
609/966-8006
Harvey C. Johnson, Exec. Dir.

CONTRACTOR'S ASSOCIATION OF BOSTON
227 Roxbury St.
Roxbury, Mass. 02119
617/442-4680
Theodore Landsmark, Exec. Dir.

*NELSON, PETERS AND ASSOCIATES
25 Halsted St.
Suite 15, 2nd Fl.
East Orange, N.J. 07018
201/676-6465/6
Gurney Nelson, Exec. Dir.

NELSON, PETERS AND ASSOCIATES
220 Delaware Ave.
Buffalo, N.Y. 14202
716/856-3145
William Taborn, Office Mgr.

NELSON, PETERS AND ASSOCIATES
Hartford Graduate Center Bldg.
275 Windsor Ave.
Hartford, Conn. 06102
203/525-3411
Rudy Mendez, Office Mgr.

NELSON, PETERS AND ASSOCIATES
Housing Investment Bldg.
416 Pnce de Leon Ave.

Hato Rey, P.R. 00918
809/764-0572 or 764-0303
Ivan Lopez, Office Mgr.

NELSON, PETERS AND ASSOCIATES
101 Park Ave., Suite 712
New York, N.Y. 10017
212/679-2857
Kirt Shah, Office Mgr.

NELSON, PETERS AND ASSOCIATES
369 Lexington Ave., Rm. 1600
New York, N.Y. 10017
212/687-6180/1
Ram Patel, Branch Mgr.

NELSON, PETERS AND ASSOCIATES
808 Powers Bldg.
Rochester, N.Y. 14614
716/232-1610
Robert Smith, Office Mgr.

NELSON, PETERS AND ASSOCIATES
415 W. Onondaga St., Suite #2
Syracuse, N.Y. 13202
315/473-6630
Robert Smith, Branch Mgr.

---

*Headquarters Office.

CONTRACTED SUPPORT SERVICES

BOONE, YOUNG AND ASSOCIATES
551 Fifth Ave.
New York, N.Y. 10017
212/661-8044
David O. Boone, Pres.

EXPERIMENT AND DEMONSTRATION

GREATER JAMAICA REVITALIZATION PROJECT
89-13 161st St.
Jamaica, N.Y. 11432
212/657-4800
Richard White, Exec. Dir.

HARLEM URBAN DEVELOPMENT CORPORATION
163 West 125th St., 17th Fl.
New York, N.Y. 10027
212/678-2460
Donald Cogsville, Gen. Mgr.

SOUTH BRONX OVERALL ECONOMIC DEVELOP-
  MENT INDUSTRIAL CENTER
370 East 149th St.
Bronx, N.Y. 10455
212/292-3113
John Patterson, Pres.

LOCAL BUSINESS DEVELOPMENT
ORGANIZATIONS

ASOCIACION PRODUCTOS DE PUERTO RICO
207 Calle O'Neil
Box 3631—San Juan
Hato Rey, P.R. 00936
809/764-8484
Edwin Gonzalez Amador, Proj. Dir.

BLACK DEVELOPMENT FOUNDATION, INC.
Minority Business Consultants
442 Pratt St.
Buffalo, N.Y. 14204
716/855-1703
Onwuka S. Nwachukwu, BDO Dir.

BROOKLYN LOCAL ECONOMIC DEVELOPMENT
  CORPORATION
1460 Fulton St.
Brooklyn, N.Y. 11216
212/493-1663
William Goodloe, Acting Pres.

CAPITAL FORMATION
2112 Broadway
New York, N.Y. 10023
212/799-6400
Benjamin Jones, Pres.

CAPITAL FORMATION, INC.
425 Broad Hollow Rd.
Melville, Long Island, N.Y. 11746
516/752-1977
Raymond Trotman, Exec. Dir.

CHINESE ECONOMIC DEVELOPMENT COUNCIL
235 Canal St.
New York, N.Y. 10002
212/925-7668
David Ho, Exec. Dir.

CONSUMER ACTION PROGRAM OF BEDFORD
  STUYVESANT
16 Court St.
Brooklyn, N.Y. 11206
212/453-7603 or 643-1580
Adolfo Alayon, Exec. Dir.

GREATER JAMAICA CHAMBER OF COMMERCE
89-13 161st St.
Jamaica, N.Y. 11432
212/657-4800
Howard Burns, Proj. Dir.

HISPANIC BUSINESSMEN'S ASSOCIATION, INC.
841 N. Clinton Ave.
Rochester, N.Y. 14605
716/546-1930
Emilio Serrano, Exec. Dir.

INTERRACIAL COUNCIL FOR BUSINESS OPPOR-
  TUNITY
24 Commerce St., Suite 524
Newark, N.J. 07102
201/622-4771
James Blow, Exec. Dir.

INTERRACIAL COUNCIL FOR BUSINESS OPPOR-
  TUNITY
2090 Seventh Ave.
New York, N.Y. 10027
212/666-9300
Preston Lambert, Exec. Dir.

JOINT ENTERPRISE TRUSTEESHIP CORPORATION
239 Central Ave.
East Orange, N.J. 07018
201/676-9700
Dudley Christie, Exec. Dir.

LOWER EAST SIDE ECONOMIC DEVELOPMENT
  ASSOCIATION
21 West 38th St.
New York, N.Y. 10018
212/354-5361
James N. Clark, Dir.

NATIONAL ECONOMIC DEVELOPMENT ASSOCIA-
  TION
10 Middle St., Park City Plaza
Bridgeport, Conn. 06610

203/333 4158
John Garcia, Area Dir.

NATIONAL ECONOMIC DEVELOPMENT ASSOCIA-
TION
Citibank Tower
252 Ponce de Leon Ave.
Hato Rey, P.R. 00918
809/765-6609
Hector Caballero, Reg. Dir.

NATIONAL ECONOMIC DEVELOPMENT ASSOCIA-
TION
19 West 44th St., Suite 407
New York, N.Y.
212/826-4734
Edwin Jorge, Area Dir.

NATIONAL ECONOMIC DEVELOPMENT ASSOCIA-
TION
1180 Raymond Blvd.
Newark, N.J. 07102
201/642-1324
Olimpio Sobrino, Area Dir.

NEW ROCHELLE COMMUNITY ACTION AGENCY/
WESTCHESTER BDO
33 Lincoln Ave.
New Rochelle, N.Y. 10801
914/576-3636/7/8
Steve Taracido, Exec. Dir.

PROGRESS ASSOCIATION FOR ECONOMIC DEVEL-
OPMENT
123 East Hanover St.
Trenton, N.J. 08608
609/396-3204
Joseph Bair, Exec. Dir.

PUERTO RICAN CONGRESS OF NEW JERSEY
313 State St.
Perth Amboy, N.J. 08861
201/442-1560
Robert Gomez, Exec. Dir.

PUERTO RICAN DEVELOPMENT FOUNDATION
Regional Distribution Center
Malecon Ave.
Ponce Playa, P.R. 00731
809/842-5382
Joaquin Yordan, Reg. Dir.

SMALL BUSINESS DEVELOPMENT CENTER
15 Court Square
Boston, Mass. 02108
617/723-8520
Geoffrey Anku, Dir.

SPANISH CHAMBER OF COMMERCE OF QUEENS
85-12 Roosevelt Ave.
Jackson Heights, N.Y. 11372
212/335-6412
Fernando Gainza, Exec. Dir.

THE BRONX CENTER FOR ECONOMIC DEVELOP-
MENT, INC.
332 East 149th St.
Bronx, N.Y. 10451
212/665-8583
David J. Burgos, Pres.

THE LOCAL BUSINESS DEVELOPMENT ORGANI-
ZATION OF THE UNIVERSITY OF NEW HAVEN
1082 Campbell Ave.
West Haven, Conn. 06516
203/932-5229
Louis Silbert, Proj. Dir.

UNITED SOUTH END SETTLEMENTS
20 Union Park
Boston, Mass. 02118
617/266-5120
Kenneth Brown, Exec. Dir.

VIRGIN ISLANDS BUSINESS DEVELOPMENT CEN-
TER
Grand Hotel Bldg., Suite 18
Charlotte Amalie, St. Thomas, V.I. 00801
809/774-7541

PRIVATE RESOURCE PROGRAMS

MINORITY BUSINESS INFORMATION INSTITU-
TION
295 Madison Ave.
New York, N.Y. 10017
212/889-8220
Earl G. Graves, Exec. Dir.

*NATIONAL PUERTO RICAN BUSINESS AND MAR-
KETING ASSOCIATION, INC.
9 East 41st St., 12th Fl.
New York, N.Y. 10017

212/682-6560
Dennis Garcia, Natl. Dir.

NATIONAL PUERTO RICAN BUSINESS AND MAR-
   KETING ASSOCIATION, INC.
100 West Monroe St., Suite 1107
Chicago, Ill. 60603
312/782-5371
Eddy Sanchez, Reg. Dir.

NATIONAL PUERTO RICAN BUSINESS AND MAR-
   KETING ASSOCIATION, INC.
252 Ponce de Leon Ave.
P.O. Box 1455
City Bank Tower, 14th Fl.
Hato Rey, P.R. 00910
809/765-0250
Rafael Torres, Exec. Dir.

NEW ENGLAND MINORITY PURCHASING COUNCIL
One State St., 13th Fl.
Boston, Mass. 02109
617/523-6280
Lynn Long, Exec. Dir.

NEW YORK MINORITY PURCHASING COUNCIL
9 West 57th St.
New York, N.Y. 10019
212/752-7220
David Whitley, Exec. Dir.

THE DEVELOPMENT COUNCIL
9 West 57th St.
New York, N.Y. 10019
212/752-7220
Margaret Richardson, Exec. Dir.

_____

*Headquarters Office.

STATE OMBE's

MASSACHUSETTS STATE OMBE
100 Cambridge St., Rm. 1303
Boston, Mass. 02202
617/727-8692
David Harris, Jr., Exec. Dir.

NEW YORK STATE OMBE
Department of Commerce
230 Park Ave.

New York, N.Y. 10017
212/949-9288
Hector I. Vazquez, Exec. Dir.

NEW YORK STATE OMBE
Department of Commerce
99 Washington Ave.
Albany, N.Y. 11245
518/949-9308
Samuel R. Johnson, Field Rep.

SAN FRANCISCO REGION

Ramon V. Romero
Regional Director
Office of Minority Business Enterprise
U.S. Department of Commerce
Federal Bldg., Rm. 15045
450 Golden Gate Ave.
San Francisco, Cal. 94102
415/556-7234

Senior Project Officer
Office of Minority Business Enterprise
U.S. Department of Commerce
2500 Wilshire Blvd., Suite 908
Los Angeles, Cal. 90057
213/688-7157

Joe Sotelo
Project Officer
Office of Minority Business Enterprise
U.S. Department of Commerce
112 N. Central Ave., Suite 515
Phoenix, Ariz. 85004
602/261-3503

BUSINESS RESOURCE CENTERS

ARCATA MANAGEMENT, INC.
1155 Broadway
P.O. Box 5471
Redwood City, Ca. 94063
415/364-3202
Buck Wong, Exec. Dir.

ARIZONA BUSINESS RESOURCE CENTER
2701 E. Thomas, Office J
Phoenix, Ariz. 85016
602/957-0860
James Salmon, Exec. Dir.

BAY AREA PURCHASING COUNCIL
Opportunity Through Ownership (OPTO)
215 Market St.
San Francisco, Ca. 94105
415/781-5560
Boyd Watkins, Exec. Dir.

MINORITY ENTERPRISE COALITION OF LOS AN-
GELES
2651 S. Western Ave.
Los Angeles, Ca. 90018
213/731-8261
Charles Smith, Exec. Dir.

BUSINESS DEVELOPMENT CENTERS

SACRAMENTO BUSINESS DEVELOPMENT CENTER
7300 Lincolnshire Dr., #210
Sacramento, Ca. 95823
916/421-2961
H.T. Blanchette, Exec. Dir.

SAN DIEGO BUSINESS DEVELOPMENT CENTER
3620 30th St., Suite E
San Diego, Ca. 92104
714/291-4631
Charles C. Shockley, Exec. Dir.

SAN JOSE BUSINESS DEVELOPMENT CENTER
Community Bank Bldg.
111 West St. John St., Suite 510
San Jose, Ca. 95113
408/288-6480
David Edmondson, Exec. Dir.

CITY OMBE

LOS ANGELES SMALL BUSINESS ASSISTANCE
PROGRAM
Room 2016, City Hall
200 N. Spring St.
Los Angeles, Ca. 90012
213/485-6142
Adrian Dove, Exec. Dir.

CONSTRUCTION CONTRACTOR ASSISTANCE CENTERS

ARIZONA CONTRACTORS' SERVICE CENTER
1800 North Central, #201
Phoenix, Ariz. 85004

602/267-7541
Martin Alvarez, Exec. Dir.

CALIFORNIA ASSOCIATION OF MEXICAN-
AMERICAN CONTRACTORS
5254 E. Pomona Blvd.
Los Angeles, Ca. 90022
213/685-4570
Edgar Cruz, Exec. Dir.

CENTRAL CONTRACTORS ASSN., INC.
2024 E. Union St.
Seattle, Wash. 98122
206/325-4554
Carl E. McCray, Exec. Dir.

MINORITY CONTRACTORS ASSOCIATION OF LOS
ANGELES
945 S. Western Ave., Suite 201
Los Angeles, Ca. 90006
213/737-7952
Ron Saenz, Exec. Dir.

MINORITY CONTRACTORS ASSOCIATION OF
NORTHERN CALIFORNIA, INC.
900 North Point, Suite C-411
Ghirardelli Square
San Francisco, Ca. 94109
415/474-3407
Benjamin J. Miller, Exec. Dir.

CONTRACTED SUPPORT SERVICES

MARISCAL AND COMPANY
4929 Wilshire Blvd., #1050
Los Angeles, Ca. 90010
213/933-8261
Robert Mariscal, Pres.

EXPERIMENT AND DEMONSTRATION

CITY OF SAN FERNANDO
117 MacNeil St.
San Fernando, Ca. 91340
213/365-3241
R.E. James, City Adm.

FOUNDATION FOR THE ADVANCEMENT OF
MINORITY ENTERPRISE
Suite 555, Park Plaza Bldg.
1939 Harrison St.

Oakland, Ca. 94612
415/893-6682
Sidney Cohen, Exec. Dir.

**LOCAL BUSINESS DEVELOPMENT
ORGANIZATIONS**

ALASKA FEDERATION OF NATIVES
550 W. 8th Ave.
Anchorage, Alaska 99501
907/274-3681
Robert Wilks, Exec. Dir.

ASIAN, INC.
1610 Bush St.
San Francisco, Ca. 94109
415/928-5910
Harold Yee, Exec. Dir.

ASIAN AMERICAN NATIONAL BUSINESS ALLI-
ANCE
1543 W. Olympic Blvd.
Los Angeles, Ca. 90015
213/382-7381
Tsutomu Uchida, Exec. Dir.

FOOTHILL ENTERPRISE DEVELOPMENT ASSO-
CIATION
118 S. Oak Knoll Ave.
Pasadena, Ca. 91101
213/792-5141

GOLDEN STATE BUSINESS LEAGUE
Wells Fargo Bldg.
333 Hegenberger Rd., Suite 203
Oakland, Ca. 94621
415/635-5900
Leon Miller, Exec. Dir.

HAWAII ECONOMIC DEVELOPMENT CORPORA-
TION
1427 Dillingham Blvd., Suite 210
Honolulu, Hawaii 96817
808/847-6502
Michael Coy, Exec. Dir.

INDIAN ENTERPRISE DEVELOPMENT CORPORA-
TION
222 W. Osborn, Suite 114
Phoenix, Ariz. 85013
602/279-2349
Marshall Christy, Exec. Dir.

INTERRACIAL COUNCIL FOR BUSINESS OPPOR-
TUNITIES
4801 S. Vermont Ave.
Los Angeles, Ca. 90037
213/753-2681
Cleveland O. Neil, Exec. Dir.

MISSION BUSINESS DEVELOPMENT CORPORATION
2390 Mission St., #11
San Francisco, Ca. 94110
415/285-0100
Mario Duarte, Exec. Dir.

NATIONAL ECONOMIC DEVELOPMENT ASSOCIA-
TION
2110 Mercede St., Suite 205
Fresno, Ca. 93721
209/266-9971
Carlos Tamayo, Exec. Dir.

NATIONAL ECONOMIC DEVELOPMENT ASSOCIA-
TION
3807 Wilshire Blvd., #800
Los Angeles, Ca. 90010
213/388-1131
Ruben Estrada, Exec. Dir.

NATIONAL ECONOMIC DEVELOPMENT ASSOCIA-
TION
1427 N. Third St., Suite 112
Phoenix, Ariz. 85004
602/263-8070
Richard Medina, Exec. Dir.

NATIONAL ECONOMIC DEVELOPMENT ASSOCIA-
TION
2725 Congress St., Suite 2M
San Diego, Ca. 92104
714/297-4041
David DeCima, Exec. Dir.

NATIONAL ECONOMIC DEVELOPMENT ASSOCIA-
TION
100 Park Center Plaza, Suite 325
San Jose, Ca. 95113
408/293-8340
Gabriel Garcia, Exec. Dir.

NATIONAL ECONOMIC DEVELOPMENT ASSOCIA-
TION
2302 E. Speedway, Suite 112
Tucson, Ariz. 85719

602/792-6386
Richard Grijalva, Exec. Dir.

NAVAJO SMALL BUSINESS DEVELOPMENT COM-
PANY
Drawer L
Fort Defiance, Ariz. 86504
602/729-5763
Joseph R. Hardy, Exec. Dir.

NEVADA ECONOMIC DEVELOPMENT CORP.
618-620 E. Carson
Las Vegas, Nev. 89101
702/384-3293
William H. Bailey, Exec. Dir.

OPERATION SECOND CHANCE
341 West 2nd St., Suite 1
San Bernardino, Ca. 92401
714/884-8764
Frances Grice, Exec. Dir.

PLAN OF ACTION FOR CHALLENGING TIMES, INC.
635 Divisadero St.
San Francisco, Ca. 94117
415/922-7150
Louis H. Barnett, Exec. Dir.

PROGRESS ASSOCIATION FOR ECONOMIC DEVEL-
OPMENT
1525 North Central Ave., Suite 206
Phoenix, Ariz. 85004
602/252-7478
Arthur Reeves, Exec. Dir.

SOUTH CENTRAL IMPROVEMENT ACTION COUN-
CIL, INC.
1930 Wilshire Blvd.
Los Angeles, Ca. 90057
213/753-3341
Louis Wilson, Exec. Dir.

THE EAST LOS ANGELES COMMUNITY UNION
1431 S. Atlantic Blvd.
Los Angeles, Ca. 90022
213/269-2131
Magdalena Aparicio, OMBE Dir.

TRI-COUNTY MEXICAN AMERICAN UNITY COUN-
CIL
109 East Alisal St.
Salinas, Ca. 93901
Albert Oliverez, Exec. Dir.

UNITED INDIAN DEVELOPMENT ASSOCIATION
1541 Wilshire Blvd., Rm. 307
Los Angeles, Ca. 90017
213/483-1460
David Lester, Exec. Dir.

UNITED INNER CITY DEVELOPMENT FOUNDA-
TION
120-23rd Ave., East
Seattle, Wash. 98122
206/325-7633
Michael Ross, Exec. Dir.

WESTERN ECONOMIC DEVELOPMENT CORPORA-
TION
Danzig Plaza Office
1430 Willow Pass Road, #290
Concord, Ca. 94523
415/689-0500
Joseph W. Gastelum, Exec. Dir.

WESTERN ECONOMIC DEVELOPMENT CORPORA-
TION
4000 Broadway
Oakland, Ca. 94611
415/652-2358
Peter Oliverez, Exec. Dir.

STATE OMBE

CAL-OMBE
Minority Enterprise Program
1823 14th St.
Sacramento, Ca. 95814
916/322-3420
Delorse Esparza, Proj. Dir.

WASHINGTON REGION

Luis Encinias
Acting Regional Director
Office of Minority Business Enterprise
U.S. Department of Commerce
1730 K St., N.W., Suite 420
Washington, D.C. 20006
202/634-7897

Field Officer
Office of Minority Business Enterprise
U.S. Department of Commerce
Federal Office Bldg., Rm. 9436

600 Arch St.
Philadelphia, Pa. 19106
215/597-9236

BUSINESS DEVELOPMENT CENTERS

BALTIMORE COUNCIL FOR EQUAL BUSINESS OP-
    PORTUNITY
Suite 110, Metro Plaza
Mondawmin Mall
Baltimore, Md. 21215
301/669-3400
Sam Daniels, Dir.

GREATER PITTSBURGH DEVELOPMENT CORPO-
    RATION
Arrott Building
301 N. Wood St.
Pittsburgh, Pa. 15222
412/391-4806
Clyde Jackson, Pres.

GREATER WASHINGTON BUSINESS CENTER
1705 De Sales St., N.W.
Washington, D.C. 20036
202/833-8960
Darryl A. Hill, Pres.

METROPOLITAN BUSINESS LEAGUE
615 N. Second St.
Richmond, Va. 23212
804/649-7473
Allen Roots, Jr., Dir.

PHILADELPHIA URBAN COALITION BUSINESS DE-
    VELOPMENT CENTER
1315 Walnut St.
Philadelphia, Pa. 19107
215/732-9222
Alexander MacKenzie, Dir.

TIDEWATER AREA BUSINESS AND CONTRACTORS
    ASSOCIATION
727 East Brambleton Ave.
Norfolk, Va. 23510
804/622-5463
Leroy S. Gaillard, Exec. Vice Pres.

CONSTRUCTION CONTRACTOR
ASSISTANCE CENTERS

ROANOKE VALLEY BUSINESS LEAGUE
720 Fairfax Ave.
Roanoke, Va. 24017
703/342-8911
Joseph L. Cason, Dir.

CONTRACTED SUPPORT SERVICES

BOONE, YOUNG AND ASSOCIATES, INC.
1525 New Hampshire Ave., N.W.
Washington, D.C. 20036
212/265-6363
Robert Foskey, Proj. Dir.

LOCAL BUSINESS DEVELOPMENT
ORGANIZATIONS

COMMUNITY ENTERPRISE DEVELOPMENT ASSO-
    CIATION
111 Cathedral St.
Anapolis, Md. 21401
301/263-8780
Leonard Blackshear, Exec. Dir.

ROANOKE VALLEY BUSINESS LEAGUE
720 Fairfax Ave.
Roanoke, Va. 24017
703/342-8911
Joseph L. Cason, Dir.

SPANISH MERCHANTS ASSOCIATION OF PHILA-
    DELPHIA
1315 Walnut St.
Philadelphia, Pa. 19107
215/546-2200
Nelson Diaz, Exec. Dir.

ZION TRUST ENTREPRENEURIAL DEVELOPMENT
    TRAINING CENTER
1501 N. Broad St.
Philadelphia, Pa. 19122
215/763-3300
Alfonso Jackson, Exec. Dir.

MINORITY BUSINESS AND TRADE ASSOCIATION

D.C. CHAMBER OF COMMERCE
1319 F St., N.W., Suite 904
Washington, D.C. 20004
202/347-7201
James Denson, Exec. Dir.

PRIVATE RESOURCE PROGRAM

URBAN BUSINESS AND ECONOMIC DEVELOP-
MENT ASSOCIATION
1625 Eye St., N.W., Suite 609
Washington, D.C. 20006
202/785-8211
Carolyn Walker, Pres.

STATE OMBEs

DELAWARE STATE OMBE
Department of Community Affairs Economic Develop-
ment
State House Annex
Dover, Del. 19901
302/678-5271
Wesley Wilson, Dir.

MARYLAND STATE OMBE
1748 Forest Drive
Annapolis, Md. 21401
301/269-2682
Henry Arrington, Dir.

PENNSYLVANIA STATE OMBE
Commonwealth of Pennsylvania
South Office Bldg., Rm. 403
Harrisburg, Pa. 17120
717/783-1127
Pamela Polk, Acting Dir.

VIRGINIA STATE OMBE
Virginia State College
Petersburg, Va. 23803
804/520-5413
John B. Harris, Dir.

WEST VIRGINIA STATE OMBE
West Virginia State Department of Commerce
State Capitol Complex, Rm. 553
Charleston, W. Va. 25301
304/348-2195
McDonald Cary, Dir.

U.S. Department of Commerce Field Offices

ALABAMA

Birmingham—Gayle C. Shelton, Jr., Director, Suite
200-201, 908 South 20th Street 35205, Area Code
205 Tel 254-1331

ALASKA

Anchorage—Sara L. Haslett, Director, 412 Hill Building,
632 Sixth Avenue 99501, Area Code 907 Tel
265-5307

ARIZONA

Phoenix—Donald W. Fry, Director, Suite 2950 Valley
Bank Center, 201 North Central Avenue 85004,
Area Code 602 Tel 261-3285

CALIFORNIA

Los Angeles—Eric C. Silberstein, Director, Room 800,
11777 San Vicente Boulevard 90049, Area Code
213 Tel 824-7591

San Francisco—Philip M. Creighton, Director, Federal
Building, Box 36013, 450 Golden Gate Avenue
94102, Area Code 415 Tel 556 5860

COLORADO

Denver—Norman Lawson, Director, Room 165, New
Customhouse, 19th & Stout Street 80202, Area
Code 303 Tel 837-3246

CONNECTICUT

Hartford—Richard C. Kilbourn, Director, Room 610-B,
Federal Office Building, 450 Main Street 06103,
Area Code 203 Tel 244-3530

FLORIDA

Miami—Roger J. LaRoche, Director, Room 821, City
National Bank Building, 25 West Flagler Street
33130, Area Code 305 Tel 350-5267

GEORGIA

Atlanta—David S. Williamson, Director, Suite 600, 1365
Peachtree Street, N.E. 30309, Area Code 404 Tel
881-7000

Savannah—James W. McIntire, Director, 235 U.S. Courthouse & P.O. Building, 125-29 Bull Street 31402,
Area Code 912 Tel 232-4321, Ext. 204

HAWAII

Honolulu—John S. Davies, Director, 286 Alexander Young Building, 1015 Bishop Street 96813, Area Code 808 Tel 546-8694

ILLINOIS

Chicago—Gerald M. Marks, Director, 1406 Mid Continental Plaza Building, 55 East Monroe Street 60603, Area Code 312 Tel 353-4450

INDIANA

Indianapolis—Mel R. Sherar, Director, 357 U.S. Courthouse & Federal Office Building, 46 East Ohio Street 46204, Area Code 317 Tel 269-6214

IOWA

Des Moines—Jesse N. Durden, Director, 609 Federal Building, 210 Walnut Street 50309, Area Code 515 Tel 284-4222

LOUISIANA

New Orleans—Edwin A. Leland, Jr., Director, 432 International Trade Mart, No. 2 Canal Street 70130, Area Code 504 Tel 589-6546

MARYLAND

Baltimore—Carroll F. Hopkins, Director, 415 U.S. Customhouse, Gay and Lombard Streets 21202, Area Code 301 Tel 962-3560

MASSACHUSETTS

Boston—Francis J. O'Connor, Acting Director, 10th Floor, 441 Stuart Street 02116, Area Code 617 Tel 223-2312

MICHIGAN

Detroit—William L. Welch, Director, 445 Federal Building, 231 West Lafayette 48226, Area Code 313 Tel 226-3650

MINNESOTA

Minneapolis—Glenn A. Matson, Director, 218 Federal Building, 110 South Fourth Street 55401, Area Code 612 Tel 725-2133

MISSOURI

St. Louis—Donald R. Loso, Director, 120 South Central Avenue 63105, Area Code 314 Tel 425-3302-4

NEBRASKA

Omaha—George H. Payne, Director, Capitol Plaza, Suite 703A, 1815 Capitol Avenue 68102, Area Code 402 Tel 221-3665

NEVADA

Reno—Joseph J. Jeremy, Director, 2028 Federal Building, 300 Booth Street 89509 Area Code 702 Tel 784-5203

NEW JERSEY

Newark—Clifford R. Lincoln, Director, 4th Floor, Gateway Building, Market Street & Penn Plaza 07102, Area Code 201 Tel 645-6214

NEW MEXICO

Albuquerque—William E. Dwyer, Director, 505 Marquette Ave., NW, Suite 1015, 87102, Area Code 505 Tel 766-2386

NEW YORK

Buffalo—Robert F. Magee, Director, 1312 Federal Building, 111 West Huron Street 14202, Area Code 716 Tel 842-3208

New York—Arthur C. Rutzen, Director, 37th Floor, Federal Office Building, 26 Federal Plaza, Foley Square 10007, Area Code 212 Tel 264-0634

NORTH CAROLINA

Greensboro—Joel B. New, Director, 203 Federal Building, West Market Street, P.O. Box 1950 27402, Area Code 919 Tel 378-5345

OHIO

Cincinnati—Gordon B. Thomas, Director, 10504 Federal Office Building, 550 Main Street 45202, Area Code 513 Tel 684-2944

Cleveland—Charles B. Stebbins, Director, Room 600, 666 Euclid Avenue 44114, Area Code 216 Tel 522-4750

OREGON

Portland—Lloyd R. Porter, Director, Room 618, 1220 S.W. 3rd Avenue 97204, Area Code 503 Tel 221-3001

PENNSYLVANIA

Philadelphia—Patrick P. McCabe, Director, 9448 Federal Building, 600 Arch Street 19106, Area Code 215 Tel 597-2850

Pittsburgh—Newton Heston, Jr., Director, 2002 Federal Building, 1000 Liberty Avenue 15222, Area Code 412 Tel 644-2850

PUERTO RICO

San Juan (Hato Rey)—Enrique Vilella, Director, Room 659-Federal Building 00918, Area Code 809 Tel 753-4343 Ext. 555

SOUTH CAROLINA

Columbia—Philip A. Ouzts, Director, 2611 Forest Drive, Forest Center 29204, Area Code 803 Tel 765-5345

TENNESSEE

Memphis—Bradford H. Rice, Director, Room 710, 147 Jefferson Avenue 38103, Area Code 901 Tel 521-3213

TEXAS

Dallas—C. Carmon Stiles, Director, Room 7A5, 1100 Commerce Street 75242 Area Code 214 Tel 749-1515

Houston—Felicito C. Guerrero, Director, 2625 Federal Bldg., Courthouse, 615 Rusk Street 77002, Area Code 713 Tel 226-4231

UTAH

Salt Lake City—George M. Blessing, Jr., Director, 1203 Federal Building, 125 South State Street 84138, Area Code 801 Tel 524-5116

VIRGINIA

Richmond—Weldon W. Tuck, Director, 8010 Federal Building, 400 North 8th Street 23240, Area Code 804 Tel 782-2246

WASHINGTON

Seattle—Judson S. Wonderly, Director, Room 706, Lake Union Building, 1700 Westlake Avenue North 98109, Area Code 206 Tel 442-5615

WEST VIRGINIA

Charleston—J. Raymond DePaulo, Director, 3000 New Federal Office Building, 500 Quarrier Street 25301, Area Code 304 Tel 343-6181, ext. 375

WISCONSIN

Milwaukee—Russell H. Leitch, Director, Federal Bldg/ U.S. Courthouse, 517 East Wisconsin Avenue 53202, Area Code 414 Tel. 224-3473

WYOMING

Cheyenne—Lowell O. Burns, Director, 6022 O'Mahoney Federal Center, 2120 Capitol Avenue 82001, Area Code 307 Tel 778-2220, ext. 2151

Small Business Administration

The Small Business Administration renders assistance in various ways to those planning to enter business as well as to those in business. This assistance includes counseling and possible financial aid.

Counseling may be by SBA specialists or retired executives under the Service Corps of Retired Executives (SCORE) program, and could include various seminars or courses, or a combination of services including reference publications.

Financial assistance may take the form of loans or the participation in, or guaranty of, loans made by financial institutions. Such assistance can be given only to those eligible applicants who are unable to provide the money from their own resources and cannot obtain it on reasonable terms from banks, franchisors, or other usual business sources.

The Small Business Administration financial support under its own legislation can provide up to $350,000 with the usual maximum maturity of six years for working capital and up to ten years for fixtures and equipment. Under some circumstances, portions of a loan involving construction can qualify for longer terms up to fifteen years. For those who qualify, loans made under Title IV of the Economic Opportunity Act can be up to $25,000 and the maturity can be up to ten years for working capital and fifteen years for fixed assets.

A list follows of Small Business Administration field offices (and the names and telephone numbers of SBA franchise representatives as of April 1st, 1977) where more detailed information regarding the various services available can be obtained.

REGIONAL OFFICES

Region 1 (Connecticut, Maine, Massachusetts, New Hampshire, Rhode Island, Vermont)
150 Causeway St., 10th Floor, Boston, MA 02203 (617) 223-2100.

Region 2 (New Jersey, New York, Puerto Rico, Virgin Islands)
26 Federal Plaza, Rm. 3930, New York, NY 10007 (212) 264-1468

Region 3 (Delaware, District of Columbia, Maryland, Pennsylvania, Virginia, West Virginia)
231 St. Asaphs Road, Bala Cynwyd, PA 19004 (215) 597-3311

Region 4 (Alabama, Florida, Georgia, Kentucky, Mississippi, North Carolina, South Carolina, Tennessee)
1401 Peachtree St., N.E., Rm. 441, Atlanta, GA 30309 (404) 526-0111

Region 5 (Illinois, Indiana, Michigan, Minnesota, Ohio, Wisconsin)
Federal Bldg., 219 South Dearborn St., Rm. 838, Chicago, IL 60604 (312) 353-4400

Region 6 (Arkansas, Louisiana, New Mexico, Oklahoma, Texas)
1720 Regal Row, Regal Park Office Bldg., Dallas, TX 75235 (214) 749-1011

Region 7 (Iowa, Kansas, Missouri, Nebraska)
911 Walnut St., 23rd Floor, Kansas City, MO 64106 (816) 374-7212

Region 8 (Colorado, Montana, North Dakota, South Dakota, Utah, Wyoming)
1405 Curtis St., Denver, CO 80202 (303) 327-0111

Region 9 (Arizona, California, Hawaii, Nevada, Pacific Islands)
Federal Bldg., 450 Golden Gate Ave., San Francisco, CA 94102 (415) 556-9000

Region 10 (Alaska, Idaho, Oregon, Washington)
710 2nd Ave., 5th Floor, Dexter Horton Bldg., Seattle, WA 98104 (206) 442-4343

DISTRICT OFFICES

Region 1
302 High St., Holyoke, MA 01040 (413) 536-8770

Federal Bldg., 40 Western Ave., Rm. 512, Augusta, ME 04330 (207) 622-6171

55 Pleasant St., Rm. 213, Concord, NH 03301 (603) 224-4041

Federal Bldg., 450 Main St., Rm. 710, Hartford, CT 06103 (203) 244-2000

Federal Bldg., 87 State St., Rm. 210, Montpelier, VT 05602 (802) 223-7472

57 Eddy St., Rm. 710, Providence, RI 02903 (401) 528-1000

Region 2
Chardon and Bolvia Sts., Hato Rey, PR 00919 (809) 763-6363

970 Broad St., Rm. 1635, Newark, NJ 07102 (201) 645-3581

Hunter Plaza, Fayette and Salina Sts., Rm. 308, Syracuse, NY 13202 (315) 473-3350

Federal Bldg., Rm. 1073, 100 South Clinton St., Syracuse, NY 13202 (315) 473-3350

111 West Huron St., Room 1311, Federal Bldg., Buffalo, NY 14202 (716) 842-3311

180 State St., Room 412, Elmira, NY 14904 (607) 734-1571

99 Washington Ave., Twin Towers Bldg., Room 922, Albany, NY 12210 (518) 472-4411

Region 3
109 North 3d St., Rm. 301, Lowndes Bldg., Clarksburg, WV 26301 (304) 623-3461

Federal Bldg., 1000 Liberty Ave., Rm. 1401, Pittsburgh, PA 15222 (412) 644-2780

Federal Bldg., 400 North 8th St., Rm. 3015, Richmond, VA 23240 (703) 782-2618

1030 15th St., N.W., 2nd Fl., Washington, DC 20417 (202) 655-4000

1500 North 2nd Street, Harrisburg, PA 17108 (717) 782-2200

20 N. Pennsylvania Ave., Wilkes-Barre, PA 18702 (717) 825-6811

844 King St., Federal Bldg., Rm 5207, Wilmington, Del. 19801 (302) 571-6294

7800 York Road, Towson, Md. 21204 (301) 962-3311

Region 4
908 South 20th St., Rm. 202, Birmingham, AL 35205 (205) 254-1000

230 S. Tryon St., Addison Bldg., Charlotte, NC 28202 (704) 372-0711

1801 Assembly St., Rm. 117, Columbia, SC 29201 (803) 765-5376

Petroleum Bldg., Suite 690, 200 Pascagoula St., Jackson, MS 39201 (601) 969-4371

Federal Bldg., 400 West Bay St., Rm. 261, Jacksonville, FL 32202 (904) 791-2011

Federal Bldg., 600 Federal Plaza, Rm. 188, Louisville, KY 40202 (502) 582-5971

2222 Ponce de Leon Blvd., 5th Floor, Miami, FL 33184 (305) 350-5011

404 James Robertson Pkwy., Nashville, TN 37219 (615) 749-5022

502 South Gay St., Rm. 307, Fidelity Bankers Bldg., Knoxville, TN 37902 (615) 637-9300

215 South Evans St., Greenville, NC 27834 (919) 752-3798

111 Fred Haise Blvd., Gulf Nat. Life Ins. Bldg., 2nd Fl., Biloxi, MS (601) 863-1972

1802 N. Trask St., Suite 203, Tampa, Fl 33607 (813) 228-2594

Federal Bldg., 167 North Main St., Rm 211, Memphis, TN 38103 (901) 521-3588

Region 5

One North Old State Capital Plaza, Springfield, IL 62701 (217) 525-4416

1240 East 9th St., Rm. 317, Cleveland, OH 44199 (216) 522-4180

34 North High St., Columbus, OH 43215 (614) 469-6860

Federal Bldg., 550 Main St., Cincinnati, OH 45202 (513) 684-2814

477 Michigan Ave., McNamara Bldg., Detroit, MI 48226 (313) 226-6075

575 N. Pennsylvania Ave., Century Bldg., Indianapolis, IN 46204 (317) 269-7272

122 West Washington Ave., Rm 713, Madison, WI 53703 (608) 252-5261

12 South 6th St., Plymouth Bldg., Minneapolis, MN 55402 (612) 725-2362

540 W. Kaye Ave., Marquette, MI 49855 (906) 225-1108

735 West Wisconsin Ave., Rm 905, Continental Bank & Trust Co., Milwaukee, WI 53233 (414) 244-3941

500 South Barstow St., Rm 16 Fed. Off. Bldg, & U.S. Courthouse, Eau Claire, WI 54701 (715) 834-9012

Region 6

5000 Marble Ave., N.E., Patio Plaza Bldg., Albuquerque, NM 87110 (505) 474-5511

One Allen Ctr., 500 Dallas Houston, TX 77002 (713) 527-4011

611 Gaines St., Suite 900, Little Rock, AR 72201 (501) 740-5011

1205 Texas Ave., Lubbock, TX 79408 (806) 738-7011

222 East Van Buren St., Harlingen, TX 78550 (Lower Rio Grande Valley) (512) 734-3011

1000 South Washington St., Marshall, TX 75670 (214) 935-5257

Plaza Tower, 17th Floor, 1001 Howard Ave., New Orleans, LA 70113 (504) 682-2611

50 Penn Place, Suite 840, Oklahoma City, OK 73118 (405) 736-4011

727 E. Durango, Rm. A-513, San Antonio, TX 78206 (512) 730-5511

1100 Commerce St., Rm 300, Dallas, TX 75202 (214) 749-1011

4100 Rio Bravo, Suite 300, El Paso, TX 79901 (915) 572-7200

3105 Leopard St., Corpus Christi, TX 78408 (512) 734-3011

Region 7

New Federal Bldg., 210 Walnut St., Rm. 749, Des Moines, IA 50309 (515) 284-4422

19th and Farnam Sts., Empire State Bldg., Omaha, NE 68102 (402) 221-4691

Suite 2500 Mercantile Tower, St. Louis, MO 63101 (314) 279-4191

110 East Waterman, Wichita, KA 67202 (316) 267-6566

Region 8

Rm 4001, Federal Bldg., 100 East B St., Casper, WY 82601 (307) 328-5330

618 Helena Avenue, Helena, MT 59601 (406) 588-6011

Federal Bldg., 653 2d Ave., North, Rm. 218, Fargo, ND 58102 (701) 783-5771

Federal Bldg., 125 South State St., Rm. 2237, Salt Lake City, UT 84111 (801) 588-5500

National Bank Bldg., 8th and Maine Ave., Rm. 402, Sioux Falls, SD 57102 (605) 782-4980

515 9th St., Federal Bldg., Rapid City, SD 57701 (605) 782-7000

Region 9

149 Bethel St., Rm. 402, Honolulu, HI 96813 (808) 546-8950

350 S. Figueroa St., Los Angeles, CA 90071 (213) 688-2000

112 North Central Ave., Phoenix, AZ 85004 (602) 261-3900

880 Front St., Rm. 4-5-33, San Diego, CA 92101 (714) 293-5444

301 E. Stewart, Las Vegas, NV 89121 (702) 385-6011

Federal Bldg., 1130 O St., Rm 4015, Fresno, CA 93721 (209) 487-5000

Region 10

1016 West 6th Ave., Suite 200, Anchorage Legal Center, Anchorage, AK 99501 (907) 272-5561

501½ 2nd Ave., Fairbanks, AK 99701 (907) 452-1951

216 North 8th St., Rm. 408, Boise, ID 83701 (208) 554-1096

1220 S.W. Third Ave., Portland, OR 97205 (503) 221-2000

Court House Bldg., Rm. 651, Spokane, WA 99210 (509) 452-2100

Internal Revenue Service, Department of the Treasury

The Internal Revenue Service offers a number of services designed to assist new businessmen in understanding and meeting their Federal tax obligations. For example, a *Mr. Businessman's Kit* (Publication 454) which contains informational publications, forms, instructions, and samples of notices which the IRS issues to business concerns is available free.

The kit is a convenient place for storing retained copies of tax returns and employee information. It also contains a checklist of tax returns and a tax calendar of due dates for filing returns and paying taxes identified on the folder. Copies of the kit may be obtained from local offices of the Internal Revenue Service. Employees of the IRS are available to explain items in the kit and answer questions about the tax forms, how to complete them, requirements for withholding, depositing, reporting Federal income and social security taxes, and the Federal unemployment tax. Copies of the kit may also be obtained by writing to the District Director who will have it delivered and explained at a mutually convenient time.

The Tax Guide for Small Business (Publication 334) may also be obtained at local offices of the IRS, the District Director, or the Superintendent of Documents, U.S. Government Printing Office, Washington, D.C. 20402. Free.

18.

BUILDING AN INSURANCE PLAN

Every franchisee—from the moment he acquires a franchise (whatever the franchise proposition may be)—assumes the status of a "small business." As such he is surrounded by the varied responsibilities of small business operations, including proper management and proper "controls."

Critical among these responsibilities is INSURANCE. In most instances, we have been accustomed to "personal" insurance (e.g., life and estate) and the protection it affords us. Business insurance, however, is much more varied and complex.

These facts are "axiomatic" . . . .

Improper insurance—or inadequate insurance—can spell the "ruination" of any franchise operation. Any one of a dozen unanticipated mishaps can completely "wipe out" the investment of the franchisee.

Proper and sufficient insurance can give all-over protection that spells continued security for the franchisee. It can "cushion" him against most mishaps—both business or personal.

In arriving at a conclusion as to how much insurance should be carried for your business, always ask yourself this question: "How much can I AFFORD TO LOSE if wiped out by a disaster, of any type, beyond my control?" Use this simple self-query as a "rule-of-thumb." For example: if the assessed value of your property is $10,000, can you afford to take only $6,000 in insurance—and absorb a loss of $4,000?

Another important thing to keep in mind as both a businessperson or franchisee, is this: On one hand, do not overinsure, burdening yourself with the expense of marginally essential or non-essential protection. On the other hand, be sure to obtain adequate insurance coverage to cover ALL your basic needs, both business and personal.

Many franchisors have what's known as a "blanket" insurance policy that in many instances may also permit their individual franchisees to come under its protection in their perspective areas. Usually, too, such blanket insurance coverage, originating from the franchisor or home office, is available to the individual franchisees at reduced rates.

Your agent or broker is prepared to render valuable assistance by an "insurance survey" or "risk analysis" which will produce the facts necessary to make intelligent insurance decisions.

The types of business coverages on which you can save money are described below. Always keep in mind, YOU are the beneficiary of insurance. As the owner, any uninsured losses would come out of *your* pocket. Fire, windstorm, explosion or death, are all recognized losses, but hidden and more disastrous losses can occur from interrupted business, terminated leases and destroyed leases. "Losses" comprise potential future damages, as well as immediate damage.

Insurance for the Franchise

1. FIRE INSURANCE: Have your property properly appraised so that it is insured for its full insurable value. Be sure that you re-examine your fire insurance periodically to see that it covers new, current value. Add to the coverage as needed.

It is also advisable that you find out to what extent, if any, the landlord's insurance covers you and then obtain added insurance in the amount you wish.

2. INVENTORY INSURANCE: It is advisable that your inventory insurance should be slightly higher than your normal inventory. To protect your "periodical inventory fluctuations," arrange to obtain periodically extended coverage from your insurance broker. Keep an accurate account of inventory so that exact replacement value is known at all times.

3. BURGLARY INSURANCE: To give yourself maximum coverage, bear in mind that this insurance includes protection against loss resulting from the following crimes:

(a) BURGLARY—which requires forcible entry. For example: your safe is broken open or a person breaks into your place of business after it is closed (carrying off merchandise or office equipment).

(b) ROBBERY—the taking of property by violence or the threat of violence.

(c) THEFT AND LARCENY—stealing property while it is un-protected;(for example) if a person finds the door of your business establishment open and steals your property. In 1960, over 1,000 places of business were entered by burglars every day (in cities of over 25,000 population). If you rent a store, the storekeeper's Burglary and Robbery Policy may answer your need. If you operate an office, you may want an Office Burglary and Robbery Policy.

4. WORKMEN'S COMPENSATION INSURANCE: This type of insurance protects employees against loss resulting from job-connected accidents and also against certain types of occupational illness. Generally, the employer is compelled by State Law to carry this insurance. Premium rates are influenced by the percentage of weekly pay allowed as a benefit. Amounts paid for medical treatment also form an important element of cost. The only way to reduce this insurance expense is to prevent accidents.

5. ACCIDENTS AND HEALTH INSURANCE: This type of insurance helps to reimburse an employee for expenses resulting from an off-the-job injury or a major illness . . . also for loss of income (while unable to work). A sound health and insurance plan will, first, act as an inducement to prospective employees; second, it will help reduce employee turnover; third, it will promote better morale and loyalty to the Company, thereby increasing productivity.

6. USE AND OCCUPANCY INSURANCE: Should your business be interrupted or suspended due to serious damage, Use and Occupancy or Earnings Insurance will provide you with the same profits as though there had been no interruption at all. A total stoppage of business is not necessary to collect. You can also collect on partial reduction of business profits resulting from designated damage.

"Shrinkage" of sales can result from: damage by fire, breaking down of machinery, vandalism by striking employees, explosions, broken water pipes and a variety of other misfortunes.

7. GENERAL LIABILITY INSURANCE: This type of insurance usually comprises two parts: (1) bodily injury, which covers claims for the accidental injury or death of persons (other than employees) and (2) property damage, which covers accidental injury to the property of others which is not being used by the insured or in his care.

Within the liability area of insurance, the following are most important:

(a) BASIC COVERAGE: This type of coverage insures liability for accidents occurring on the business premises or arising out of the use of the premises for business purposes. This is, ordinarily, obtainable through the Owner's, Landlord's and Tenant's Liability Policy. The premium is normally figured on the number of square feet in the area to be insured with, in some cases, an additional charge for frontage.

(b) OTHER TYPES OF LIABILITY COVERAGE: Products liability arising from any dangers through use of products or services. For example: accidents from defective electrical apparatus, poisoning from food or from dyes in textiles, and many miscellaneous hazards.

(c) AUTOMOBILE INSURANCE: There are two principal forms of automobile insurance: (1) Automobile Liability and (2) Automobile Physical Damage. The first form protects the car owner or operator against damage suits arising out of automobile accidents. The second form reimburses the owner for loss of or damage to his own car. There are three types of physical damage insurance within the category of automobile insurance: (1) fire; (2) theft; (3) collision.

(d) CONTRACTUAL LIABILITY: This type of insurance covers liability imposed by law for negligence.

(e) The most popular type of insurance policy to cover all these areas is the COMPREHENSIVE GENERAL LIABILITY POLICY which provides automatic coverages for many of the new, unanticipated hazards that may develop after you have purchased your policy.

8. BUSINESS LIFE INSURANCE: This is necessary protection for a business, or for the family of the businessman. Uninsured financial loss can occur due to the death of someone associated with the business. Such insurance maintains business continuity and your full value in a business for your family. Main types of coverages are:(1) Key-man protection—reimburses the business for loss upon the death of a key employee; (2) Partnership insurance—retires a partner's interest at death; (3) Corporation insurance—buys out a shareholder's interest at death; (4) Proprietorship insurance—provides for maintenance of business upon the death of a sole proprietor; (5) Insurance to aid a firm's credit status—covers the owner or key-man during the period of a loan or the duration of

a mortgage; (6) Where the estate of a businessman consists almost entirely of his interest in a business, insurance on his life is payable to his family on his death, providing them with cash and aid in liquidation of his interest in the business.

9. FIDELITY INSURANCE: Protects you against losses of property and money because of fraud or dishonesty by one or more employees. Your best coverage could be a "blanket bond," which covers losses resulting from the dishonest act of any employee.

Insurance Checklist

Here is a helpful insurance checklist for use in reviewing with your agent or broker. All the phases of protection may not be required in your business, but it would be well for you to be fully familiar with all types of insurance protection offered:

Buildings:

Fire (building and contents)
Improvements and betterments
Extended coverage
Vandalism and malicious mischief
Earthquake and flood
Sprinkler leakage and water damage
Glass
Business interruption (Contingent B.I. agreed amount)
Extra expense
Rent and leasehold
Replacement cost
Debris removal
Demolition

Business:

Key-man life
Business continuation
Life: Proprietorship, partnership, closed corporation

Employees (Protection of Human Life Values):

Group life
Salary savings
Pension plan
Group disability

Medical payment
Workmen's compensation
Non-occupational disability
Unemployment compensation

Liability Against Wrongful Actions:

Owners, landlords and tenants
Manufacturers
Contractual
Contingent
Elevator
Comprehensive general

Merchandise:

Inland marine
Transportation, parcel post
Salesmen's samples
Exhibition floater
Robbery and safe burglary
Installment sales floater
Ocean marine cargo
Burglary, robbery and theft
Open stock burglary
Money and Securities, 3-D broad form

Equipment:

Boiler and machinery
Auto physical damage
Aircraft damage
Marine hull
Auto liability
Non-ownership
Neon sign
Use and occupancy

Protection Against Human Failure:

Honesty, ability, and financial strength
Supply bond
Contract bond
License and permit bond
Schedule position bond
Blanket position bond
Depositors forgery bond

19.

HOW TO ASSURE YOURSELF OF THE CONTINUING "BUSINESS HEALTH" OF YOUR FRANCHISE

The objective of your franchise acquisition is to establish a profitable business. Step #1 is selecting the right franchise. Step #2 is proper, dedicated management and application to your enterprise. Step #3—usually the most neglected phase of your business—is the most critical phase. We refer to the business aspects of your franchise.

This is so important that, in a recent statistical survey, a governmental agency comments that over 50% of small business failures are caused by poor arithmetic control—or lack of proper record keeping.

One fallacy of business is that, often, the small businessman thinks he is doing well because he has been very busy all year, perhaps working as many as 12 hours a day. Imagine his consternation when, at the end of the year, he discovers that he has actually lost money. Pathetically, he asks why?

The reasons are usually based on the lack of arithmetic control of his business. He has not properly allocated expenses versus income, at every step, to determine whether or not he is making a profit. He has failed to give himself a month-by-month awareness of exactly how he is doing—to assure himself that he is in a profitable position and to correct any weakness promptly, before it's too late!

For example, most small businessmen have no idea as to the Break-Even point of their business—what it is and how it can alert them relative to their business.

Within the scope of this chapter, we will endeavor to explain the things you should know to give you adequate, continuing control of the business phases of your protection. This chapter comprises:

a. Proper record-keeping systems
b. Knowing the Break-Even point of your business
c. Knowing your business ratios

Record-keeping for Your Franchised Business

As a general rule, franchisees shun the arithmetic aspects of their business. These are considered necessary "negatives" which they prefer not to see—in fact such figures are "shoved" under some hypothetical "carpet" to be ignored.

This reminds us of a story about newlyweds we knew. Seems that the bride had prepared her first meal for hubby. He registered disapproval and kept registering it several times. "I wish you would stop bringing up that meal again," his wife exclaimed with great exasperation. "I would like very much not to," the husband replied, coyly, "however, it keeps coming up—all by itself!"

The same with your business arithmetic. You can forget it—"shove" it under the "carpet"—however, it will "keep coming up—all by itself." When it does come up, its reaction may be explosive. You may suddenly discover:

. You are not in adequate control of what you're doing.

. You may be over-paying for certain things, where, in actuality, you can avoid as much as half the cost without impeding your business progress. For example: rent, personnel, and advertising.

. You may be under-paying for certain things that can help to expedite business expansion.

. You may be over-inventoried . . . or under-inventoried (both of which can prove damaging to your business).

. You may be under-paying on taxes (subjecting you to severe penalties) or you may be over-paying these taxes (again throttling your business progress or earning potential).

. You may have a series of wasteful "leakages" in your business—enough of them to permanently "sink your ship."

All these possible hazards refer to record keeping, the way you maintain your books and the day-by-day awareness you have of your business activities and status.

What are the things that a proper record-keeping system should do for a franchisee? Below is a partial list:

1. How much total business is he doing?

2. How much cash does he have in the bank and on hand?

3. Is the latter amount sufficient?

4. Is there any cash shortage?

5. How much inventory does he have on hand?

6. How much merchandise is he taking out of the business for personal or family use?

7. How much money does he owe to wholesalers and others?

8. How much gross profit does he earn?

9. How much were his expenditures for any given period?

10. How much net profit is he making?

11. How much is he obligated to pay in taxes?

12. What is his net worth; that is, what is the value of his proprietorship?

13. What are the trends in his sales, expenses, profits, net worth? How is his business progressing from month-to-month, and year-to-year?

14. How does this business compare with similar-type businesses?

The answers to the above questions are, in effect, "directional" signals. They tell the small businessman where he is going and whether he should do something to change the direction of the business. Once he understands the conditions which exist, the franchisee can take the necessary action to improve his position.

Basic requisites of a successful record-keeping system are the following:

. It should be simple

. It should be quick and easy to maintain

. It should provide easy procedures for day-by-day figure compilation

. It should provide a periodic summation—enabling an "at-a-glance" perspective of the business

. It should require very little time to transcribe pertinent figures, usually during the evening

. It should be so simple that the franchisee can control the system . . . irrespective of any professional accountant used.

Fortunately for the franchisee, a number of such simplified systems are available—making quick transcription, easy awareness and continuing control of the business arithmetic a relatively simple matter. In most instances, these services will go so far as to prepare the tax statements for clients. This service would include related data, estimates of income, Social Security figures and the Profit-and-Loss statement. All this—at moderate cost—geared to the nature of small businesses.

A record-keeping system of this type enables precise tax compilation. Most important, it acts to avoid costly over-payments on taxes. It is estimated that 6 out of 10 small businessmen overpay on their taxes!

In addition to providing these all-important advantages, an effective record system also provides certain "fringe" benefits. For example, a franchisee who wished to apply for a loan will need an accurate Balance Sheet to present to the bank. A good set of records can provide such a Statement quickly and accurately.

Examples of simplified record-keeping form are pictured and described at the end of this chapter. They are extracted from a record-keeping system for small businesses offered by General Business Services, Washington, D.C.—one of the organizations referred to previously. For the same package fee they also prepare the tax returns for small businesses. In examining these forms you'll note the simplicity of the day-by-day business entries . . . the all-inclusive picture it gives of the business status.

In sum: to assure that the business is being operated successfully, to achieve the kind of earnings expected when you took on your franchise, maintenance of good records is a "must." It is, in fact, considered every bit as important as sales for the continued "health" of the business.

One of the most vital elements in assuring the continued success of your franchise is knowing the Break-Even point of the business. As the term implies, it is that particular point in the business operation where you neither lose nor make money but have just covered your expenses.

To make that still clearer, it is the particular point where your gross sales exactly equal the total of your fixed plus controllable expenses.

Assume, for example, that you have a shop with a potential for doing a maximum business of $5200 a month and you want to determine your Break-Even point. This, of course, is a hypothetical figure used as an example. Most franchise operations are expected to gross much more.

Here is what you would do:

FIRST: Ask yourself, what are your FIXED EXPENSES? They would include your rent, utilities, insurance, depreciation, various taxes you must pay—all the items that remain constant change no matter what amount of business you do. Jot down your total fixed expenses, for example, as being $800 a month.

SECOND: Note your maximum sales potential per month. That, as previously stated, is $5200.

THIRD: Figure your VARIABLE EXPENSES—in other words, the expenses that usually increase as your sales volume increases. These would include outside labor, operating supplies, advertising, bad debts, repairs and maintenance, car and delivery, legal and miscellaneous expenses.

Now, let us assume that your records indicate that your average sales for the month should amount to 80% of your maximum potential—in other words, about $4200. Then further determine your variable expenses at, let us say, 67% of $4200—or about $2800.

FOURTH: Add together your fixed expenses ($800) plus your variable expenses ($2800) and you arrive at a total expense of $3600.

Knowing these figures, you are now ready to make up your Break-Even chart. This should show you the point where your business will reach a Break-Even spot—neither making nor losing money—under a given set of conditions.

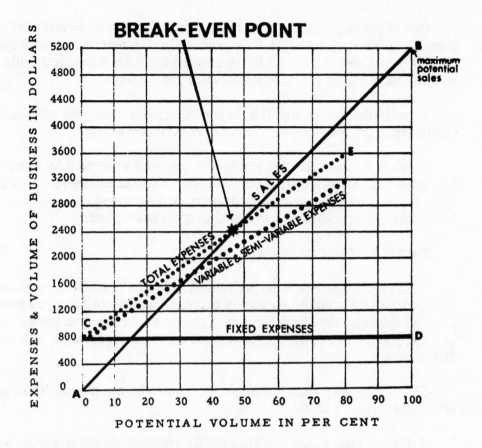

BREAK-EVEN POINT

POTENTIAL VOLUME IN PER CENT

Instructions for Preparing Your Break-Even Chart

1. Draw a blank chart like that shown on above, with equal horizontal divisions numbered 0, 10, 20, 30, 40 and so on to 100—these figures representing 0% to 100%.

2. Your vertical divisions, in this case, run from $00 to $5200. So let's decide to make the vertical division represent sales in hundreds of dollars, with the bottom line representing $0, the next line $400, the next line $800, then $1200, $1600, etc.

3. Rule a diagonal line running from $0 on the lower left corner, to $5200 in the upper right corner, the line we show as A-B. Label this line SALES.

4. Now rule a horizontal line across at the $800 mark. This indicates your fixed expenses, which remain approximately the same every month, no matter what your sales. This line is shown here as line C-D and is labeled FIXED EXPENSES.

5. We stated above that the average expected sales would be 80% of maximum potential and that total expenses would amount to $3600. So place a dot at the point where the vertical line at 80% meets the horizontal line at $3600. This we show as point E on your chart.

6. Now draw a line from $800 at 9% diagonally up to point E. This is indicated as line C-E, and we label it TOTAL EXPENSES.

7. Where lines A-B and C-E intersect, is your Break-Even point. This we show as point X.

8. Point X in our example falls at $2400—which is a little better than 45% of maximum sales potential. This signifies that you must do $2400 worth of business in order to "break-even." At this point you are neither making nor losing money, but just about covering your expenses.

How Your Break-Even Chart Can Help You

You can learn, from this particular chart, that for any month, in order to make a profit, you must do a sales volume in excess of $2400. The chart can help control your budget by indicating changes that may be necessary, in order to bring expenses into line with income.

When your sales aren't all they should be, the chart will indicate this too, telling you that you should do something about your sales methods, your merchandise or your staff.

Here are some other things the Break-Even chart can show you:

   . How much business you can afford to lose before you run the risk of disappearing profits.

   . What would take place if you increased or reduced prices.

   . Whether you can afford to incur the added expense of making improvements.

   . Which lines and items you should "push" and which you might be wise to drop.

Before the start of each month, learn how much business you must do that month by making a Break-Even chart. This will help you plan your way to bigger, more consistent profits and will tell you which way you are heading, at all times.

What Are Your Business Ratios?

Franchisees often tell us that they would appreciate some "yardsticks" that would help give them a valid, continuing "picture" of their business progress.

RATIO analysis is one proven method to help you judge the financial condition of your business and financial changes that may occur. In most cases, you will be able to detect the start of any small trouble and stop it before it has a chance to do your business genuine financial harm. The ratio will show you the relationship between two items; usually between a complete item and one or more of its parts, or between two or more parts of the same item.

When you apply the ratio to your Balance Sheet or your Profit and Loss statement, you can compare items that are part of the same statement or compare various items from different statements. You can also use this method to compare your business status with others in the industry—for there are available "standard" ratios for most types of business.

Below are listed examples of ratios and how they can be applied to your business. In all examples, use the largest number that will divide each number evenly.

1. CURRENT RATIO: A comparison between current assets and current liabilities.

Current assets are those which will flow into cash during a normal business cycle, usually one year. They include: cash, notes and accounts receivable, inventory and other assets intended to be converted into cash within one year. Current liabilities will include bills due within one year, such as notes, accounts payable for merchandise, bank notes and taxes.

For example; a grocer has current assets totaling $3600 and total current liabilities of $3000. The ratio would be found by computing as follows: $3600/$3000 or 6/5. Therefore, his ratio would be 6 to 5, meaning that for every $6 of assets, he has $5 of liabilities. The difference between current assets and current liabilitiers or $600 is the working capital of the business.

2. NET PROFIT MARGIN: Compares net profits to total net sales.

A druggist has monthly net sales of $1800 and the net profit from these sales is $600. Comparison may be made as follows: $1800/$600 equals 3/1. In this example, then, the net profit margin would be 3 to 1, $3 of sales for every $1 of net profit or 33%.

When a comparison of your ratio is made with those of other firms in the same business, results of ratios for a few years back can often be as useful as very recent ratios. The important thing is to get started with a comparison standard.

3. GROSS EARNINGS RATIO: Comparison of total net sales to gross earnings (mark up).

In the last example, we have assumed that the druggist's total net sales were $1800. If his gross earnings were $1200, this ratio would be: $1800/$1200 or 3/2. This ratio shows that for every $3 of net sales, there are $2 of gross earnings.

Your cost of goods sold may affect this, as well as other ratios. Costs of goods may seem high simply because of a low selling price. For example: if sales are $10,000 and cost of goods is $8,000, then your gross profit on your sales is 20% and the cost of goods sold is 80%.

Now, if your gross profit was increased to 25% and the cost of the goods remained the same, your sales would be $10,666 and the $8,000 figure would represent only 75% of sales.

4. UNIT COST RATIO: Comparison of the costs of production and the physical volume produced.

If a manufacturer finds that his actual production costs come to $300 for every 1,500 cases of merchandise sold, the example can be compared as: $1500/$300 or 5/1. Therefore, for every 5 cases of merchandise, the manufacturer has production costs of $1.

5. CAPITAL EMPLOYED RATIO: Comparison showing how much capital was invested to produce net profits.

In example 2, the net profits were $600. If this businessman invested $500 to obtain these profits, the ratio can be figured as: $600/500 or 6/5. Thus, $6 of profits are received for every $5 of invested capital or a return of 120%.

If you compare your ratio to that of another business in the same line and you find that the gross profit should be 25%, this does not mean that you must average 25% gross profit for every single item you sell.

Your competition may force you to lower your profit margin on some items. There may be other excellent reasons in your business for your Company to be higher or lower than your competitor on certain items or ratios.

However, a sound and well-balanced pricing policy will enable you to obtain the same margin of profit on your over-all business.

6. FIXED PROPERTY RATIO: Fixed assets (furniture, fixtures, property) compared to total net sales.

A plumber has fixed assets totaling $3600. His total net sales are $12,000. Therefore, to find how much was invested to produce each dollar of net sales, the example would be: $12,000/$3600 or 10/3. Thus, the plumber, finds that $10 of sales were produced for each $3 invested in fixed assets.

Knowing fixed assets ratios can become very useful to a businessman because it answers these questions: (a) how much business is being generated by every dollar invested in equipment? and (b) can I increase business by further investment in fixed assets?

The application of the ratio, for comparing various items connected with the operation of your business, can be most helpful. You will be able to "spot" any weak points of your business with these comparisons. You can check back on possible "leakages" or inefficiencies if you find that your sales figures come too close to production costs. You will be able to readjust any items that you find are becoming costly in the operation of your business.

Because the operating ratio is such an important one, here is a list of some of the classifications usually covered by operating ratios:

MANAGEMENT WAGES: In most small businesses it is often the practice to compute profits before allowing any compensation to the owner or owners. After all other deductions are made, the earnings left usually represent their compensation. However, it is recommended that the business allot a salary to the owner for his services—as a more valid yardstick for measuring his business progress.

EMPLOYEE WAGES AND SALARIES: Wages and salaries vary, depending on the type of business. In grocery stores, for example, they're as low as 2½% of gross receipts. In laundry plants they're as high as 40%. To assure that you are not overpaying—or underpaying—it's advisable to study basic rates paid by others in your line.

OCCUPANCY COSTS: Rent or occupancy costs are an important factor in your financial statement. It's advisable not to overpay. It's equally advisable not to underpay. Often low-rent locations require commensurately large outlays in advertising to draw traffic so that, in effect, you are paying a penalty for a low-rent location. Analyze: Do you have the type of business that depends on passerby-impulse traffic . . . or will customers ordinarily seek you out?

ADVERTISING: As you know, advertising is a powerful factor in attracting customers. As a rule of thumb, the larger the number of turnovers in your business, the more you should spend on advertising. Set aside a definite portion of your budget and increase it as your business volume increases. Check with other people in the same line of business as to what percentage of expenditures is spent on advertising.

CREDIT: Most small businesses must extend some credit to realize their maximum sales potential. Properly controlled, credit can stimulate sales, encourage large orders and build goodwill. A recent survey showed that over 75% of small businesses extend credit. Credit requests range from occasional "charges" to regular installments or budget sales. In setting up a credit program, it is vital that it be organized methodically and carefully maintained. A good program can hold credit losses to 1% or less.

Here are some steps that should be taken to set up an effective credit program:

First: At the time an account is opened, inform the customer clearly of your collection policy—exactly when payment is expected. Do not vary your procedures.

Second: Send out statements promptly. Follow up with additional statement if the account is not paid promptly.

Third: Set a specific credit limit for each customer and do not exceed this limit at any time.

Fourth: If you deal with people who are transient and unknown to you, have them fill out a financial statement. This lists personal and financial references. Check the references carefully in advance.

Fifth: Maintain proper credit records.

CASH-FLOW PROJECTIONS

Based on a set of assumptions and educated guesses, a Cash-Flow Projection is a study and analysis of the expected flow of *actual* cash through a business. Cash-Flow is *not* concerned with accounts receivable, accounts payable, depreciation, or any other accrual factor which is not a reflection of the immediate cash situation.

Ideally, a Cash-Flow Projection could be prepared to illustrate the flow of cash in such small increments as one day at a time. This, however, is not practical and is not really necessary. The time increment usually used is one month with annual recaps.

The principal objectives of a Cash-Flow Projection are to determine the following:

1. The amount of investment and borrowings necessary to finance the business at the assumed rate of growth.

2. The rate of growth that is comfortably financeable or that can be accomplished within the limitations of cash generated by the business.

3. Approximately when further infusions of cash may be needed.

4. When there will be sufficient cash surplus to start drawing a salary from the business and approximately how much may be drawn.

5. The volume level and timing at which employees can be engaged.

6. When commitments for additional space, equipment, inventory, etc., can be made within the financial capability of the business.

7. Whether the entire business concept is practical and feasible from the financial viewpoint.

In preparing a Cash-Flow Projection, it is important to include *all* income and disbursements when they actually occur. In other words, if you are considering a business which must sell on credit, you cannot enter the income from sales until the period when the customers normally pay their bills. In a cash business, this is of little or no concern. Regarding disbursements, you enter them in the periods in which you must pay the bills. The longer the credit terms you are able to negotiate, the more favorable will be your cash-flow situation.

Many businesses fail even though their Operating Statements reflect profits and that assets are greater than liabilities. The cause of this is usually a negative cash-flow, making it impossible to pay bills, meet payrolls and pay taxes. Conversely, a business having large, depreciable assets that are income producing, might show little or no profit in the accountant's operating statement yet can pay handsome salaries to owners while remaining in business forever. Typical of this anomaly is the real estate business wherein the operating statement of a large building (and its tax returns) might reflect "paper" losses resulting from theoretical "depreciation" of the building.

Since rental income is not directly affected by depreciation and such depreciation is not an actual cash disbursement, cash-flow is not affected adversely.

In working up a Cash-Flow Projection for a business you are thinking of establishing or purchasing, be as thorough and realistic as possible. A carefully drawn Cash-Flow Projection can help you make important business decisions. It is also a valuable planning tool and an excellent exhibit to present to financial sources when obtaining financing.

CASH-FLOW PROJECTION

(NO PROVISION FOR TAXES)

	1	2	3	4	5	6
Sales	Start-up Period None	First Month $500	Second Month $1,000	Third Month $3,000	Fourth Month $5,000	Fifth Month $6,000
INCOME						
From Investment	$ 5,000					
From Loans	5,000					
From Sales			500	1,000	3,000	5,000
Other						
Total Income	10,000	-0-	500	1,000	3,000	5,000
DISBURSEMENTS						
Rent Security	200					
Rent	100	100	100	100	100	100
Utility Securities	100					
Gas & Electric	75	75	75	75	75	75
Telephones	50	50	50	50	50	50
Leasehold Imprv.	1,000					
Furniture	500					
Equipment	1,000					
Stationery	250					
Merchandise	5,000			200	500	2,000
Payroll						
Officers				400	400	600
Salesmen						500
Secretary						
Driver						300
Payroll Taxes (10%)				40	40	140
Advertising	500		100	100	100	100
Selling Exp.				50	50	75
Maintenance		50	50	50	50	50
Postage	100	25	25	25	45	45
Petty Cash	100	25	25	25	25	25
Misc.	50	50	50	50	50	50
Accountng	100	50	50	50	50	50
Legal	500					
Total Disbursements	9,625	425	525	1,215	1,535	4,160
Cash Ahead (Behind) For Period	375	(425)	(25)	(215)	1,465	840
Accumulated Cash	375	(50)	(75)	(290)	1,175	2,015

Sales and Income For _December_ 19___

Page 1

DATE	DAY	1. TOTAL MONEY RECEIVED	2.		3. TOTAL SALES	4.	5.	6.	7.	8.
1	TUE.	104 75								
2	WED.	106 25								
3	THU.	117 55								
4	FRI.	129 36								
5	SAT.	132 43								
6	SUN.	——→	590 84							
7	MON.	110 40								
8	TUE.	100 75								
9	WED	128 60								
10	THU.	112 80								
11	FRI.	121 05								
12	SAT.	118 70								
13	SUN.	——→	692 30							
14	MON.	131 15								
15	TUS.	124 50								
16	WEA	129 07								
17	THU.	127 70								
18	FRI.	134 85								
19	SAT.	120 20								
20	SUN.	——→	767 47							
21	MON.	129 90								
22	TUS.	126 65								
23	WEO.	128 05								
24	THU.	136 20								
25	FRI.	CHRISTMAS								
26	SAT.	129 70								
27	SUN.	——→	650 50							
28	MON.	127 30								
29	TUE.	120 68								
30	WEB	132 60								
31	THU.	98 12								
		——→	478 70							
TOTAL		3719 81								

Money Received from Other Sources

9. Sale of Equipment		
10. Money Borrowed for the Business		
11. Other		
12. Total This Month (add items 9, 10, 11)		
13. Total Previous Months (item 14 previous month)		
14. Total Year to Date (item 12 plus 13)		

Accounts Receivable Control

15. Accounts Receivable Due from Customers beginning of Month		
16. Add total sales for Month (col. 3)		
17. Sub-Total		
18. Subtract Total Money Received (col. 1)		
19. Balance Due from Customers End of Month		
20. Adjustments		
21. Balance carried forward SHOULD EQUAL ACCOUNTS RECEIVABLE SUMMARY SHEET TOTAL		

GBS FORM 5001

MONTHLY RECORD OF SALES AND INCOME

Indicates daily cash receipts from business plus all additional funds received from other sources.

The record-keeping charts contained on this and subsequent pages have been furnished through courtesy of Bernard Browning, president of General Business Services, 51 Monroe Street, Rockville, Maryland.

Business Expenses For _DECEMBER_ 19____

Page 2

(1) OPERATING SUPPLIES		(2) OFFICE SUPPLIES		(3) GROSS EMPLOYEES SALARIES (ENTER MONTHLY TOTALS FROM PAYROLL RECORDS)		(4) RENT		(5) INTEREST AND BANK CHARGES		(6) BUSINESS TAXES LICENSES ITEM			(7) EMPLOYER'S SHARE SOCIAL SECURITY
612	33 60	2	1 85			599	200 —	601	10 40	607 County License		58 40	
3	6 40	3	5 —	31	400 —					619 State License		73 40	(8) UNEMPLOYMENT
26	10 12	18	3 —										
						TOTAL 200 —		TOTAL 10 40		TOTAL 131 80			TOTAL

						(9) REPAIRS AND MAINTENANCE		(10) INSURANCE		(11) PROFESSIONAL FEES		(12) COMMISSIONS		(13) TRAVEL
						618	12 50		84 50	604	150 —			
						1	10 —							
TOTAL 50 12		TOTAL 9 85		TOTAL 400 —		TOTAL 22 50		TOTAL 84 50		TOTAL 150 —		TOTAL		TOTAL

(14)		(15) AUTO - TRUCK		(16) DUES AND SUBSCRIPTIONS		(17) LAUNDRY AND UNIFORM		(18) TELEPHONE		(19) TRADING STAMPS		(20) ENTERTAINMENT		(21)
		613	27 80	605	25 —	1	3 30	603	12 30	602	20 —	11	4 —	
		624	44 —	625	12 —	8	3 30							
		1	3 —			14	3 30							
		5	3 —			22	3 30							
		9	3 —			29	3 30							
		17	3 —	TOTAL 37 —		TOTAL 16 50		TOTAL 12 30		TOTAL 20 —		TOTAL 4 —		TOTAL
		21	3 —	(22) ADVERTISING		(23) ELECTRIC - FUEL GAS - WATER		(24)		(25) CONTRACT SERVICES		(26) MISCELLANEOUS ITEM		
		24	3 —							617	15 —			
		28	3 —	614	48 —	621	27 85			2	5 —			
				17	10 —	622	12 70			14	2 —			
										18	5 —			
										28	2 —			
TOTAL		TOTAL 92 80		TOTAL		TOTAL		TOTAL		TOTAL 29 —		TOTAL		

GB&FORM 500?

MONTHLY BUSINESS EXPENSE
All payments are listed by expense category.
Provides an immediate check on comparative expense items.

Monthly Summary For ___DECEMBER___ 19___

WITHDRAWALS & PERSONAL EXPENSES OF PARTNERS OR OWNER

DATE		DATE	
2	100 —		
9	100 —		
16	100 —		
23	100 —		
30	100 —		
	500 —		
	3000 —		
	3500 —		

OTHER PAYMENTS
Loans — Notes — Fixtures — Equipment — Deposits

INTEREST PAYMENTS SHOULD BE ENTERED ON PAGE 2 ITEM 5

DATE	ITEM	AMOUNT
601	C.S. BANK	89 60
616	ADDING MACH.	23 30
623	AUTO	85 10
← Total This Month's →		198 —
← Total Previous Months →		1602 —
← Total Year To Date →		1800 —

MONTHLY PROOF & BALANCE

TOTAL MONEY AVAILABLE THIS MONTH:

1. Beginning of Month: CASH (Including Receipts not yet deposited in bank) — 50 —
   CHECK BOOK BALANCE — 1843 20
2. Total received from customers this month (Colum 1, Page 1) — 3179 81
3. Money received from other sources (Item 12, Page 1)
4. Total (Sum of Lines 1, 2, 3) — 5073 01

TOTAL MONEY SPENT THIS MONTH:

5. Total Business Expenses this month — 1369 32
6. Less: Employees Taxes & other items withheld — 43 32
7. Net Business Expenses — 1326 —
8. Total Resale Purchase Payments — 1557 55
9. Total other Payments on Loans, Notes, Fixtures & Equipment — 198 —
10. Total Withdrawals and Personal Expenses of Partners or Owners — 500 —
11. Payments of Employees Tax Withheld (Fed $____ State $____)
12. Payments of Other Items Withheld ($____)($____)
13. This Month's Expenditures (Sum Lines 7-12) — 3581 55
14. Total money which should be available end of month (Line 4 minus Line 13) — 1491 46
15. Actually Available—End of Month
    CASH (including receipts not yet deposited in Bank) — 327 45
    CHECK BOOK BALANCE — 1164 01 — 1491 46
16. Overage or Shortage—Difference between 14 and 15

PROFIT AND LOSS

ITEMS	TOTAL THIS MONTH	TOTAL PREVIOUS MONTHS	TOTAL YEAR TO DATE	%
BUSINESS INCOME:				
a. Total money received	3179 81	28768 89	31748 70	100
b.				
c. Resale Purchase Payments	1557 55	15033 70	16591 25	
d.				
e. GROSS PROFIT (a. minus c.)	1622 26	13135 19	14757 45	
BUSINESS EXPENSES:				
1 OPERATING SUPPLIES	50 12	359 33	409 45	
2 OFFICE	9 85	284 25	294 10	
3 EMPLOYEE SALARIES	400 —	3240 —	3640 —	
4 RENT	200 —	2200 —	2400 —	
5 INTEREST & BANK CHARGES	10 40	101 30	111 70	
6 BUSINESS TAXES LICENSES, ETC	131 80	46 55	178 35	
7 EMPLOYER'S SHARE SOCIAL SECURITY		113 75	113 75	
8 UNEMPLOYMENT		84 20	84 20	
9 REPAIRS AND MAINTENANCE	22 50	203 50	226 —	
10 INSURANCE (Business only)	84 50	80 50	165 —	
11 PROFESSIONAL FEES	150 —	75 —	225 —	
12 COMMISSIONS		80 —	80 —	
13 TRAVEL		61 50	61 50	
14				
15 AUTO TRUCK	92 80	645 34	733 14	
16 DUES & SUBSCRIPTIONS	37 —	106 85	143 85	
17 LAUNDRY & UNIFORMS	16 50	180 90	197 40	
18 TELEPHONE	12 30	121 25	133 55	
19 TRADING STAMPS	20 —	200 —	220 —	
20 ENTERTAINMENT	4 —	25 30	29 30	
21				
22 ADVERTISING	58 —	310 75	368 75	
23 ELEC FUEL-GAS-WATER	40 55	338 67	379 22	
24				
25 CONTRACT SERVICES	29 —	331 —	360 —	
26 MISCELLANEOUS		12 31	12 31	
f Total Business Expenses	1369 32	9402 25	10771 57	
g NET PROFIT (e. minus f.)	252 94	3732 94	3985 88	

MONTHLY SUMMARY

**Show on one page, all income, expense and withdrawals and provide a monthly and "total-to-date"
profit and loss analysis. Also include a Proof and Balance form for reconciling cash.**

Analysis Sheet For _____

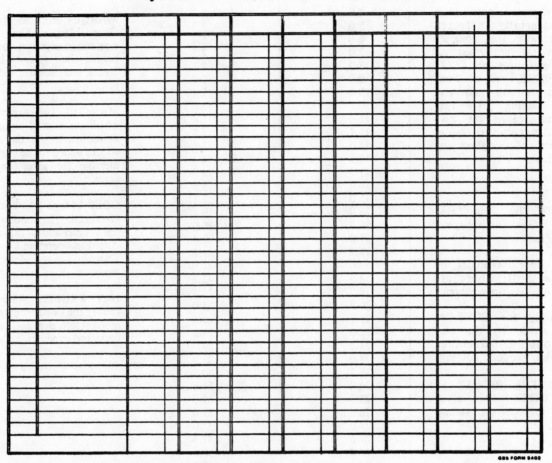

GBS FORM 5402

ANALYSIS SHEET
Allows for the analysis of additional business breakdowns
i.e.: Retail and wholesale sales; cash and credit sales; etc.

RETAILERS' QUICK-REFERENCE TABLES
HOW TO COMPUTE YOUR CORRECT SELLING PRICES

MARGIN & MARKUP	MARGIN DESIRED % of Selling Price	MARKUP REQUIRED % of Cost
	4.8	5.0
	5.0	5.3
	6.0	6.4
	7.0	7.5
	8.0	8.7
	9.0	10.0
	10.0	11.1
	10.7	12.0
	11.0	12.4
	11.1	12.5
	12.0	13.6
	12.5	14.3
	13.0	15.0
	14.0	16.3
	15.0	17.1
	16.0	19.1
	16.7	20.0
	17.0	20.5
	17.5	21.2
	18.0	22.0
	18.5	22.7
	19.0	23.5
	20.0	25.0
	21.0	26.6
	22.0	28.2
	22.5	29.0
	23.0	29.9
	23.1	30.0
	24.0	31.6
	25.0	33.3
	26.0	35.0
	27.0	37.0
	27.6	37.5
	28.0	39.0
	28.5	40.0
	29.0	40.9
	30.0	42.9
	31.0	45.0
	32.0	47.1
	33.3	50.0
	34.0	51.5
	35.0	53.9
	35.5	55.0
	36.0	56.3
	37.0	58.8
	37.5	60.0
	38.0	61.3
	39.0	64.0
	39.5	65.5
	40.0	66.7
	41.0	70.0
	42.0	72.4
	42.8	75.0
	44.4	80.0
	46.1	85.0
	47.5	90.0
	48.7	95.0
	50.0	100.0

Your expected profit can be materially affected by the way you compute markup. *Margin must always be figured on SELLING PRICE, not on Cost.* Markup on cost may give you a selling price that will not realize the necessary margin to cover your cost of operation and net profit.

How To Use This Table To Get Correct Selling Price

1. Find your MARGIN or gross profit percentage in the first column.

2. Multiply the COST of the article by the corresponding percentage in the second column.

3. ADD THE RESULT to the COST. This gives you the correct selling price.

EXAMPLE:
Assume that you buy an item at cost price of $1.20. Also assume that you need a margin of 25% to cover your cost of operation and net profit. You look for your margin of 25% in the first column of this table. The corresponding percentage in the second column is 33.3%. Multiplying the cost ($1.20) by 33.3% (.333) gives you .399. Add .399 to the cost ($1.20). This gives you your correct selling price: $1.599 (or $1.60).

EXPLANATION OF TERMS USED

MARGIN or Gross Profit, or Gross Margin. The sum of operating expenses and net profit. The "spread" between cost of merchandise and selling price.

MARKUP. The percentage by which the cost of an article is multiplied to get the amount which, added to the cost of the merchandise, gives the selling price.

OPERATING EXPENSES or Overhead. The amounts paid out for any and all expenses incurred in operating a business. These do not include cost merchandise.

NET PROFIT. Amount of money the business earns—the amount left, over and above all costs and expenses.

20.

116 DIFFERENT TYPES OF FRANCHISED BUSINESSES

(A Business to Fit Every Capacity)

We have discussed the merits of franchises, how to judge a franchise and a franchise contract, what can be expected of both the franchisee and franchisor and how to achieve the "right start" in a franchised business. In addition, we have suggested many ways for promoting business, for answering sales objections and for assuring the continued health of your business. But which business? What types of franchises are available?

Here is a list of businesses that offer franchises:

Business and Industrial Aids, Services and Equipment:

1. Record-keeping and tax preparation
2. Accounting
3. Data-processing equipment
4. Employment agencies
5. Office equipment and systems
6. Business directories
7. Audio-visual equipment
8. Locate missing persons
9. Collection plans and agencies
10. Signs and displays
11. Car and truck rental
12. Heavy-equipment rental
13. Office and building cleaning
14. Heating systems
15. Theft-prevention systems
16. Fire-prevention systems
17. Closed-circuit TV systems
18. Industrial lubricants
19. Hot-beverage machines
20. Photo murals
21. Window frosting and tinting
22. Lighting equipment and bulbs
23. Telephone-answering devices
24. Mechanics' tools
25. Labels
26. Insect and pest control

Home Equipment and Services

27. Swimming pools
28. Water softening
29. Pre-cut log cabins and homes
30. Protective equipment
31. Insect-killing devices
32. Lawn services
33. Cookware
34. Wall-covering materials
35. Air-purification equipment
36. Furnace and chimney cleaning
37. Sewer cleaning

General Services:

38. Credit-card plans
39. Dry cleaning
40. Laundry
41. Furniture restoring
42. Rental—party equipment
43. Rug and upholstery cleaning
44. Photo finishing
45. Modeling

Personal—Health—Beauty Care:

46. Cosmetics
47. Hearing aids
48. Massaging equipment
49. Physical conditioning equipment
50. Baby furniture and equipment
51. Bed-wetting correction
52. Sickroom supplies rental
53. Wigs and hairpieces
54. Foot comfort shop

Recreation:

55. Bowling
56. Miniature bowling
57. Miniature golf
58. Trampoline equipment
59. Children's fun centers
60. Cycle exercise equipment

61. Electronic games
62. Teen clubs
63. Ice skating school
64. Dance studio

Instruction

65. Bar-management training
66. Data-processing school
67. Beauty culture school
68. Civil Service exam courses
69. Business courses
70. Language instruction
71. Speed reading
72. Motel-management training
73. Teaching machines
74. Sales training

Retailing—General

75. Florist
76. Rack merchandising
77. Candy store
78. Greeting cards
79. Variety store
80. Cheese store
81. Fashion shop
82. Beauty bar
83. Fabric store
84. Floating houseboat restaurant
85. Miniature supermarket
86. Paperback bookstore
87. Shoe store
88. Bedding and sleep products
89. Paint store

Food Shops

90. Pancakes
91. Hamburgers
92. Doughnuts
93. Take-out chicken
94. Take-out Chinese food
95. Pizza
96. Root beer

97. Juice
98. Ice cream
99. Coin-op restaurant
100. Barbecue
101. Popcorn

Automotive

102. Auto-supply store
103. Brake service
104. Muffler shop
105. Gas station
106. Seat-cover shop

107. Claim adjustor
108. Car wash
109. Car rental
110. Parking lot

Mobile (Truck Mounted)

111. Ice cream
112. Pizza
113. Chinese food
114. Shoe repair
115. Lawn spray
116. Frankfurters

21.

381 SPECIFIC FRANCHISE OPPORTUNITIES FOR YOUR SELECTION

In this chapter are listed 381 specific franchise opportunities covering the following types of franchise offerings:

1. Store-type franchises—Those in which the franchisee establishes a location to which customers or clients come in order to avail themselves of his services or products.

2. Sales-type franchises—The franchisee operates either from an office or his home and utilizes a sales force to contact prospective customers and clients at their homes or places of business.

3. Service-type franchises—Inclusive of automotive services, mobile services, restaurants, employment agencies, etc.

4. Institutional-type franchises—Inclusive of motels.

These names have been compiled from the Handbook of Business Opportunities, published by the Department of Commerce.

Important: The listing of these franchise availabilities does not constitute an endorsement or recommendation by the author or by the Department of Commerce.

Franchised Business Opportunities

The following franchised business opportunities are selected from the

"Franchise Opportunities Handbook" of the U.S. Department of Commerce and International Business Administration, and other sources.

They are classified according to the "General Business Categories" so that you may select the category that best suits your desires and individual requirements.

Bear in mind that, in addition to franchise investment, the franchisee, in most instances, should also have "reserve funds" to cover unexpected expenses and contingencies, and to support himself for at least the first six months or until adequate cash flow is generated from the business itself.

In all instances, "investigate before you invest."

AUTOMOTIVE PRODUCTS/SERVICES

AAMCO Automatic Transmissions, Inc.
408 East Fourth Street
Bridgeport, Pennsylvania 19405

Repair, recondition and rebuild automatic transmissions

ABC Mobile Systems
9240 Telstar Avenue
El Monte, California 91731

Specially designed mobile vans doing brake service and muffler repair at service stations and automotive repair shops

Bernardi Bros., Inc.
101 South 38th Street
Harrisburg, Pennsylvania 17111

Car washes

Car-Matic Systems, Inc.
P. O. Box 12466
Norfolk, Virginia 23502

Rebuilt transmissions and engines

Collex, Inc.
512 Pennsylvania Avenue
Fort Washington, Pennsylvania 19034

Collision service

Cook Machinery Company
Div. ALD, Inc.
4301 South Fitzhugh Avenue
Dallas, Texas 75226

Car Wash

Endrust Marketing Organizations
1725 Washington Road
Suite 406
Pittsburgh, Pennsylvania 15241

Automotive rustproofing

The Firestone Tire & Rubber Co.
1200 Firestone Parkway
Akron, Ohio 44317

Tires, auto and home supplies

B. F. Goodrich Tire Company
500 South Main Street
Akron, Ohio 44318

Tires and related merchandise

The Goodyear Tire & Rubber Co.
1144 East Market Street
Akron, Ohio 44316

Tire and automotive service and
home-related merchandise

Insta-Tune, Inc.
17755 Sky Park East
Irvine, California 92714

Automotive tune-ups

Kwik Kar Wash
11351 Anaheim Drive
Dallas, Texas 75229

Car wash

Lee Myles Associates Corporation
325 Sylvan Avenue
Englewood, New Jersey 07632

Transmission centers

MAACO Enterprises, Inc.
381 Brooks Road
King of Prussia, Pennsylvania 19406

Auto paint & body centers

Midas-International Corp.
222 South Riverside Plaza
Chicago, Illinois 60606

Exhaust system, brakes, shock absorbers,
and front-end alignment

National Auto Glass Company, Inc.
3434 West 6th Street
Los Angeles, California 90020

Auto-glass installation centers

OTASCO
11333 East Pine
P. O. Box 885
Tulsa, Oklahoma 74102

Home and auto supplies, sporting goods,
major appliances

RAYCO, Division of FDI, Inc.
3250 West Market Street
Akron, Ohio 44313

Installation & repair of tires, exhaust, seat
covers, tops, brakes, front end, etc.

Regal Car-Care Centers, Inc.
15 Ridgewood Lane
Manchester, New Hampshire 03102

Specialty automotive after-market services include exhaust, rustproofing, shocks, brakes, etc.

Robo-Wash, Inc.
2330 Burlington
North Kansas City, Missouri 64116

Automatic, high-pressure carwash

Tuff-Kote Dinol, Inc.
P. O. Box 306
Warren, Michigan 48090

Automotive rustproofing

Valley Forge Products Company
150 Roger Avenue
Inwood, New York 11696

Auto replacement parts, mobile distributors

Western Auto
2107 Grand Avenue
Kansas City, Missouri 64108

Retails automotive, hardware, sporting goods, tools and wheel goods, appliances, televisions, radios, etc.

White Stores, Inc.
3910 Call Field Road
Wichita Falls, Texas 76308

Retails tires, batteries, automotive parts and accessories, TV, stereo & other electronics, housewares, sporting goods, tools and summer goods

Ziebart Rustproofing Company
1290 East Maple Road
Troy, Michigan 48084

Rustproofing auto and truck bodies

AUTO/TRAILER RENTALS

Budget Rent-A-Car Corporation
35 East Wacker Drive
Chicago, Illinois 60601

Auto rental

Dollar Rent-A-Car Systems, Inc.
6141 West Century Boulevard
Los Angeles, California 90045

Auto & truck rental

Econo-Car International, Inc.
4930 West 77 Street
Suite 260
Edina, Minnesota 55435

Auto rental

Hertz Corporation   Auto & truck rental
660 Madison Avenue
New York, New York 10021

National Car Rental System, Inc.   Auto rental
5501 Green Valley Drive
Minneapolis, Minnesota 55437

Thrifty Rent-A-Car System   Auto rental
P. O. Box 51069
2400 North Sheridan Road
Tulsa, Oklahoma 74151

BEAUTY SALONS/SUPPLIES

Edie Adams Cut & Curl   Beauty salons
125 South Service Road
Long Island Expressway
Jericho, New York 11753

Hair Replacement Centers   Hair center
P. O. Box 16150
Plantation Branch
Ft. Lauderdale, Florida 33318

Harper Method Incorporated   Beauty salons
1700 Broadway
New York, New York 10019

BUSINESS AIDS/SERVICES

H & R Block, Inc.   Prepare individual income-tax returns
4410 Main Street
Kansas City, Missouri 64111

Comprehensive Accounting Corp.   Monthly computerized bookkeeping,
901 East Galena Boulevard   accounting & tax service to small and
Aurora, Illinois 60505   medium-sized business

Credit Service Company   Medical-dental-hospital collection
101 Miles Building   service
2025 Canal Street
New Orleans, Louisiana 70112

General Business Services, Inc.
51 Monroe Street
Rockville, Maryland 20850

Businesses counseling, financial management, & tax services for the small business

Marcoin, Inc.
7887 Katy Freeway
Suite 108
Houston, Texas 77024

Counseling & other services primarily to small businesses

Muzak Corporation
100 Park Avenue
New York, New York 10017

Lease of special work & public area music programs to businesses of all kinds

Safeguard Business Systems
470 Maryland Drive
Fort Washington, Pennsylvania 19034

Offers a complete basic accounting function

Success Motivation Institute Inc.
500 Lake Wood Drive
Waco, Texas 76710

Management, sales, & personal development programs to individuals, companies, governments

Telecheck Services, Inc.
49 South Hotel Street, Suite 314
Honolulu, Hawaii 96813

Personal-check-verification system

Whitehill Systems
Div. Small Business Advisors, Inc.
48 West 48th Street
New York, New York 10036

Advising of businesses on bookkeeping systems, computerized programs and tax service

Edwin K. Williams & Company
5324 Ekwill Street
P. O. Box 6406
Santa Barbara, California 93111

Business management counseling & computerized bookkeeping services to small businesses

CAMPGROUNDS

Jellystone Campgrounds, Ltd.
236 Michigan Street
Sturgeon Bay, Wisconsin 54235

Camp-resort developments & operation & economy family motor inns

Kamp Dakota, Inc.
220 Bartling Building
Brookings, South Dakota 57006

Campgrounds for tents and trailers

Kampgrounds of America, Inc.
P. O. Box 30558
Billings, Montana 59114

Campgrounds with facilities—for recreational vehicles

Safari Campgrounds
United Safari International, Inc.
1111 Northshore Drive
Drawer 203, Suite 201
Knoxville, Tennessee 37919

Luxury camping & recreational facilities

CHILDREN'S STORES/FURNITURE/PRODUCTS

Baby-Tenda Corporation
909 State Line
Kansas City, Missouri 64101

Line of baby safety equipment

CLOTHING/SHOE STORES

Formal Wear Service
639 V.F.W. Parkway
Chestnut Hill, Massachusetts 02167

Sale & rental of men's formal clothes

Gingiss International, Inc.
180 North LaSalle Street
Chicago, Illinois 60601

Sale & rental of men's formal clothes

Just Pants
310 South Michigan Avenue
Chicago, Illinois 60604

Sell quality branded jeans, slacks, tops & accessories

Lady Madonna Management Corp.
36 East 31st Street
New York, New York 10016

Women's maternity apparel

Mode O'Day Company
2130 North Hollywood Way
Burbank, California 91505

Ladies' apparel specialty store

Modern Bridal Shoppes, Inc.
600 Route 130 North
Cinnaminson, New Jersey 08077

Bridal apparel & cocktail formal wear

Pauline's Sportswear, Inc.
3525 Eastham Drive
Culver City, California 90230

Ladies' sportswear store

Red Wing Shoe Company
419-427 Bush Street
Red Wing, Minnesota 55066

Men's sport & work shoes

Sally Wallace Bride's Shop, Inc.
232 Amherst Street
East Orange, New Jersey 07018

Bridal shop and bridal service

CONSTRUCTION/REMODELING—MATERIALS/SERVICE

Eldorado Stone Corporation
P.O. Box 125
Kirkland, Washington 98033

Manufacture & sell simulated stone & brick building products

General Energy Devices, Inc.
1753 Ensley Avenue
Clearwater, Florida 33516

Solar energy system distribution

Homewood Industries, Inc.
17641 South Ashland Avenue
Homewood, Illinois 60430

Renovating of existing kitchen cabinets

Marble-Crete Products, Inc.
3439 - 3441 Northwest 19th Street
Lauderdale Lakes, Florida 33311

Manufacture simulated marble

Marble-Flow Industries, Inc.
3439 NW 19th Street
Lauderdale Lakes, Florida 33311

Sell & install seamless "marble" floors

New England Log Homes, Inc.
2301 State Street
P. O. Box 5056
Hamden, Connecticut 06518

Dealer sells hand-peeled, pre-cut log homes from model-home "office."

Perma-Stone Company
2495 Bancroft Street
Columbus, Ohio 43211

Sales & application of Perma-Stone to owners' property

The Permentry Company
37 Water Street
P.O. Box 347
West Haven, Connecticut 06516

Leases franchisee steel molds which will precast in one piece, outside basement stairwell entrances

Poraflor, Inc.
2300 Shames Drive
Westbury, New York 11377

Sells & installs seamless flooring

Shawnee Steps of America, Inc
250 Tolland Street
East Hartford, Connecticut 06108

Manufacture, sell & install concrete pre-cast steps

COSMETICS/TOILETRIES

Fashion Two Twenty, Inc.
1263 South Chillicothe Road
Aurora, Ohio 44202

Sell cosmetics through party plan

DRUG STORES

Medicine Shoppes Intl., Inc.
100 Progress Parkway
Maryland Heights, Missouri 63043

Retail sales of pharmaceuticals and medicines

Rexall Drug Company
3901 North Kings Highway Blvd.
St. Louis, Missouri 63115

Retail sales of pharmaceuticals, medicines, cosmetics & vitamins

Union Prescription Centers, Inc.
105 West Michigan Street
Milwaukee, Wisconsin 53203

Retail pharmacies

EDUCATIONAL PRODUCTS/SERVICES

Barbizon Schools of Modeling
689 Fifth Avenue
New York, New York 10022

Modeling & personal development schools

Butler Learning Systems
1325 West Dorothy Lane
Dayton, Ohio 45409

Audio-visual training program for salesmen, supervisors, women in business & industry

The Image of Loveliness, Inc.
1581 - 40th Northwest
Salem, Oregon 97304

A personal improvement course for women

John Robert Powers Finishing & Modeling School
9 Newbury Street
Boston, Massachusetts 02116

Finishing, self-improvement, drama, modeling, & fashion merchandising to women

Mary Moppet's Day Care Schools, Inc.
7120 East Oak Street
Scottsdale, Arizona 85257

Day-care school for children

Mind Power, Inc.
P. O. Box 1464
Bethlehem, Pennsylvania 18018

Speed reading & memory operation

EMPLOYMENT SERVICES

Adia Temporary Services, Inc.
(Part time Division)
64 Willow Place
Menlo Park, California 94025

Temporary office, technical & marketing personnel

Bailey Employment System, Inc.
51 Shelton Road
Monroe, Connecticut 06468

Chain of cooperating employment-service offices

Baker & Baker Employment Service, Inc.
P.O. Box 364
114½ Washington Avenue
Athens, Tennessee 37303

Employment-service agencies for small towns of 20,000 population and city suburbs

Dr. Personnel, Inc.
2045 Franklin Street
Denver, Colorado 80205

Employment system providing paramedical & paradental personnel to physicians and dentists

Dunhill Personnel System, Inc.
1 Old Country Road
Carle Place, New York 11514

Sales, administrative & technical as well as skilled clerical

Employers Overload Company
EO Building
8040 Cedar Avenue South
Minneapolis, Minnesota 55420

Complete range of business & temporary help services

F-O-R-T-U-N-E Franchise Corp.
505 Fifth Avenue
New York, New York 10017

Middle management/executive personnel service

Harper Associates, Inc.
Division of Sanford Rose Assoc.
265 Main Street
Akron, Ohio 44308

Specialized management placement services

Kogen Personnel, Inc.
202 Whitemarsh Plaza
15 East Ridge Pike
Conshohocken, Pennsylvania 19428

Full-range permanent placement service for clerical & entry-level technical, administrative & sales applicants; career placement service for middle management, engineering and scientific

Management Recruiters Intl., Inc.
1015 Euclid Avenue
Cleveland, Ohio 44115

Personnel placement service

Management Search, Inc.
229 Peachtree Street, N.E.
500 Cain Tower
Atlanta, Georgia 30303

Professional & clerical placement

Manpower, Inc.
5301 North Ironwood Road
Milwaukee, Wisconsin 53217

Complete line of temporary help

The Olsten Corporation
1 Merrick Avenue
Westbury, New York 11590

Temporary office & industrial personnel

Personnel Pool of America, Inc.
521 South Andrews Avenue
Fort Lauderdale, Florida 33301

Domestic personnel pool furnishing temporary domestic help; labor pool furnishing temporary industrial help; medical personnel pool; office personnel pool furnishing temporary sales, office and clerical help

Place Mart Franchising Corp.
20 Evergreen Place
East Orange, New Jersey 07018

Employment agency

Republic Personnel Service System
4989 Cleveland Street
Virginia Beach, Virginia 23462

A total professional service to applicants & employers alike

Richard P. Rita Personnel System, Inc.
One Weybosset Hill
Providence, Rhode Island 02903

Complete personnel services

S-H-S International
The Schneider-Hill-Spangler Network
Western Savings Bank Building
Broad & Chestnut, Suite 710
Philadelphia, Pennsylvania 19107

Accounting, EDP, sales, marketing, technical, engineering, clerical & secretarial fields, mid-management area

Sales Consultants International
A Division of Management Recruiters
International, Inc.
1015 Euclid Avenue
Cleveland, Ohio 44115

Placement of salesmen, sales managers, sales engineers, & marketing people

Sanford Rose Associates, Inc.
265 South Main Street
Akron, Ohio 44308

Broad spectrum of personnel placement

Snelling & Snelling, Inc.
Executive Offices
Snelling Plaza
4000 South Tamiami Trail
Sarasota, Florida 33579

Full range of employment activity in both blue-collar and white-collar fields

Staff Builders International, Inc.
122 East 42nd Street
New York, New York 10017

Temporary help for office, medical, industrial, technical, data-processing, & marketing operations

EQUIPMENT/RENTALS

Taylor Rental Corporation
570 Cottage Street
Springfield, Massachusetts 01104

A general-purpose rental business

Time Tool & Equipment Rentals, Inc.
10795 North Irma Drive
Denver, Colorado 80233

Full line general equipment centers

United Rent-All, Inc.
10131 National Boulevard
Los Angeles, California 90034

General rental stores

FOOD-DONUTS

Country Style Donuts
8370 Woodbine Avenue, RR 2
Gormley, Ontario LOH 1GO Canada

"Special" blend of coffee and over 56 varieties of donuts

Donutland, Inc.   Retail coffee and donuts
P. O. Box 409
Marion, Iowa 52302

Dunkin' Donuts of America, Inc.   Coffee & donut shops with drive-in and
P. O. Box 317   walk-in units
Randolph, Massachusetts 02368

Mister Donut of America, Inc.   Donut & coffee shops: drive-ins and
Subsidiary of International   walk-in units
Multifoods Corporation
1200 Multifoods Building
Minneapolis, Minnesota 55402

Southern Maid Donut Flour Co., Inc.   Donut shops
3615 Cavalier Drive
Garland, Texas 75042

Spudnuts, Inc.   Retail donut shop
450 West 1700 South
Salt Lake City, Utah 84115

Tastee Donuts, Inc.   Coffee & donut shops with drive-in and
P. O. Box 2708   walk-in units
Rocky Mount, North Carolina 27801

FOOD-GROCERY/SPECIALTY STORES

Cheese Shop International, Inc.   Fine cheese, gourmet foods, related gift
23 Amogerone Crossway   items & wines where permissible
Greenwich, Connecticut 06830

The Circle K Corporation   Convenience-type food stores
Contract Operations
P. O. Box 20230
Phoenix, Arizona 85036

Convenient Food Mart, Inc.   Complete lines of top-name national-
John Hancock Center   brand merchandise
875 North Michigan Avenue, Ste. 1401
Chicago, Illinois 60611

Hickory Farms of Ohio, Inc.   Selling packages & bulk specialty food
1021 North Reynolds Road   featuring the Hickory Farms BEEF
Toledo, Ohio 43615   STICK Summer Sausage, a variety of
                                        imported & domestic cheeses, candies &
                                        other related food products under the
                                        Hickory Farms label

ISCO, Ltd.
International Services Company, Ltd.
4760 Interstate Drive
Cincinnati, Ohio 45246

Specialty food shops featuring cheese, meat, specialty foods & related products

Jitney-Jungle, Inc.
440 North Mill Street
Jackson, Mississippi 30207

Convenience food store

King's Chicken
P. O. Box 15202
Salt Lake City, Utah 84115

Fried chicken take-home service

Li'l Shopper, Inc.
811 East State Street
Sharon, Pennsylvania 16146

Convenience grocery stores

Mr. Dunderbak, Inc.
P. O. Box 912
Rocky Mount, North Carolina 27801

A Bavarian Pantry specializing in cheeses, sausages, gourmet foods, deli-type sandwiches & German sausages

Open Pantry Food Marts
3055 East 63rd Street
Cleveland, Ohio 44127

Miniature supermarkets open from early morning to midnight every day

Quick Shop Minit Marts, Inc.
P. O. Box 1748
Vancouver, Washington 98663

Stores sell name-brand groceries, some with self-serve gasoline, sandwiches, deli, etc.

Quick Stop Markets, Inc.
P. O. Box 1745
Fremont, California 94538

Retail convenience grocery store

The Southland Corporation
2828 North Haskell Street
Dallas, Texas 75204

Convenience grocery stores

Sunnydale Franchise System, Inc.
400 Stanley Avenue
Brooklyn, New York 11207

Retail convenience food store

Swiss Colony Stores, Inc.
51 Alpine Park
Monroe, Wisconsin 53566

Domestic & imported cheeses, sausage, European-style pastries, candy, specialty foods & gifts

Telecake International
2265 East 4800 South
Salt Lake City, Utah 84117

National cake by phone service. Franchisee is usually a retail bakery

Tiffany's Bakeries, Inc.   Fresh baked pastries & breads
40 University Avenue
Toronto, Ontario M5J 1T1 Canada

White Hen Pantry Division   Convenience-type food store
Jewel Companies, Inc.
666 Industrial Drive
Elmhurst, Illinois 60126

FOOD-ICE CREAM/CANDY/POPCORN/BEVERAGES

Baskin-Robbins, Inc.   Retail ice cream store
1201 South Victory Boulevard
Burbank, California 91506

Bresler's 33 Flavors, Inc.   Specialty ice cream shops
4010 West Belden Avenue
Chicago, Illinois 60639

Calico Cottage Candies, Inc.   Fudge shops or departments
11 Crescent Street
Hewlett, New York 11557

Carvel Corporation   Retail ice cream shops
201 Sawmill River Road
Yonkers, New York 10701

Dairy Isle & 3 In One Restaurants   Soft ice cream stores & fast-food
Commissary Corporation   operation
45237 Cass - P.O. Box 162
Utica, Michigan 48087

Karmelkorn Shoppes, Inc.   Sell popcorn, popcorn confections, a
101 31st Avenue   variety of kitchen candies & related snack-
Rock Island, Illinois 61201   food items

Mister Softee, Inc.   Soft ice cream products from a mobile
901 East Clements Bridge Road   unit
Runnemede, New Jersey 08078

Swensen's Ice Cream Company   Old-fashioned ice cream parlors
915 Front Street
San Francisco, California 94111

Swift Dairy & Poultry Company   Dipper Dan retail ice cream shoppe
115 West Jackson Boulevard
Chicago, Illinois 60604

Zip'z   Zip'z features soft ice cream - soft frozen
P. O. Box 5630   yogurt & the Zip'z "Make Your Own
4470 Monroe Street   Sundae Bar"
Toledo, Ohio 43613

FOODS-PANCAKE/WAFFLE/PRETZEL

General Franchising Corporation   French restaurants, specializing in
1350 Avenue of the Americas   crepes (French pancakes)
Suite 2700
New York, New York 10019

International House of Pancakes   Fast-food family-style restaurants—
6837 Lankershim Boulevard   pancakes, steak & chicken dinners,
North Hollywood, California 91605   sandwiches

Perkins Cake & Steak Restaurants   Restaurant with full menu. Specializes
4917 Eden Avenue   in pancakes
Edina, Minnesota 55424

Village Inn Pancake House, Inc.   Pancake house restaurants
400 West 48th Avenue
Denver, Colorado 80216

FOODS-RESTAURANTS/DRIVE-INS/CARRY-OUTS

A & W International, Inc.   Drive-in-walk-in restaurants
922 Broadway
Santa Monica, California 90406

Arthur Treacher's Fish & Chips, Inc.   Arthur Treacher's Fish & Chips
1328 Dublin Road
Columbus, Ohio 43215

Bonanza International, Inc.   Bonanza Sirloin Pit restaurants
1000 Campbell Centre
8350 North Central Expressway
Dallas, Texas 75206

Boy Blue Stores, Inc.
10919 West Janesville Road
Hales Corners, Wisconsin 53130

Soft serve, frozen yogurt & limited menu stores

Brown's Chicken
800 Enterprise Drive
Oak Brook, Illinois 60521

Sit-down/carry-out restaurants, specialty "chicken"

Burger Chef Systems, Inc. TA-2
College Park Pyramids
P.O. Box 927
Indianapolis, Indiana 46206

Limited menu restaurants

Burger King Corporation
P.O. Box 520783
Miami, Florida 33152

Self-service walk-in restaurant, specializing in hamburgers

Burger Queen Enterprises, Inc.
P. O. Box 6014
4000 Dupont Circle
Louisville, Kentucky 40206

Fast-food restaurant

Captain D's
P. O. Box 1260
1724 Elm Hill Pike
Nashville, Tennessee 37202

Seafood & hamburger restaurant

Casey Jones Junction, Inc.
6235 West Kellogg
Wichita, Kansas 67209

Family restaurant, catering to smaller children

Chicken Delight
227 East Sunshine
Suite 119, P. O. Box 23757
Springfield, Missouri 65807

Restaurant featuring chicken, shrimp, fish, BBQ ribs and pizza

Chicken Unlimited Family Restaurants
One Salt Creek Lane
Hinsdale, Illinois 60521

Quick-service dining, featuring fried chicken

Chip's Hamburgers
114 Grand Avenue
Wausau, Wisconsin 54476

Carry-out fast food, limited to hamburgers, fish & dessert

Cozzoli's Deli - Pizzeria
Cozzoli Corporation
1110 Brickell Avenue
Suite 606
Miami, Florida 33131

Full meal, sandwich shops, fast-food take-out units & pizza

Country Kitchen Intl., Inc.
7800 Metro Parkway
Minneapolis, Minnesota, 55420

Family-style sit-down restaurant 16/24 hour operation

Dairy Sweet Company
610 Des Moines Street
Ankeny, Iowa 50021

Fast-food drive-in & carry-out restaurants featuring sandwiches, shrimp, chicken, soft drinks & soft ice cream

Dairy King Distributors
1140 Yuma Street
Denver, Colorado 80204

Fast-food, drive-in, window service restaurant

Der Wienerschnitzel Intl., Inc.
4440 Von Karman Avenue
Newport Beach, California 92660

Fast-food restaurant specializing in hot dogs

Dino's Inc.
2085 Inkster Road
Garden City, Michigan 48135

Pizzeria restaurants-carry-out and parlors

Dog N Suds, Inc.
Subsidiary of Frostie Enterprises
1420 Crestmont Avenue
Camden, New Jersey 08101

Drive-in & family sit down

Domino's Pizza, Inc.
2865 Boardwalk Drive
Ann Arbor, Michigan 48104

Pizza stores

El Taco Restaurants, Inc.
24001 Alicia Parkway Business Center
Suite 221
Mission Viejo, California 92675

Mexican food drive-thru restaurants & inside seating

Famous Recipe Fried Chicken, Inc.
11315 Reed Hartman Highway
Suite 200
Cincinnati, Ohio 45241

Fried chicken take-home and sit-down restaurants

Farrell's Ice Cream Parlour Restaurant
Div. of Marriott Corporation
5161 River Road
Washington, D.C. 20016

Gay 90's style dining & ice cream parlour

Frostop Corporation 12 First Street Pelham, New York 10803	Fast-food drive-ins serving Frostop root beer & limited American fast-food menu
Golden Skillet Companies 5905 West Broad Street Richmond, Virginia 23230	Fried-chicken restaurants
Happy Joe's Pizza & Ice Cream Parlors 1875 Middle Road Bettendorf, Iowa 52722	Old-fashioned pizza & ice cream parlors
The Happy Steak, Inc. 1118 North Fulton Street Fresno, California 93728	Family-type steak house
Hardee's Food Systems, Inc. P. O. Box 1619 1233 North Church Street Rocky Mount, North Carolina 27801	Fast-food hamburger restaurants
Howard Johnson Company 220 Forbes Road Braintree, Massachusetts 02184	Full service restaurants
International Blimpie Corporation 720 Fifth Avenue New York, New York 10019	Specialty sandwiches (Blimpie)
International Dairy Queen, Inc. P.O. Box 35286 Minneapolis, Minnesota 55435	Soft serve dairy products, hamburgers & beverages
J's Restaurants Intl., Inc. 8478 Central Avenue N.E. Minneapolis, Minnesota 55432	Family-style sit-down 16/24 hour restaurant
Jake's International, Inc. 1204 Carnegie Street Rolling Meadows, Illinois 60008	Carry-out & delivery pizza
Japanese Steak Houses, Inc. Suite 415C Plaza Executive Center 7370 N.W. 36th Street Miami, Florida 33166	Japanese steak houses

Jerry's Restaurants
Jerrico, Inc.
P.O. Box 11988
Lexington, Kentucky 40579

Coffee shops & dining-room operations. Family oriented, informal

KFC Corporation
P. O. Box 32070
Louisville, Kentucky 40232

Colonel Sanders' Kentucky Fried Chicken

Little Caesar Enterprises, Inc.
38700 Grand River Avenue
Farmington Hills, Michigan 48024

Pizza carry-out stores & parlors; family restaurants featuring pizza & other Italian foods

Long John Silver's Inc.
Jerrico, Inc.
P. O. Box 11988
Lexington, Kentucky 40579

Fast-food restaurants, self-service, carry-out or seating in a wharf-like atmosphere

Love's Enterprises, Inc.
6837 Lankershim Boulevard
North Hollywood, California 91605

Barbecue restaurant & cocktail lounge

Lum's Restaurant Corporation
8410 N.W. 53rd Terrace, Ste. 200
Miami, Florida 33166

Fast-food family restaurant with waitress service & carry-out service

Maid Rite Products, Inc.
100 East Second Street
Muscatine, Iowa 52761

Fast-food limited menu sandwich-type operation

McDonald's Corporation
1 McDonald's Plaza
Oak Brook, Illinois 60521

Hamburgers, cheesburgers, special sandwiches

Minute Man of America, Inc.
P. O. Box 828, 701 Collins
Little Rock, Arkansas 72205

Broiled hamburgers, 12 types of sandwiches and hot pies

Mr. Pizza, Inc.
560 Sylvan Avenue
Englewood Cliffs, New Jersey 07632

Family-style restaurant

Mr. Steak, Inc.
International Headquarters
P. O. Box 5805 T.A.
5100 Race Court
Denver, Colorado 80217

Full-service, sit-down family-type restaurant

Orange Julius of America
3219 Wilshire Boulevard
Santa Monica, California 90403

Fast-food operation, featuring the brand drink, "Orange Julius"

Pacific Tastee Freez, Inc.
1101 South Cypress Street
La Habra, California 90631

Fast-food drive-in restaurant, featuring hamburger, Mexican food, ice cream & beverages

Pappy's Enterprises, Inc.
300 East Joppa Road
Towson, Maryland 21204

Restaurant features sandwiches, steaks, pizza and beer in a family-oriented atmosphere

Pasquale Food Company, Inc.
19 West Oxmoor Road
Birmingham, Alabama 35209

Pizza, spaghetti, ravioli and a line of Italian-style sandwiches

The Peddler, Inc.
P. O. Box 1361
Southern Pines, North Carolina 28387

Quality steak house, featuring a unique salad bar

Pedro's Food Systems, Inc.
Box 622
Columbus, Mississippi 39701

Mexican-style restaurants

Pepe's Incorporated
1325 West 15th Street
Chicago, Illinois 60608

Tacos fast food Mexican restaurants

Pioneer Take Out Corporation
3663 West 6th Street
Los Angeles, California 90020

Featuring eat-in & take-out fried chicken, fish & shrimp by the bucket or by the piece

The Pizza Inn, Inc.
2930 Stemmons Freeway
P. O. Box 22247
Dallas, Texas 75222

Pizza restaurants

Ponderosa System, Inc.
P. O. Box 578
Dayton, Ohio 45401

Cafeteria-style fast-food steak house

Reaban's Inc.
10726 Manchester Road
Kirkwood, Missouri 63122

Fast-food operation, featuring hamburgers, chicken, etc.

The Red Barn System
Div. of Servomation Corporation
6845 Elm Street
McLean, Virginia 22101

Fast-food, self-service restaurant with indoor & outdoor seating facilities

Red Devil
Div. of Messina Meat Products, Inc.
614-B East Edna Place
Covina, California 91723

Pizza restaurants & other Italian foods

The Round Table Franchise Corp.
1101 Embarcadero Road
Palo Alto, California 94303

Pizza, sandwiches, hamburgers, salads

Shakey's Incorporated
5565 First Intl. Building
Dallas, Texas 75202

Pizza parlors resemble night clubs for the whole family, live entertainment (piano & banjo), singing and fun

Sir Beef Limited
4300 Morgan Avenue
Evansville, Indiana 47715

Fast-food; roast beef, fish & chips

Sir Pizza International, Inc.
700 South Madison Street
Muncie, Indiana 47302

Retail & commissary operations, selling pizza, sandwiches, etc., for both on-premises consumption and carry-out

Sizzler Family Steak Houses
12731 West Jefferson Boulevard
Los Angeles, California 90066

Popular-priced family steak house

Stand'n Snack of America, Inc.
Suite 200, Ribault Building
1851 Executive Center Drive
Jacksonville, Florida 32207

Fast-food operation

Stewart's Drive-ins
Div. of Frostie Enterprises
1420 Crestmont Avenue
Camden, New Jersey 08103

Drive-in restaurants, with or without dining room with car-hop service

The Straw Hat Restaurant Corp.
6400 Village Parkway
Dublin, California 94566

Pizza restaurant

Stuckey's, Inc.
P. O. Box 370
Eastman, Georgia 31023

A one-stop center for the traveler on the interstates & main U.S. highways, food, candies, souvenirs, gasoline

Subway
25 High Street
Milford, Connecticut 06460

Foot-long sandwiches (submarines)

Sveden House International
a Div. of Intl. Multifoods Corp.
1200 Multifood Building
Minneapolis, Minnesota 55402

Smorgasbord restaurants

Taco Hut, Inc.
3621 South 73rd East Avenue
Tulsa, Oklahoma 74145

Mexican foods, convenient for either dine-in or carry-out operation

Woodson-Holmes Enterprises, Inc.
"Taco John's"
P. O. Box 1589
Cheyenne, Wyoming 82001

Mexican food operation

Taco Time International, Inc.
P. O. Box 2056, 3880 West 11th
Eugene, Oregon 97401

Mexican food restaurants

Tastee Freez Big T Family
Restaurant Systems, Tastee Freez
Int'l., Inc.
1515 South Mount Prospect Road
Des Plaines, Illinois 60018

Fast-food services family restaurant

Texas Tom's Inc.
P. O. Box 4592
Kansas City, Missouri 64124

Variety of food items on the menu & homemade recipies. Both sit-down & carry-out service is available & also call-in service

Tippy's Taco House, Inc.
2853 West Illinois
Dallas, Texas 75233

Fast food to take home, using drive-thru & inside seating. Mexican food

Wendy's Old-Fashioned Hamburgers
c/o Wendy's International, Inc.
P. O. Box 256
4288 West Dublin-Granville Road
Dublin, Ohio 43017

Hamburgers featuring plush dining rooms & a unique "pick up" window

Wiener King Corporation
1610 East Morehead Street
Charlotte, North Carolina 28207

Fast-food restaurant specializing in hot dogs and chili

GENERAL MERCHANDISING STORES

Ben Franklin
Div. City Products Corporation
1700 South Wolf Road
Des Plaines, Illinois 60018

General merchandise operation

Coast to Coast Stores
Central Organization, Inc.
P. O. Box 80
Minneapolis, Minnesota 55440

Retail "total hardware" store

Gamble-Skogmo, Inc.
Gamble Stores Division
5100 Gamble Drive
Minneapolis, Minnesota 55416

Retail store operation: hardware, automotive, sporting goods, major appliances, furniture, electrical, housewares, paints & supplies, lawn & garden, plumbing, electronics, carpet and floor covering

Montgomery Ward
One Montgomery Ward Plaza
Chicago, Illinois 60671

Retail sales of all merchandise in Montgomery Ward catalogs

Rasco Stores
Div. of Gamble-Skogmo, Inc.
2777 North Ontario Street
Burbank, California 91504

Two types of franchises: Rasco Variety (a family store) and Toy World (toy specialty stores)

HEALTH AIDS/SERVICES

Diet Control Centers, Inc.
1021 Stuyvesant Avenue
Union, New Jersey 07083

Weight-loss classes & programs

The Diet Workshop
111 Washington Street
Brookline, Massachusetts 02146

Group weight control

Gloria Stevens Figure Salons
10 Forbes Road
Braintree, Massachusetts 02184

Women's figure-control salons

Health Clubs of America
Box 4098
Waterville, Connecticut 06714

Health and slenderizing salons

MacLevy Products Corporation 92-21 Corona Avenue Elmhurst, New York 11373	Health club and salon
Medicab International, Inc. 68 - 72 Runyon Avenue Yonkers, New York 10701	Transportation for handicapped and disabled
Quality Care Inc. 65 Roosevelt Avenue Valley Stream, New York 11580	Provide nursing, health care & paramedical personnel
Staff Builders Medical Services 122 East 42nd Street New York, New York 10017	Supply medical services personnel

HEARING AIDS

RCI, Inc. P. O. Box 16223 Minneapolis, Minnesota 55416	Hearing aids in Montgomery Ward retail stores

HOME FURNISHINGS/FURNITURE—RETAIL/REPAIR/SERVICES

Abbey Carpet Company 6643 Franklin Boulevard Sacramento, California 95823	Specialty store, retail carpets
Best Bros., Inc. 9 Kulick Street Clifton, New Jersey 07011	Retail home decorator stores
Carpeteria, Inc. 1122 North Vine Street Hollywood, California 90038	Retail carpet outlets
Castro Convertibles 1990 Jericho Turnpike New Hyde Park, New York 11040	Exclusive line of convertible sleep sofas & other allied products
Chem-Clean Furniture Restoration Center Union, Maine 04862	Furniture stripping & refinishing

Crossland Furniture Restoration
Studios
10009 East Toledo Road
Blissfield, Michigan 49228

Furniture stripping & refinishing service and retail furniture refinishing products

Decorating Den
American Drapery Consultants, Inc.
P. O. Box 68165
5753 West 85th Street
Indianapolis, Indiana 46268

Sell custom-made draperies, carpeting, wallcovering, other related decorating items from samples. Business does not require inventory or retail store

Delhi Chemicals, Inc.
22 South Street
Stamford, New York 12167

Service to commercial, industrial & family accounts in the removal of finishes from articles made of wood, metal, glass, marble, alabaster, tin, copper, brass, bronze, etc.

Flex-cote Products Corporation
103 East Hawthorne Avenue
Valley Stream, New York 11580

Reconditioning and re-coloring of upholstery finishes such as leather, vinyl, plastic and cloth

G. Fried Carpetland, Incorporated
800 Old Country Road
Westbury, New York 11590

Retail floor-covering stores

Guarantee Carpet Cleaning & Dye
Company
2953 Powers Avenue
Jacksonville, Florida 32207

Carpet & upholstery-cleaning business

Pro-Strip, Inc.
P. O. Box 179
136 Center Point Road, South
Hendersonville, Tennessee 37075

A furniture-stripping system

Rug Crafters
3895 South Main Street
Santa Ana, California 92707

Yarn craft stores

Spring Crest Company
505 West Lambert Road
Brea, California 92621

Retail draperies, drapery hardware and accessories

Stanley Steamer International, Inc.
4654 Kenny Road
Columbus, Ohio 43220

Carpet & furniture cleaning

Steamatic Incorporated
1601 109th Street
Grand Prairie, Texas 75050

Carpet-cleaning service & portable in-home dry-cleaning service for upholstery & drapes

Vinylife, Inc.
2628 Pearl Road
Medina, Ohio 44256

Range of services including vinyl repair, recoloring, and general restoration

LAUNDRIES, DRY CLEANING-SERVICES

A Cleaner World
1213 Dorris Street
High Point, North Carolina 27262

Dry cleaning & shirt laundry

Big B Franchise, Inc.
P.O. Box 1000
Richmond, Kentucky 40475

Fast-service laundry and dry-cleaning stores.

Bruck Distributing Company, Inc.
9291 Arleta Avenue
Arleta, California 91331

Drapery dry cleaning, 40% of business done under name of major department stores

Coit Drapery & Carpet Cleaners, Inc.
897 Hinckley Road
Burlingame, California 94010

Supply & maintenance of draperies & other window furnishings

Comet International Corporation
178 North County Road
Palm Beach, Florida 33402

Fast-service laundry & dry-cleaning

Cook Machinery Company
Division ALD, Inc.
4301 South Fitzhugh Avenue
Dallas, Texas 75226

Laundry & dry-cleaning stores

Dutch Girl Continental Cleaners
175 Express Street
Plainview, New York 11803

On-the-premises boutique dry-cleaning store

Gigantic Cleaners & Laundry, Inc.
401 East 17th Avenue
Denver, Colorado 80203

Fast-service laundry & dry-cleaning plants

Martinizing
Franchise department
McGraw-Edison Company
5050 Section Avenue
Cincinnati, Ohio 45212

Fast-service "Martinizing" dry-cleaning stores

LAWN AND GARDEN SUPPLIES/SERVICES

Lawn-A-Mat Chemical & Equipment Corporation
153 Jefferson Avenue
Mineola, New York 11501

Sell lawn products and service lawns at no additional cost

Lawn Doctor Incorporated
P. O. Box 186, Conover Road
Wickatunk, New Jersey 07765

Automated lawn service

Lawn King, Inc.
14 Spielman Road
Fairfield, New Jersey 07006

Automated lawn service

Lawn Medic, Inc.
1024 Sibley Tower Building
Rochester, New York 14604

Automated lawn service

Superlawns, Inc.
17032 Briardale Road
Rockville, Maryland 20855

Automated lawn-care service

MAINTENANCE/CLEANING/SANITATION-SERVICES/SUPPLIES

ABC Maintenance Development Corp.
18850 Ventura Boulevard
Suite 214
Tarzana, California 91356

Commercial building maintenance services

Chem-Mark International, Inc.
200 South Cypress Street
Orange, California 92666

Market commercial dishwashing machines, glass-washing equipment, cleaning and sanitation products for restaurants and institutions

Chemical Franchising Corporation
3515 St. Augustine Road
Jacksonville, Florida 32207

Manufactures and sells commercial cleaning products

Diversified Cleaning Services, Inc.
5050 Newport Drive
Suite 8
Rolling Meadows, Illinois 60008

Nightly cleaning of offices, banks, etc.

Domesticare, Inc.
190 Godwin Avenue
Midland Park, New Jersey 07432

Complete on-location residential cleaning services, including fire damage restoration, soot and smoke removal, water damage cleanup

Duraclean International
Duraclean Building
Deerfield, Illinois 60015

On-location cleaning of carpet and upholstery fabrics

General Sewer Service, Inc.
P.O. Box 83
Iselin, New Jersey 08830

Residential and commercial electric sewer cleaning

Lien Chemical Company
9229 West Grand Avenue
Franklin Park, Illinois 60131

Sanitation service for commercial, industrial and institutional restrooms

Mr. Rooter Corporation
4220 N.W. 23rd Street
Oklahoma City, Oklahoma 73107

Sewer and drain cleaning

National Chemical and Services, Inc.
480 Wrightwood Avenue
Elmhurst, Illinois 60126

Commercial and industrial washroom-cleaning and sanitation supplies

National Surface Cleaning Corp.
4959 Commerce Parkway
Cleveland, Ohio 44128

Distribute specialized chemicals and equipment to clean exterior of masonry (stone or brick) buildings

Port-O-Let Company, Inc.
Subsidiary of Thetford Corp.
2300 Larsen Road
Jacksonville, Florida 32207

On-the-site temporary toilet facilities for construction sites, etc.

Roto-Rooter Corporation
300 Ashworth Road
West Des Moines, Iowa 50265

Sewer and drain cleaning service

Servicemaster Industries, Inc.
2300 Warrenville Road
Downers Grove, Illinois 60515

Cleaning of homes, offices, plants, public buildings and institutions, covering carpets, furniture, walls, floors and fixtures

Servpro Industries, Inc.
11357 Pyrites Way
Rancho Cordova, California 95670

Cleaning, including carpets, furniture, walls, floors, drapes; deodorizing, flood and fire damage

Sparkle Wash, Inc.
177 East Washington Street
Chagrin Falls, Ohio 44022

Mobile power cleaning services for a diverse market, including: truck fleets, mobile and residential homes; commercial, governmental and industrial buildings; industrial and farm machinery, aircraft, etc.

Von Schrader Manufacturing Co.
1600 Junction Avenue
Racine, Wisconsin 53403

Commercial cleaning of rugs, carpets, furniture, automobile interiors, and interior painted walls and ceilings with electrically operated automatic machines

MOTELS, HOTELS

Admiral Benbow Inns, Inc.
Affiliate of Morrison Incorporated
P. O. Box 2608
Mobile, Alabama 36625

Motor inns

Days Inns of America, Inc.
2571 Buford Highway, N.E.
Atlanta, Georgia 30324

"Budget-Luxury" motels and restaurants

Downtowner/Rowntowner System
P.O. Box 171807
Memphis, Tennessee 38117

Diversified food service/lodging company

Econo-Travel Motor Hotel Corp.
20 Koger Executive Center
P. O. Box 12188
Norfolk, Virginia 23502

Econo-Travel Motor Hotels and Econo Lodges

Family Inns of America, Inc.
1111 Northshore Drive
P. O. Box 2191
Knoxville, Tennessee 37901

Motels with food and beverage facilities

Holiday Inns, Inc.
3796 Lamar Avenue
Memphis, Tennessee 38118

Hotels and restaurants

Howard Johnson's Motor Lodge
220 Forbes Road
Braintree, Massachusetts 02184

Motor hotels and hotels with food

Quality Inns, Intl., Inc.
10750 Columbia Pike
Silver Spring, Maryland 20901

Motor inns with food and beverage facilities

Ramada Inns, Inc.
3838 East Van Buren Street
Phoenix, Arizona 85008

Hotels and motor hotels

Red Carpet Inns of America, Inc.
Master Hosts Inns
444 Seabreeze Boulevard
P. O. Box 2510
Daytona Beach, Florida 32015

Franchising and operation of motels

Regal 8 Inns
P. O. Box 1268
Mt. Vernon, Illinois 62864

Motels

Rodeway Inns of America
2525 Stemmons Freeway
Suite 800
Dallas, Texas 75207

Motor hotels offering full services

Sheraton Inns, Inc.
470 Atlantic Avenue
Boston, Massachusetts 02210

Operate franchised inns

Super 8 Motels, Inc.
224 Sixth Avenue, S.E.
Aberdeen, South Dakota 57401

Budget motels

Travelodge International, Inc.
Travelodge Drive
El Cajon, California 92090

Motor motels

Treadway Inns Corp.
140 Market Street
Paterson, New Jersey 07505

Motor inns

PAINT AND DECORATING SUPPLIES

Davis Paint Company
1311 Iron Street
North Kansas City, Missouri 64116

Retail paint and wallpaper stores

Mary Carter Industries, Inc. 1191 Wheeling Road Wheeling, Illinois 60090	Retail stores handling paint, wallpaper, floor tiles and do-it-yourself supplies

PET SHOPS

Doctor Pet Centers, Inc. Dundee Park Andover, Massachusetts 01810	Retail pets, supplies, accessories and grooming services

PRINTING/COPYING

Big Red Q Quickprint Centers 3131 Douglas Road Toledo, Ohio 43614	Instant printing and copying services, etc.
Creative Copy Cats, Inc. 1256 East Tallmadge Avenue Akron, Ohio 44310	Instant printing centers with while-you-wait copying service
Curry Copy Centers of America, Inc. 43 Harvard Street Worcester, Massachusetts 01608	Instant printing and copying centers
Insty-Prints, Inc. 417 North Fifth Street Minneapolis, Minnesota 55401	Instant litho printing centers
Kopy Kat, Inc. National Franchise Division Executive Plaza Fort Washington, Pennsylvania 19034	Instant printing center
Kwik-Kopy Corporation 5525 Hollister Houston, Texas 77040	Rapid printing
Minuteman Press Intl., Inc. 1640 New Highway Farmingdale, New York 11735	Instant printing
(PIP) Postal Instant Press 8201 Beverly Boulevard Los Angeles, California 90048	While-you-wait printing

Sir Speedy Instant Printing Centers
P. O. Box 1790
Newport Beach, California 92663

Instant printing centers

RECREATION/ENTERTAINMENT/TRAVEL SERVICES/SUPPLIES

Corner Pockets of America, Inc.
1445 Broadwater Avenue
Billings, Montana 59104

Billiard lounges, featuring beverages, specialized foods, pocket billiard tables, football tables, and other amusement games

Disco Factory
405 Park Avenue
New York, New York 10022

Mobile discotheque called Murray the K's Disco on Wheels

Empress Travel Franchise Corp.
293 Madison Avenue
New York, New York 10017

Travel agency

Fascination, Ltd.
1950 East Estes
Elk Grove, Illinois 60007

Coin-operated video games in cocktail-table format

Fun Services, Inc.
50 East Rawls Road
Des Plaines, Illinois 60016

Professional Fun Fairs for the leisure-time and recreational industries

Golf Players, Inc.
5952 Brainerd Road
Chattanooga, Tennessee 37421

Miniature golf courses

Lomma Enterprises, Inc.
Lomma Building
1120 South Washington Avenue
Scranton, Pennsylvania 18505

Prefabricated miniature golf courses that can be used indoors or outdoors

Putt-Putt Golf Courses of America, Inc.
P. O. Box 35237
Fayetteville, North Carolina 28303

Miniature-golf facilities

RETAILING—NOT ELSEWHERE CLASSIFIED

Bathtique International Ltd.   Bath specialty shop
1304 Long Pond Road
Rochester, New York 14626

Bunning the Florist, Inc.   Retail florist shops
144 East Las Olas Blvd.
Fort Lauderdale, Florida 33301

Budget Tapes & Records, Inc.   Retail tapes and records
10625 East 47th Avenue
Denver, Colorado 80239

Famous French Galleries, Ltd.   Art gallery
Box 181
Saluda, Virginia 23149

Flowerama of America, Inc.   Turnkey retail flower shops & shopping
3165 West Airline Highway   mall, flower kiosks.
Waterloo, Iowa 50701

Flower World of America, Inc.   Retail flowers, plants, gifts and related
1655 Imperial Way   items
Mid-Atlantic Park
West Deptford, New Jersey 08086

Golden Dolphin, Inc.   Bath boutique specialty shops
29 East Rawls Road
Des Plaines, Illinois 60018

Lafayette Electronics Sales, Inc.   Retailing consumer and hobby electronics
P. O. Box L
Syosset, New York 11791

Little Professor Book Centers, Inc.   Book stores
33200 Capital
Livonia, Michigan 48150

Miss Bojangles, Inc.   Fashion jewelry operation locating ex-
P.O. Box 14589   clusively in enclosed malls
2762 Continental Drive
Baton Rouge, Louisiana 70808

Open Book Marketing Corp.   Book stores
2966 Biddle
Wyandotte, Michigan 48192

Paperback Booksmith 420 D Street Boston, Massachusetts 02210	Book & record stores
Photo Plaza P. O. Box 52 North Hackensack Station River Edge, New Jersey 07661	Drive-up kiosk units providing photo-developing service, including sales of cameras and related equipment and supplies
The Ringgold Corporation 9513 Dalecrest Houston, Texas 77080	Picture framing and art shops
Sport Shacks, Inc. Route 2, P. O. Box 349 Lindstrom, Minnesota 55045	Retailing of sporting goods
Team Central, Inc. 720 - 29th Avenue S.E. Minneapolis, Minnesota 55414	Retail electronics stores specializing in consumer-oriented entertainment products
The Tinder Box International, Ltd. P. O. Box 830 Santa Monica, California 90406	Retail pipes, tobacco, cigarettes, cigars and gifts, primarily in regional shopping centers
Wicks 'N' Sticks, Inc. 6937 Flintlock P. O. Box 40307 Houston, Texas 77040	Candle store
World Bazaar Munford, Inc. 68 Brookwood Drive, N.E. Atlanta, Georgia 30309	Sale at retail of imported goods, i.e., art objects, furniture, home decorative items, etc.

SECURITY SYSTEMS

Crusader Security Corporation P. O. Box 1488 Salisbury, North Carolina 28144	Sales & installation of patented security products
Dictograph Security System P. O. Box 96 Florham Park, New Jersey 07932	Burglar, fire & smoke, holdup and security devices for residential, commercial, institutional and industrial application as well as closed-circuit TV and camera-surveillance equipment as deterrents against shoplifting, pilferage and theft

Honor Guard Security Service
1725 Eye Street, N.W.
Suite 304
Washington, D. C. 20006

Uniformed security guards

Rampart Industries Inc.
One Oxford Valley
Langhorne, Pennsylvania 19047

Residential/small commercial security alarms

Telcoa International Corp.
16 Church Street
Greenwich, Connecticuit 06830

Wholesale & retail distributors of burglar and fire alarm equipment

SOFT DRINK/WATER BOTTLING

Bubble-up Company
2800 North Talman Avenue
Chicago, Illinois 60618

Issued to soft-drink bottlers. Sell only one item to franchisees, and that is DAD's concentrate, from which is produced DAD's Root Beer finished product

Double-Cola Company
3350 Broad Street
Chattanooga, Tennessee 37402

Manufacture and sale of soft drinks

Mission of California
197 Chatham Street
New Haven, Connecticut 06513

Soft-drink extracts, dairy flavor bases, fountain syrup. Franchises are available for bottlers/canners

Mountain Valley Spring Company
150 Central Avenue
Hot Springs, Arkansas 71901

Distributing Mountain Valley Water from Hot Springs, Arkansas, & imported bottled waters

SWIMMING POOLS

Blue Dolphin Pools, Inc.
4013 Woodville Highway
P. O. Box 6326
Tallahassee, Florida 32301

Aluminum wall, vinyl-lined, inground swimming pools

Cascade Industries, Inc.
Talmadge Road
Edison, New Jersey 08817

Sell and install swimming pools

Fort Wayne Pool Equipment, Inc.
4611 Newaygo Road
Fort Wayne, Indiana 46808

Sell and install swimming pools

San Juan Products, Inc.
831 N. E. Northgate Way
Seattle, Washington 98125

Once-piece fiberglass swimming pool, in various sizes, to installing dealers who have construction experience either in the swimming-pool industry or general construction

Sylvan Pools
Route 611
Doylestown, Pennsylvania 18901

Servicing, repair and maintenance of swimming pools

TOOLS, HARDWARE

Mac Tools, Inc.
P. O. Box 370
South Fayette Street
Washington Court House, Ohio 43160

Complete inventory of over 9,000 tools, calling directly on mechanics and light industry

Snap-on Tools Corporation
2801 - 80th Street
Kenosha, Wisconsin 53140

Sales of hand tools and equipment to garages and service stations. Dealer travels his territory using a truck or a similar vehicle

Vulcan Tools
United-Greenfield Div. of TRW, Inc.
2300 Kenmore Avenue
Buffalo, New York 14207

Tools sold from van to garages, fleets, car dealers, airports, shops, etc.

VENDING

American Juice Corporation
1500 East Little Creek Road
Suite 210
Norfolk, Virginia 23518

Distributor of vending products; pure fruit juices for sale through self-service vending machines; distributor routes

Ford Gum & Machine Co., Inc.
Division Automatic Service Co.
Newton & Hoag Streets
Akron, New York 14001

Distributor of chewing gum, candy, and candy-coated confections for sale through self-service vending machines

S & S Distributors, Inc.
2060 Concourse Drive
St. Louis, Missouri 63141

"Profit Machine" designed exclusively for the vending of Fruit of the Loom Pantyhose. S & S Distributors Inc. will secure locations for the operation

WATER CONDITIONING

Chemical Engineering Corp.
P.O. Box 246
Churubusco, Indiana 46723

Sales, rentals and servicing of water-conditioning equipment

Culligan International Co.
One Culligan Parkway
Northbrook, Illinois 60062

Franchisee sells leases, maintains and repairs water-conditioning equipment for domestic, commercial, and industrial consumers

Ecodyne Corporation
The Lindsay Division
P.O. Box 43420
St. Paul, Minnesota 55164

Residential (sales & rentals), commercial and industrial water-conditioning equipment

Rainsoft Water Conditioning Co.
1225 East Greenleaf Avenue
Elk Grove Village, Illinois 60007

Sell, lease and rent home, commercial and industrial water-treatment equipment

Watercare Corporation
1520 North 24th Street
Manitowoc, Wisconsin 54220

Water-conditioning sales, rental and service; domestic, industrial, institutional and commercial

Water Purification Systems, Inc.
6502 N.W. 16th Street
Plantation, Florida 33313

Water-purification system attaches under the sink and to the ice maker in the consumer's home

Water Refining Company
500 N. Verity Parkway
Middletown, Ohio 45042

Water-conditioning sales, rentals, service

MISCELLANEOUS WHOLESALE AND SERVICE BUSINESSES

Bar-Master, International
2206 Beverly Boulevard
Los Angeles, California 90057

Sell soft-drink and liquor dispensers

Commercial Mobile Services, Inc.   Mobile van appliance repair service
850 Stanton Road
Burlingame, California 94010

COVCO   Mobile "factory on wheels" for
360 Lafayette Avenue   the purpose of making boat-cover repairs
Hawthorne, New Jersey 07506   or custom installations

Diversified Arts   Part-time distributor - requires 8-10
15 Palmer Road   hours per week to service accounts to
Waterford, Connecticut 06385   whom paintings are consigned, also will
                                          aid in setting up of full-time galleries

Hydrophonics Industries, Inc.   Factory-built home greenhouses and
95 Rio Grande Boulevard   hydrophonic greenhouses—distributor
Denver, Colorado 80223   of related hydrophonic garden products

Key Korner Systems, Inc.   Complete business includes all phases
3420 Kenyon Street   of key cutting, lock repairing, engraving,
San Diego, California 92110   rubber stamps. All shops located at the
                                          entrance of major retail shopping centers

Meistergram   Monogram embroidery equipment and
310 Lakeside Avenue, West   supplies sold to department stores and
Cleveland, Ohio 44113   manufacturers

Nationwide Exterminating   U-do-it pest control product for sale to
A Division of Nationwide Chemical   the general public
P. O. Box 3027
Hamilton, Ohio 45013

Nationwide Fastener Systems, Inc.   Supply nuts, bolts, screws, etc., for
240 Laura Drive   industrial use from mobile warehouse
Addison, Illinois 60101

Parking Company of America   Self-service parking lots and garages
1515 Arapahoe Street
3 Park Central, Room 1031
Denver, Colorado 80202

Redd Pest Control Company, Inc.   Pest and termite control
4114 Northview Drive
Jackson, Mississippi 39206

Selectra-Date Corporation   Computer-dating
2175 Lemoine Avenue
Fort Lee, New Jersey 07024

Tepco, Inc.
2705 Industrial Lane
Garland, Texas 75041

Electronic air-cleaning and air-pollution-control equipment

Terminix International, Inc.
855 Ridge Lake Blvd.
P. O. Box 17167
Memphis, Tennessee 38117

Termite- and pest-control services to commercial and residential customers

United Air Specialists, Inc.
6665 Creek Road
Cincinnati, Ohio 45242

Commercial electronic air cleaners

22. FRANCHISE LAW SUMMARY

by VERNON W. HAAS

INTRODUCTION

THIS booklet has been prepared for your use as a general guideline. It is not meant to be a definitive work which covers every topic, but is intended as a very general overview of the subject and is designed to give you insight as to potential problem areas. Your legal staff should be contacted should it appear your activities might come within the jurisdiction of one or more of these laws.

ABOUT THE AUTHOR

VERNON W. HAAS is a practicing attorney who makes his home in Ventura, California. In 1951 Mr. Haas founded Engineering Corporation of America (ECA), an ongoing franchise organization. As the owner and operator of ECA for now in excess of 25 years, Mr. Haas was involved in franchising before there were any franchisise laws. He saw the first franchise full disclosure law develop in California, and since he has personally experienced the same problems many franchisors are now experiencing, he has an understanding of business problems possibly not realized by most practicing attorneys.

With many states now requiring franchise registration, Mr. Haas has devoted a great deal of time and energy to the field of franchise law. He has worked with the small franchisors just starting in business to the large publicly held international corporations.

TABLE OF CONTENTS

FRANCHISE LAW SUMMARY

Importance of the Definition of a Franchise

Prior to 1971 the definition of a franchise had little, if any, legal significance. In 1971, California passed the first franchise investment law in the United States. There are now 12 or 13 states that have registration laws, depending on what one terms a registration. In addition, there are another 7 states which have laws affecting other aspects of the franchise operation which include terminations and renewals, multi-level (or pyramid) sales marketing schemes, deceptive practices and unfair trade practices. Therefore, the definition of a franchise has become very important from a legal standpoint. Any operation which is classified as a franchise under the law must comply with a complicated set of rules and regulations.

In passing the franchise laws, as is so often the case, the state legislators left the details of the law to be defined and refined by administrative bodies and the courts. In a recent Minnesota case involving the sale of an unregistered franchise, the sole issue was "What is the definition of a franchise?" The State of California's administrative body interpreted the operation as not being a franchise while Minnesota's administrative body interpreted the same operation as being a franchise. To illustrate the newness of these franchise laws, in preparing the Minnesota case with the aid of the West Computer, the case law of every state was researched in an attempt to find cases in which the definition of a franchise was in issue. Not one case was found.

Until the courts have ruled and resulting precedents have been set, no one knows for sure what the final definition of a franchise may be. It appears one thing is certain, every state which has a franchise law has a different definition of what constitutes a franchise and as the courts define and refine the definition of a franchise, each state's definition will be further modified.

Problems of Operating Under the Franchise Laws

First, the cost of filing fees ranges from $25 to $500 per state. The current total filing fee for the 12 states is $4,225. Each registration must be renewed each year and the fee for renewal ranges from $10 to $250. The current cost of renewal in the 12 states is $1,785. In some of the states, each amendment requires a fee. These fees can go as high as $100 each and the simple act of adding a salesman can require the filing of an amendment before the salesman can start work.

Second, since each state has a different franchise law it may be necessary to prepare several prospectuses. Several states have stated (see chart, center of this book) they will accept the Uniform

295

Franchise Offering Circular. However, some accept this only with additional changes. Printing costs increase with the requirements for several different prospectuses and changes each year can also add to the cost of the prospectus, because the prior year's prospectus is discarded and a new one is prepared.

Third, each year one incurs time and expense in preparing an *audited* financial statement. Usually the prospectus and the registration application require changes as well. The agency responsible for the renewal approval may be slow in reviewing and renewing the re-registration, and, if the current registration expires before the renewal becomes effective *all sales activities must stop.* The company is faced with the question of what to do with the current sales leads and sales staff.

Fourth, the requirements of the states vary, but all require that the prospectus and contract be delivered to a prospective buyer anywhere from 2 to 7 days (depending on the state) before the signing of the contract or the payment of any money. The prospectus must state the franchise fee and give a complete breakdown of all costs. These cannot be negotiated and cannot be raised or lowered without changing the prospectus, registration and contract. The same offer must be made to all and this offer must be clearly stated in the prospectus. If financing is available, the terms must be clearly stated and be equally available to all.

Fifth, before any advertisement can be published the ad copy must be submitted to each state's administrative body 3 days to 10 business days before the date of publication. As a general rule, the states will not allow words like, "profit," "secure future," "secure investment," etc., and by the time the states approve an ad, obtaining any results are doubtful. With few exceptions, advertising costs are greatly increased.

Sixth, several states have fairness doctrines. Simply stated, should the state find that, in its opinion, a franchise contract is not fair the state official has the power to issue a Cease and Desist Order, thereby causing the franchisor to stop selling the franchise.

In Minnesota the person having this power has been an employee of the state for less than two years, is not even admitted to practice law in the State of Minnesota, and yet can and did tell McDonald's that their contract was unfair and stopped the sale of McDonald's franchises. This order was later revised by a court order.

It would appear no one in the McDonald's organization believes the franchise agreement to be unfair because there are several legal actions pending in which McDonald's franchisees are attempting to retain their franchise and others in which people are trying to force McDonald's to grant them a franchise, and no wonder with the average franchise net profit, that is in-pocket profit after all expenses, of $17,000 per each unit each month.

Seventh, all the states requiring registration, with the exception of Virginia, have provisions whereby the state can impound *all* the funds received by the franchisor from the franchisee until the franchisor has performed *all* his duties under the franchise agreement. Seven of the states requiring registration have another provision which gives the state the option of requiring a surety bond from the franchisor in lieu of the impound condition. How many companies can operate with *all* their income impounded? And for how long? Just like the old saying about borrowing money from a bank, "If you can prove you don't need it, they will loan it to you." Here all that is needed to get the funds released is to prove you don't need them, because if you need these funds, in most cases, the funds will not be released.

This may cause the franchisor to go broke which prevents the franchisor from performing under the contract and thus it puts both the franchisor and franchisee out of business. The franchisee loses his investment in time and effort and this may be greater than the amount which has been impounded. This law is supposed to protect the franchisee?

What Constitutes a Franchise

The definition of a franchise varies from state to state. California, being the first state to pass a franchise law, defines a franchise as follows:

"'Franchise' defined — 'Franchise' means a contract or agreement, either expressed or implied, whether oral or written, between two or more persons by which:

(a) A franchisee is granted the right to engage in the business of offering, selling or distributing goods or services under a marketing plan or system prescribed in substantial part by a franchisor; and

(b) The operation of the Franchisee's business pursuant to such plan or system is substantially associated with the franchisor's trademark, service mark, trade name, logotype, advertising or other commerical symbol designating the franchisor or its affiliate; and

(c) The franchisee is required to pay, directly or indirectly, a franchise fee."

Note: In California all petroleum distribution agreements are classified as franchises.

The states of Illinois, Indiana, North Dakota, Rhode Island, Virginia and Wisconsin have generally followed the California definition of a franchise. However, one must be careful because each is a little different.

The states of Hawaii, Minnesota, South Dakota and Washington have replaced the "marketing plan" clause with a "community of interest" clause. Furthermore, to be classified as a franchise in Michigan the agreement need only provide for a marketing plan and the payment of a fee *or* the use of the name along with the payment of a fee.

Large franchisors may be exempted from the registration requirement (see chart, center of this book). To qualify for the exemption, however, the states (although they differ) generally require the franchisor to have a net worth of at least Five Million Dollars ($5,000,000) or One Million Dollars ($1,000,000) and be 80% owned by a company having a net worth of over Five Million, and to have had twenty-five (25) franchisees for five years.

What State Law Applies?

The sale of a franchise may be controlled by four state laws simultaneously: (1) the domicile of the franchisee, (2) where the offer is made, (3) where the offer is accepted, and (4) where the franchise is to be operated.

California defines "In this State" as follows: "An offer or sale of a franchise is made in this state when an offer to sell is made in this state, or an offer to buy is accepted in this state, or if the franchisee is domiciled in this state, the franchised business is or will be operated in this state."

"(b) An offer to sell is made in this state when the offer either originated from this state or is directed by the offeror to this state and received at the place to which it is directed. An offer to sell is accepted in this state when acceptance is communicated to the offeror in this state; and acceptance is communicated to the offeror in this state when the offeree directs it to the offeror in this state reasonably believing the offeror to be in this state and it is received at the place to which it is directed."

"(c) An offer to sell is not made in this state merely because, (1) the publisher circulates or there is circulated on his behalf in this state any bona fide newspaper or other publication of general, regular, and paid circulation which has had more than two-thirds of its circulation outside this state during the past 12 months, or (2) a radio or television program originating outside this state is received in this state."

Guidelines for Determining Whether an Agreement Constitutes a "Franchise" Under California Law

Four Elements: Four elements are essential for an agreement to constitute a "franchise" within the definition of California Law.

(1) A *right* must be granted to the franchisee to engage in the business of offering, selling or distributing goods or services.

(2) The *right* must be granted to engage in the business under a marketing plan or system prescribed in substantial part by the franchisor.

(3) The operation of the franchisee's business must be substantially associated with an advertising or other commercial symbol designating the franchisor or an affiliate of the franchisor such as a trademark, service mark, trade name or logotype.

(4) The franchisee must be required to pay, directly or indirectly, a fee or charge, known as a "franchise fee," for the right to enter into the business.

Area Franchise: According to California law, and the laws of several other states, "franchise" unless otherwise stated, includes an "area franchise." An "area franchise" is generally defined as an agreement by which a franchisor for a consideration grants to a subfranchisor the right to sell or negotiate the sale of franchises in the name of or on behalf of the franchisor. Therefore, when an agreement with a distributor constitutes a franchise in California, and in most states, the distributor's agreement granting to a subdistributor the right to appoint lower level subdistributors for a consideration is an "area franchise" and is subject to the registration requirement.

Franchisee Engaged in Business : For an agreement to be a franchise, the franchisee must be granted the right to engage in the business of offering, selling, or distributing goods or services. It is important to note that an agreement which grants the franchisee the right to engage in a business identified with the franchisor's commercial symbol, is no less a franchise by reason of the fact that the franchisee previously on his own and without reference to the franchisor's plan and symbol, had been engaged in the particular line of business. Furthermore, the grant of the right by the franchisor to the franchisee to solicit others to join in the franchise operation, or to solicit sales of other franchises does itself constitute the right to engage in business. If the agreement does not grant the franchisee the right to engage in business, it is not a franchise. Thus, an agreement by which a person designated as "franchisee," for a fee designated as "franchise fee," is given the right to participate in the profits of a business, but given no right to participate in the operation of the business, is not a franchise, but is a profit participation or investment contract which may be subject to the qualification requirements of the Securities Law.

Business Operated Under a Marketing Plan or System Prescribed in Substantial Part by Franchisor: For the agreement to constitute a "franchise," the business in which the franchisee is granted the right to engage, must be operated under a marketing plan or system prescribed in substantial part by the franchisor.

If no marketing plan or system is prescribed and the franchisee is left entirely free to operate the business according to his own marketing plan or system, the agreement is not a franchise. Thus, a distribution agreement by which a manufacturer or wholesaler for a fee grants the right to a distributor or retailer to sell a trademarked item or product purchased from the manufacturer or wholesaler is not a franchise, if the distributor or retailer may sell the product according to his own plan without express or implied limitations on the method or mode of sale, as discussed below, except where the business includes the soliciting of others to purchase further franchises which may itself constitute a marketing plan.

In making the determination whether there is a prescribed marketing plan or system, it is necessary to keep in mind the objective of the law to deal with a multiplicity of business establishments created by the franchisor which he then presents to the public as a unit or marketing concept, and for all of which it ostensibly assumes responsibility by causing them to be operated with the appearance of some centralized management and uniform standards regarding the quality and price of goods sold, services rendered and other material incidents of the operation. The marketing plan or system as prescribed by the franchisor is one of the important means by which the appearance of centralized management and uniform standards is achieved.

(1) **Significant Provisions:** If a franchisor, in his advertising to prospective franchisees, claims to have a successful marketing plan available, the element of a marketing plan presumably will be present. In other cases, arrangements designed to establish uniformity of prices and marketing terms are significant. These might include provisions which contemplate a nation-wide or area-wide distribution grid on an exclusive or semi-exclusive basis, possibly with multiple levels of jurisdiction, such as regional and local distributorships. Control which is reserved by a franchisor over terms of payment by customers, credit practices, warranties and representations in dealings between franchisees and their customers, suggest a uniform marketing plan. Provisions concerning collateral services which may or may not be rendered, or prohibiting or limiting the sale of competitive or non-competitive goods are consistent with, though certainly not in and of themselves determinative of, a prescribed marketing plan. Significance is attached to provisions which impose a duty of observing the licensor's directions or obtaining his approval with respect to the selection of locations, the use of trade names, advertising, signs, sales pitches, sources of supply, or concerning the appearance of the licensee's business premises and the fixtures and equipment utilized therein, uniform of employees, hours of operation, housekeeping, and similar decorum.

The implementation of these procedures, and other similar directions, for inspection by, and reporting to, the franchisor with respect to the conduct of the franchised business, and the right on the part of the franchisor to take corrective measures, possibly at the expense of the franchisees, are indicative of the franchisor's control over the franchisee's operation and consequently indicative of a marketing plan prescribed by franchisor. A comprehensive advertising or other promotional program of the franchisor, with or without an obligation on the part of the franchisees to bear part of the expense of such program, is indicative of a marketing plan prescribed by the franchisor, especially if the advertising or promotional material identifies the locations of the franchisees, and the more so if individual advertising or promotional activities by franchisees are prohibited or require the prior approval of the franchisor.

(2) **Prescribed "In Substantial Part":** Agreements which grant to a person the right to engage in business subject to some restrictions but with a measure of freedom regarding the plan or system under which the grantee's business is to be operated present close questions of interpretation. In this respect, to be a franchise, the marketing plan or system must be prescribed by the franchisor "in substantial part." Whether or not the directions given to the franchisee in the agreement are "substantial" in this sense, is a question which necessarily must be determined with respect to each agreement. The determination must be based upon an appraisal of all provisions contained therein and the effect which they have as a whole upon the ability of the person engaged in the business to make decisions without being subject to restrictions or having to obtain the consent or approval of other persons. The determination must be made in the light of applicable principals of general law and of customs prevailing in the particular trade or industry.

(3) **Marketing Plan "Prescribed" by Implication:** A marketing plan or system may be "prescribed" within the meaning of the law when a specific sales program is outlined, suggested, recommended, or otherwise originated by the franchisor, even if there is no obligation on the part of the franchisee to observe it. Thus, a sales program may be "prescribed" by the franchisor when he supplies the franchisee with sales aids or props (such as demonstration kits, films, or detailed instructions for personal introduction and presentation of the product, possibly including the text of a sales pitch) especially when such a program is supported by training materials, courses or seminars. By such means a non-mandatory program may attain the force of a "prescribed" one, particularly when there are negative covenants against the use of specified modes of distribution, such as a prohibition of sales to retail stores. Therefore, a provision in the agreement which states that the franchisee is to be considered an independent contractor or that the franchisor is not concerned with the means employed by the franchisee to make sales, or with the manner in which the business of the franchisee is conducted, does not preclude the possibility that the franchisor's business is, actually and in fact,

	REGISTRATION										ADVERTISING			UNIFORM OFFERING CIRCULAR	
	FILING FEE	RENEWAL FEE	AMENDMENT FEE	OPINIONS	OPINION FEE	TIME BETWEEN FILING AND EFFECTIVENESS	RENEWAL REVIEW TIME	TIME BETWEEN PRESENTATION AND SIGNING	LARGE FRANCHISOR EXEMPTION	DATE OF THE LAW	ADVANCE SUBMISSION OF COPY FOR ADVERTISING APPROVAL	FEE	LARGE FRANCHISOR EXEMPTION	1974	1975
CALIFORNIA	$250	$50	$50	YES	—0—	15 b.d.	15 days	48 hrs.	YES	1971	3 b.d. ##	NO	YES	YES	YES
HAWAII	$500	$100	$100	YES	—0—	15 b.d.	15 days	48 hrs.	YES	1975	7 b.d. ##	NO	YES	YES	YES
ILLINOIS	$500	$250	$25*	YES	$50	20 b.d.	20 days	7 days	NO	1974	5 days ##	NO	NO	YES	YES
INDIANA	$500	$250	—0—	YES	$50	30 days	30 days	3 days	YES	1975	5 days	NO	YES	YES	YES
MICHIGAN	$500	$250	—0—	YES	—0—	30 days	30 days	1 week	YES	1974	10 b.d. ##	NO	YES	NO	YES
MINNESOTA	$250	$100	$50	YES	$25	**	30 days	7 days	NO	1973	3 days	NO	NO	YES	NO
N. DAKOTA	$250	$100	$50	YES	$50	15 days	15 days	7 days	YES	1975	5 b.d.	NO	YES	NO	YES
OREGON	INFORMATION MUST BE SUBMITTED TO THE STATE PRIOR TO A SALE OR OFFER TO SELL														
RHODE ISLAND	$200	$50	$50	YES	—0—	15 b.d.	15 days	*	YES	1973	3 b.d.	NO	YES	YES	YES
S. DAKOTA	$100	$10	$20	YES	$25	indef.	30 days	7 days	YES	1974	3 b.d.	NO	YES	YES	YES
VIRGINIA	$25	$25	—0—	No specific provisions	No specific provisions	No specific provisions	3-4 mos.	72 hrs.	NO	1972	No specific provisions			No specific provisions	
WASHINGTON	$500	$100	$100	YES	—0—	15 b.d.	15 days	48 hrs.	YES	1972	7 days	NO	NO	NO	YES
WISCONSIN	$400	$250	$100	YES	$20	15 b.d.	15 days	48 hrs.	YES	1972	5 days ##	YES	NO	NO	YES
ALBERTA, C.	$250	$250	***	No specific provisions	No specific provisions	Within 30 days	30 days	4 days	YES	1971	No specific provisions				

b.d. = business days
* $100 if the change is a material one
** No specified time. Registration becomes effective upon issuance of an order for registration.
*** There are 13 categories of amendments ranging from $25 to $50 per amendment
\# 48 hours before signing and 72 hours before giving consideration
\#\# Does not include "tombstone" ads which consist or a limited amount of information specifically prescribed by statute or regulation.

NOTE: Registrations are for one (1) year from date of approval except for Virginia where registrations must be renewed each June 30.

SUMMARY OF NON-REGISTRATION STATES' STATUTES AND REGULATIONS

ARKANSAS: Limited requirements which are subject to the interpretation of the State Attorney General.

CONNECTICUT: Statutes controlling the termination/renewal of franchises and unfair and deceptive practices. Franchises and subsequent renewals must be for periods of not less than three (3) years.

DELAWARE: Statute controlling termination/renewal of franchises.

FLORIDA: Rules and statutes controlling deceptive and nfair trade practices, referral sales, multi-level (pyramid) sales marketing schemes and fraudulent misrepresentation.

MISSISSIPPI: Statutes controlling and specifically prohibiting pyramid sales and profit projections.

MISSOURI: Statutes controlling termination/renewal of franchises and prohibition of pyramid sales.

NEW JERSEY: A "Franchise Practices Act" regarding termination/renewal of franchises as well as other activities of franchisors and franchisees.

**ALTHOUGH THIS INFORMATION IS BELIEVED TO BE RELIABLE
THESE LAWS CHANGE RAPIDLY
AND LEGAL COUNSEL IS RECOMMENDED**

operated pursuant to a marketing plan or system prescribed in substantial part by the franchisor, and such an agreement, if other requirements of the definition are satisfied, may be a franchise.

(4) Normal Routines No Marketing Plan: On the other hand, the requirement of a marketing plan or system prescribed in substantial part by the franchisor is not satisfied merely because the agreement imposes procedures or techniques on the operator of the business which are customarily observed in business relationships in the particular trade or industry, even though they may restrict the freedom of action or the discretion of the operator to some extent. Thus, an obligation imposed upon a distributor to use his best efforts to make or increase sales of the licensor's product is too general a requirement to amount to a marketing plan or system. When a television station is licensed to produce a copyrighted game show there is no marketing plan or system merely because the station is required to follow the format of the show and use props provided by the licensor. When a restaurant is authorized to be conducted under a trade name without the imposition of any other marketing plan or system, a requirement that public liability insurance be maintained in a certain amount does not characterize the agreement as a franchise. Such a requirement is not a substantial limitation, and is normal and customary in an agreement exposing the licensor to public liability which may result from acts authorized therein. Likewise, when a manufacturer is licensed by an inventor, or when a retail store is licensed to distribute trademarked articles subject to a royalty, maintenance of records and accounts by the licensee for verification of the royalty due under the agreement is not a substantial limitation. Also specifications to be observed by a licensee in the manufacture of a patented device designed to protect the quality of the product are normal in such circumstances.

These requirements, therefore, in and of themselves, do not amount to a marketing plan or system. While any one of the restrictions which have been (or many others which could be) mentioned may not amount to "a marketing plan or system prescribed in substantial part by a franchisor," several such restrictions taken together may be sufficient to amount to such a plan or system.

Operation Substantially Associated with Franchisor's Commerical Symbol: To constitute a franchise, the operation of the franchisee's business must be substantially associated with the franchisor's commercial symbol, such as a trademark, service mark, trade name or logotype. An agreement does not constitute a franchise if that business is not substantially associated with a commerical symbol of the franchisor or its affiliate, even if it prescribes a detailed marketing plan or system for the operation of the business authorized thereby. Again it must be remembered that the objective of the law is to deal with a multiplicity of business establishments presented to the public as a unit or marketing plan and moreover, under the coverage of a common symbol. Therefore, if the other requirements are satisfied, if the franchisee is granted the right to use the franchisor's symbol, the franchise concept is satisfied, even if he is not obligated to display the symbol.

In addition, in line with the objective of the law as above stated, for the operation of the franchisee's business to be substantially associated with the symbol it must be communicated to the customers of the franchisee. A commercial symbol which a supplier of goods or services only uses on his invoices or on his advertising to distributors but which he does not permit the distributors to show in dealing with their customers is not, in the eyes of the public, substantially associated with the operation of the supplier.

However, when the trademark is communicated to the customers of the supplier the appearance of a unified operation is established, and it is immaterial whether the advertising containing the trademark is originated, distributed, or paid for by the franchisor or by the franchisee. In resolving the question whether there is substantial association between the licensee's business and the licensor's commercial symbol, it is necessary to consider whether or not that commerical symbol is brought to the attention of the licensee's customers to such an extent that they would regard the licensee's establishment as one in a chain identified with the licensor. Thus, in one case, the shape devised by a franchisor for the franchisee's restaurants amounted to a commercial symbol.

Franchise Fee: For the agreement to constitute a franchise it must call for the payment of a franchise fee by the franchisee.

(1) **Definition:** Most Franchise Investment laws contain a broad definition of "franchise fee." Included in the definition is any fee or charge that a franchisee is required to pay or agrees to pay for the right to enter into a business under a franchise agreement. In accordance with this definition, any fee or charge which the franchisee is required to pay to the franchisor or an affiliate of the franchisor for the right granted him to engage in business is a franchise fee regardless of the designation given to, or the form of, such payment. Whether or not a fee or charge is "required" and whether it is made "for the right to enter into a business," is a mixed question of fact and law. The legal aspects of the question call for a consideration of all pertinent facts.

(2) **Types of Franchise Fees:** A franchise fee may be payable in a lump sum or in installments. The amount of installment payments may be made to depend on gross receipts or net profits in the form of a royalty, or it may be charged on units of merchandise ordered or sold by the franchisee. A franchise fee thus may be contained in the price charged by the franchisor or an affiliate of the

franchisor for goods or services supplied to the franchisee or in the rental payable by the franchisee for business premises or equipment rented from the franchisor or an affiliate of the franchisor.

(3) **Bona Fide Wholesale Price of Goods:** Under some state laws, there is an exemption from the definition of franchise fee for a payment on account for the purchase of goods in an amount not exceeding the bona fide wholesale price of such goods. This exemption is based on the rationale that no substantial prejudice will come to a person buying a business and paying only the bona fide wholesale price for merchandise which he proposes to sell in that business. Such payment is not deemed to be made for the right to enter into the franchised business and the goods purchased are considered adequate consideration for the payment. In line with this rationale, "bona fide wholesale price" means the price at which goods are purchased and sold by a manufacturer or wholesaler to a wholesaler or dealer where there is ultimately an open and public market in which sales of goods are effected to consumers of the goods. "Bona fide wholesale price" does not include the price of goods for which there is no such open and public market, and the goods are sold primarily to a person engaged in their redistribution.

(4) **Goods:** The bona fide wholesale price exemption is applicable only to the purchase of goods which the franchisee is authorized to distribute by the franchise agreement. The exemption does not apply to payments which the franchisee is required to make under the franchise agreement in return for benefits other than goods, such as payments for real estate, services or for rental payments. Furthermore, it is not applicable to fixtures, equipment or other articles such as display cases, tools and equipment which are to be utilized in the operation of the franchised business. In the case of a restaurant franchise, for instance, such items as table linen, napkins, flatware and other service utensils do not fall under the exemption.

Some laws exempt from the registration requirement, though not from other provisions of the Franchise Investment Law, the offer or sale of a franchise which is subject to registration solely because the agreement obligates the franchisee to pay a sum not exceeding $1,000 (amounts vary from state to state) annually on account for the purchase price or rental of fixtures, equipment or other tangible property to be utilized in, and necessary for, the operation of the franchised business, if the price or rental so charged does not exceed the cost which would be incurred by the franchisee acquiring the item or items from other persons in the open market.

Furthermore, some laws exempt from the registration requirement, though again not from other provisions of the law, the offer or sale of a franchise which is subject to registration solely because the franchisee is required, directly or indirectly, to make a payment, no matter for what purpose, as long as on an annual basis it does not exceed $100 (amounts vary from state to state). Under the aforementioned rationale, the exemptional provision with respect to "goods" does not include an idea or program, whether or not the same is offered or distributed by word of mouth (through instructions or lectures) or in the form of written or printed material, or by a combination of both. Rather, the communication of such an idea or program is in the nature of a service to which the exemption and the provisions are not applicable.

(5) **Question of Fact:** Whether the price which the franchisee is required to pay under the agreement for goods exceeds their bona fide wholesale price (or exceeds it by an amount in excess of the tolerance allowed) is a question of fact. Most states will not resolve this question in an interpretive opinion because such opinions are limited to the interpretation and determination of legal questions arising under the law. However, there are some legal considerations applicable to the determination of the bona fide wholesale price which are as follows:

(a) The bona fide wholesale price of goods which are marketed under a trademark or other commercial symbol may vary depending on the degree to which such trademark or symbol has attained public acceptance. The price charged for trademarked articles does not necessarily exceed their bona fide wholesale price when non-trademarked articles of equal or comparable quality are wholesaled at a lower price, because products with little or no market identification usually have a lower bona fide wholesale price than items, though of comparable quality, which have a marketing history and a ready identity in the market. Therefore, if, as a matter of fact, at the time of the franchise agreement the trademarked articles command a premium price in the market place by virtue of the trademark, such premium does not characterize the payment as a franchise fee. However, sales to distributors who are all within the common enterprise or marketing system do not suffice to substantiate the ultimate marketability and market identification, and consequently do not serve to support the bona fide wholesale price of the product being sold.

(b) The bona fide wholesale price of goods may vary at different levels of the distributing system, or vary depending on the quantity of goods sold. Thus, a variance in the price paid by franchisees selling goods at different levels of distribution, such as jobbers selling to wholesalers, and wholesalers selling to retailers, does not necessarily lead to the conclusion that the higher price paid by franchisees on the lower level constitutes a franchise fee. In a layered system of distribution, the price paid by a person engaged in distribution of the goods on one level may be a bona fide wholesale price even though it is at variance with the bona fide wholesale price paid for the same goods by a distributor on another level.

(c) If the distributors under the agreement with the franchisor are required to purchase specified amounts of goods or to purchase such specified amounts within a specified period, the bona fide wholesale price exemption is not available when the amount so required to be purchased exceeds the quantity which a reasonable business man normally would purchase by way of a starting inventory or supply or to maintain as a going inventory or supply. Because payment for such excessive purchases is made by the franchisee by agreement and not because he has a need for the goods, it is understandable only as a method by which he secures the right to sell the goods under the franchise agreement, and for that reason it constitutes a franchise fee.

(d) According to most state laws, the franchisor has the burden of proving that the price at which he sells goods to the franchisee does not exceed the bona fide wholesale price of such goods. Similarly he must prove the facts to support any other exemption on which he wishes to rely.

(6) **"Required" to Pay:** The law does not include in the definition of "franchise fee" payments which the franchisee is not required to make but which are optional with him and required only if he elects to purchase, lease or rent merchandise, equipment or other property from the franchisor or an affiliate of the franchisor. In the absence of an obligation or a condition in the franchise agreement compelling action on his part, or the necessity for undertaking such obligation in order to successfully operate the business, such voluntary payments are not "required" under the agreement, and therefore are not within the statutory definition of "franchise fee." Also, such voluntary payments presumably are not made for the right to enter into the franchised business, and for that reason do not meet that definition. However, while a truly optional payment is not a franchise fee, a payment by a franchisee, though nominally optional, may in reality be a required one if the article for which the payment is made is essential, or if the franchisor intimates or suggests that it is essential, for the successful operation of the business.

(7) **Payments to Franchisor or Others:** Payments which the franchisee is required to make under the franchise agreement for the account of the franchisor are equivalent to payments made to the franchisor. It makes no difference whether payments for the rental of premises are required to be made by the franchisee to the franchisor as the owner and lessor of the premises, or to a third party owner where the franchisor is the lessee and the franchisee his sublessee. Also, payments required in the franchise agreement to be made by the franchisee for advertising and promotion to enhance the good will of the franchisor's business, even though they also benefit the operation of the franchisee, may be deemed made for the account of the franchisor. This is especially

true when the agreement gives the franchisor discretion to determine the manner and content of the publicity.

A payment to or for the account of third parties who are not affiliated with the franchisor is not a "franchise fee" within the meaning of most state codes. Even in cases in which the franchisee is required by the agreement to make such payment and even if the franchisor collects it from the franchisee on behalf of the third party, if such payment is not made for the right to enter into the business it is not a "franchise fee." However, if the agreement is a franchise due to other payments required of the franchisee amounting to a franchise fee, the obligation to make payments to the franchisor in whole or in part on behalf of third parties, must, in most states, be disclosed by the franchisor in the prospectus.

Conclusion of What Constitutes a Franchise under California Law

These guidelines demonstrate the complexities of the question whether an agreement constitutes a "franchise" under the California Franchise Law. As stated above, these guidelines do not hold true in all the states. Therefore, when it is not clear that an agreement is not a franchise, it is recommended that an interpretive opinion of the Franchise Investment Law be obtained from each state before a sale or offer to sell is made.

Interpretive Opinions

The principal purpose of Interpretive Opinions is to provide a procedure by which members of the public can protect themselves against liability for acts done or omitted in good faith in reliance upon an administrative determination made under the Franchise Investment Laws. There is a fee of up to $50 for these requests and each request must fully set forth the legal questions presented and the particular facts and circumstances of the transaction concerning which the opinion is requested, including the names of all parties to the transaction, because each interpretive opinion is applicable only to the transaction identified in the request and may not be relied upon in connection with any other transaction. Requests submitted by public agencies or by attorneys at law must set forth the views of such agencies or attorneys with reference to the legal questions presented.

Submission of contract and advertising materials is generally required and some states will not issue an opinion if any sales have been made in the state using the contract in question or a similar contract. Generally, once a state issues an interpretive opinion, minor changes in the contract will not change the interpretive opinion. However, operations that differ in any substantial way from the procedures submitted when the request was made, will not be covered by the opinion even though no changes were made in the contract. The states are under no legal obligation to issue interpretive opinions and most codes state "the State in its discretion may honor requests from interested parties for interpretive opinions." Once a company requests and receives an interpretive opinion which classifies it as a franchise, there is little chance that the state will reconsider its ruling even if substantial changes are made in the operation. It is, therefore, *essential* that the original request be made properly and that all changes in the operation be made prior to such request to ensure that if a favorable ruling can be obtained it will be.

Bad Advice

As a participant in the four major "Own Your Own Business" shows, I have come in contact with many company representatives, and have heard person after person make statements, similar to the following, which reflect an ignorance of, or indifference to, the franchise laws.

Statement #1: "I have never had any problems, so why should I worry?"

Comment: Since many of the franchise laws are new, they have not been enforced due to the governmental agency feeling its way with the new law. Sometimes the agency has only recently received a budget to enforce these laws. These state agencies work together and one complaint can start a chain reaction.

Statement #2: "When I have a problem I will do something about it."

Comment: When a state files a notice of violation it normally demands the following: (1) that you stop selling franchises forthwith and until registered; and (2) that you refund all monies received, reimburse any expenditures of money made and pay for the time the buyer has spent on the deal. Further, sometimes, if there was a projected profit, this may also have to be paid. How many companies can refund all money that has been received? Further, failure to comply may result in criminal charges against all officers, directors and each person connected with the sale of the unregistered franchise.

Statement #3: "Our operation is not a franchise because we state it is a dealership." Or, "It is stated in the contract this is not a franchise."

Comment: It makes no difference what *you* call it. The question is, "Does it fall under the definition of a franchise in that state?"

Statement #4: "Our operation does not have a marketing plan because it states there is no obligation to follow our advice, systems, procedures, etc."

Comment: Even if the franchisee is not obligated to follow a suggested course of action it will not necessarily mean that there is no marketing plan. Carefully read the section of this booklet which deals with marketing plans.

Statement #5: "Our company does not charge a fee."
Comment: You may actually be charging a fee and not realize it. Read carefully the section of this booklet which deals with franchise fees.

Statement #6: "The local person does not use our name."
Comment: Lack of use of a name alone will not exempt anyone from this provision of the law. This particular subject is very complex and the section of this booklet which deals with trademarks, trade names, commercial symbols, etc., should be carefully read.

General Considerations Regarding Territory and Other Restraints

The general restraint of trade laws, starting with the law which makes price fixing illegal, have been around for a long time and fill many books and will not be discussed here. The antitrust laws apply to all businesses whether the business is classified a franchise or not. Only the newer applications of these laws that affect franchising will be covered in this summary.

Different courts and different judges view these new applications to franchising differently. Therefore, there may be problems in this area regardless of how carefully the agreement is drafted. The following comments are to be considered generally applicable, but will not hold true in all applications.

If the business is such that exclusive territories are necessary for a viable distribution system, they may be granted provided they are limited to what is necessary for such viability. If the grant is achieved by implementing a company policy, rather than by formal contract, it must be unilateral. A company cannot discuss with other franchisees the exclusion or admission of new franchisees. Even the *appearance* of a veto power vested in the other franchisees can lead to problems. In phrasing the contract, and in practice, care must be taken that an exclusive grant is a restraint against the company, not the franchisee. It must be clear that the franchisee is not prohibited from selling and trans-shipping from his area to other areas. It is illegal to undertake to prevent other franchisees outside the area from shipping into the franchisee's exclusive area. It is also illegal just to represent that you may legally do so.

"Primary area of responsibility" clauses (or quotas in connection with them) may be enforceable if the area is demographically and geographically sound and the quota or best efforts requirement is realistic. Otherwise, the arrangement may be classified as a territorial restriction and illegal. Location restrictions in proper cases may be used, and exclusive areas in proper cases may be used in connection with location restrictions. A franchisor should take care not to compete or authorize other locations to other franchisees in an exclusive marketing area. When a company has a request for an additional franchised location, and the company intends to deny the request, this should *not* be discussed with other franchisees.

Price-Fixing

A franchisor may not control resale prices either by arrangements with his franchisees (vertical price-fixing) or by arrangement with his competitors (horizontal price-fixing). Price fixing is illegal regardless of whether the price controlled is a minimum price, fixed price or maximum price. It makes no difference whether the intent is to raise, lower or maintain prices, it is illegal.

Exclusive Dealings

Exclusive dealing arrangements are arrangements whereby the franchisee is required to purchase exclusively from the franchisor or a source approved by the franchisor. These are not illegal per se. The rule of reason is applied and the exclusive dealing arrangement becomes illegal when competition in a substantial share of a relevant geographical and product market is foreclosed.

Tie-in Sales

"Tie-in" is a term which means the franchisor conditions the sale of one desired product or service upon the franchisee's purchase of some other distinct product or service (the tie-in product) he may or may not want. This practice is illegal.

Independent Contractors

Most franchisors undoubtedly intend their relations with franchisees to be that of independent contractors. The franchise agreement should generally disclaim agency, or employee relationships, and clearly state that the franchisee is an independent contractor. There is a growing trend in government agencies which is directed toward imposing vicarious liability on franchisors for acts or omissions of franchisees on quasi-agency or quasi-employee theory. The National Labor Relations Board (NLRB) once held that franchisees were employees entitled to bargain with employers (franchisors) because of extensive controls;

then the NLRB held in later cases that franchisees were independent contractors. The degree of franchisor control was a factor in each of the decisions.

Franchisor Controls Over Franchisee

In the agreement and in practice, preclude use of franchisor's trade name in franchisee's business name. When a franchisee uses an assumed name, the agreement should require registration of the owner's (franchisee's) name where required or permitted by public law.

Avoid excessive controls and limit them to those reasonably ancillary to protecting the marks and goodwill. In particular, franchisors should avoid: control over financial institutions to be used by the franchisee; the right of franchisor to accumulate a fund from the franchisee and hold and control it, with unlimited right to use it in settling cases against franchisee or franchisor at the latter's discretion; control over employment policy with the right to direct the discharge of employees of the franchisee (this should be expressly disclaimed); avoid excessive controls of the type most frequently attacked under anti-trust laws.

Take steps to notify third parties of the nature of the relationship and disclaim any agency "publicly." For example: Have a sign on the premises as to the franchisee's status. The relationship does not have to be "thrown in the face" of a customer. Any serious liability to him will probably be insurable. In the back or business office, the sign should be quite explicit and obvious. Business forms, including letterheads, purchase orders and invoices should indicate the franchisee's own business name and the fact that he is a franchisee or licensed operator under franchisor's system. Some franchisors require indication of independent ownership in telephone book advertising. Others find this impracticable and excessively negative in a public relations sense. Where it is practicable to use a short form of employment agreement, franchisor may consider including in it an acknowledgement by the franchisee's employees that the franchisee is not an agent of the franchisor and that the latter has no control over the employees, is not responsible to them and that they may not look to the franchisor for payment of their wages or payroll taxes. Franchisor may consider requiring approval of sources of supply conditioned on notice to the supplier that franchisee alone will be liable for payment for his purchases. Check all franchisor and franchisee advertising copy to make certain it is not unfair, misleading or deceptive.

Franchise Terminations

"Termination" includes cancellation for cause stated in the franchise agreement and the failure to renew same on expiration of the term. Under the common law, franchisors and franchisees were generally permitted to terminate the franchise relationship for material breaches of the franchise agreement. In addition, neither party was obligated to renew the franchise upon expiration according to the terms of the franchise agreement. In recent years the courts have been reconsidering the common law rule in order to limit the contractual right of the franchisor to terminate the franchise relationship.

Securities

While it is not the intent of this summary to cover securities problems, it should be mentioned that, under recent court decisions, where any advance payment, deposit or franchise fee on which credit will be given for future purchases or on which any future credit of any kind is given, care should be taken. This does not include payments where merchandise is to be shipped immediately. Anytime a company uses a franchisee's money for its operating expenses, there may be a security violation. As of this time, franchise fees have not been classified as a security, but overpayment for merchandise has been so classified.

Also, in passing, it is worthwhile to note that efforts have been made to employ the use of joint ventures and general partnerships in an attempt to avoid being classified as a franchise and thereby skirt the franchise laws. In at least one state, these arrangements are being scrutinized, and while they may enable a business to remain free of franchise regulations, such agreements may be classified as securities and, thus, be subject to additional qualification under the complex and technical state securities law.

The California Department of Corporations is concerned with whether these arrangements meet the legislative mandate of "fair, just and equitable." In making such a determination, numerous substantive issues may be raised.

California's Corporate Securities Law of 1968 defines "security" to include any certificate of interest or participation in any profit-sharing agreement, transferable share, investment contract or any interest or instrument commonly known as a "security." Joint venture interests and interests in both general and limited partnerships are securities within this definition; however, a limited exemption is provided for such interests where the offer and sale of the interests does not involve a public offering. The exemption may not be available in certain situations where a business intends to employ joint venture or partnership agreements for the joint ownership and operation of an enterprise. There is a strong possibility that the sale of a venture security to one individual in certain business organizations may be viewed as a sale to all of the investors in the business in their individual capacity, therefore involving a public offering of the joint venture security.

Furthermore, the presence of the joint venture or partnership agreement may give rise to the creation of an investment contract. An investment contract has been characterized as a transaction which contemplates the conduct of a public enterprise by other than the purchasers, in the profits and proceeds of which the purchasers share. The Hawaii Supreme Court has stated: "An investment contract is created whenever; (1) an offeree furnishes initial value to an offeror; (2) a portion of this initial value is subjected to the uses of the enterprise, (3) the furnishing of the initial value is induced by the offeror's promises on representations which give rise to a reasonable understanding that a valuable benefit of some kind, over and above initial value, will accrue to the offeree as a result of the operation of the enterprise and (4) the offeree does not receive the right to exercise practical and actual control over the managerial decisions of the enterprise." In this connection, it should be noted that the Securities Law does not provide an exemption for the sale of investment contracts.

There are other potential related problems with the use of joint ventures. If the parties to the joint venture constitute "sponsors" under the Securities Law, the aggregate compensation paid to all such persons and their affiliates is subject to limitations. In addition, among other problems, there is the difficulty in providing the investor with adequate disclosure of the complex terms of the joint venture agreement.

Clearly from the above, avoidance of the franchise laws may well place a business under a much more intricate and restrictive set of rules. Given the choice, it appears that the burden of the franchise laws is substantially less upon a business than are the securities laws and careful consideration must be given to the ramifications of either choice.

Penalty for Violation of Franchise Law

All the states have penalties for violation of the franchise law. The California Corporation Code reads as follows:

"Any person who willfully violates any provision of this law, or who willfully violates any rule or order under this law, shall upon conviction be fined not more than ten thousand dollars ($10,000) or imprisoned in the state prison for not more than 10 years or in a county jail for not more than one year, or be punished by both such fine and imprisonment; but no person may be imprisoned for the violation of any rule or order if he *proves* that he had no knowledge of the rule or order."

A Closing Thought Relative to the Burden of Proof

Most state laws contain a provision similar to the California statute: "In any proceeding under this law, the burden of proving an exemption or an exception from a definition is upon the person claiming it."

Read carefully the section dealing with the four elements of a franchise and then decide how you would like to try to explain to a jury of little old ladies how or why your operation is not covered by the franchise law.

23.

IN CONCLUSION . . . .

It is our hope that this book has succeeded in conveying a detailed evaluation of the franchising field that enables you to form better judgment in the selection of a franchise or, if presently a franchisee, to best adjust your business procedures to increase your earnings.

The questions and answers below may help to further "sum up" the "pros" and "cons" of franchising . . . and your suitability for this field.

Q. Is it advisable to be a franchisee, as contrasted with going into business by myself?

A. In most instances, yes . . . provided you select a franchise that fits your capabilities, financial capacities and "comfortableness." Also, provided that you have carefully checked out the integrity and dependability of the franchisor and the "record" of successes achieved by other franchisees.

Q. What do you mean by "comfortableness"?

A. Any business you enter is one that you live with for a great portion of your day and your life. To the extent that you are comfort able—and actually *look forward*—to the work you are doing, to that extent will you be successful. Hence, if you are mechanically inclined, you may not be comfortable with a sales-oriented franchise. If you are office-inclined, you may not be comfortable with a mechanics-oriented "dirty-hands" type of business. If you are travel-inclined, you may not be comfortable with a sedentary type of business. Any "non-adaptability" could impede your success.

Q. How much should I pay for a franchise?

A. A franchise business is not purchased on the basis of "bargain price." Generally (as in everything else) you get exactly what you pay for. The measure of what you pay is based on value received and earnings potential. Most important, it is based on what you are able to afford to pay without running into "scared money." Normally, you should allow yourself enough operating capital to cover your living costs for a *minimum* of six months. You should also select the type of franchise that can yield sufficient earnings to support your particular standard of living.

Q. Whose advice should I seek in making the decision to acquire a franchise?

A. First of all, that of your wife (she'll have to "live" with this business almost as much as you). Second, other franchisees. Third, similar businessmen. Fourth, your banker. Fifth, your lawyer. Sixth, your accountant.

Best wishes for your success!

INDEX